Dear Bear—
HAPPY _____ DAY

_____

Rabbit

THE
CULTURE
BARONS

THE
CULTURE
BARONS

BY

FAYE LEVINE

THOMAS Y. CROWELL COMPANY
Established 1834/NEW YORK

Designed by S. S. Drate

Manufactured in the United States of America

Library of Congress Cataloging in Publication Data

Levine, Faye.
    The culture barons.

    Includes index.
    1. Art patronage—United States.   2. Arts—United
States—Management.   I. Title.
NX711.U5L48   338.4′7′700973   75-43877
ISBN 0-690-01098-2

1 2 3 4 5 6 7 8 9 10

CONTENTS

Tables, Charts, and Lists

Acknowledgments

A great many people helped me on this book. First of all, I would like to thank the assistants and secretaries: Liz Shaw for Blanchette [Mrs. John D.] Rockefeller; Cecelia Mescall for Tom Hoving; Joan Dayton and Dick Porter for David Keiser; Jean White and Simone Crockett for Dick Clurman; Gail Merrifield for Joe Papp; Annette Meyers for Hal Prince; Roberta Barrows for Howard Stein; Kathi Gorringe for Ron Delsener; Natasha for Bill Graham; Annette Berg and the late Virginia C. Lavelle for McNeil Lowry; Eric Barnes for Otto Preminger; and Charles Franz for Oliver Smith. Betty Hom helped me with research, and Sheila LaLima of the Thomas Y. Crowell Company gave me her time generously.

I am very grateful, of course, for the interviews granted me by the Culture Barons themselves and others in New York, Los Angeles, Pittsburgh, Boston, and Texas. Of these, Mr. Lowry of the Ford Foundation took the most active and generous interest in the ultimate correctness of the book.

I wish I could thank everyone. But for now only an especial thanks to my sweet parents, Lillian Haft Shulman Levine and the Honorable Seymour R. Levine, and to my editor, Jay Acton, and my agent, Elaine Markson, without whose special characters this book would not have come into being at all.

PREFACE:

A Fantasy of
Culture Barons

THE big guns, the heavies, the head honchos of the U.S. have gathered in the meeting room of an inconspicuous office building somewhere in Manhattan. Except for a blow-up, pop poster style, of Jack and Jackie Kennedy radiant, stepping off an airplane in Dallas, there are no visual distractions. In the outer office, a bald transvestite screens the lower doors and elevators on a closed circuit TV.

"All right, men," says Huntington Hartford, only moments after the last chair has been filled, standing up again and slapping both fistfuls of minicomputers and assorted combi-implements on the elliptical segment of the free-form urethaned mahogany conference table next to him.

"How's the A&P, HH?" croons E. Howard Hunt, in an attempt to heckle the chain grocery store magnate. Paul Mellon chuckles appreciatively, chucking an unsmiling Shah of Iran on the back.

"Andjyer bimbo's dialyzer—!" Hartford replies without missing a beat, and the gathering is quieted. But just to make sure, he kicks a pointed boot against the nearest bit of apparent wood and smiles quietly at the ungodly sound. He is wearing a ten-gallon creased Wyoming rustler's hat, and a red, green, and blue plaid jumpsuit with design researched pockets in ten different sizes and clotures.

1

*John D. Rockefeller 3rd, Bob Moses, Du Pont #732, and Mel-
lon are eyeing Hartford's implements, absentmindedly smoothing
a fold in their own flannels, or consulting a fobbed watch, politely silent.*

*"O now I dunno how t' tell it," Hartford suddenly complains,
and, lapsing into a brief fit of sobbing, clumsily retrieves from
one of his jumpsuit's open pockets a small flat box of plasticized
metal, a half inch by two inches square, and thrusts it down onto
the table amid his heap of trashy-looking killer-toys. The tape recorder begins playing, upon impact. He takes his seat, quietly
whimpering.*

*Crystalline, Hartford's voice nuncupates: "Men. All right,
men: not a word of this leaves this room or the talker dies. You
know I mean that—" At this, slightly revived, the seated Hartford
picks up his little gas trajectant in the shape of a pistol and wig-
gles it playfully. None of the other men smile. They respect each
other's money. "Not a word. Not a whisper to the bimbo. No noise
from your fat lips! I am building—hold your hats, now, Yankees"
(and one hand actually went to a pheasant-feathered Abercrom-
bie homburg, for the owner of the hat was used to obeying all authoritative commands) "—I am stone upon stoning what we can
call 'The New York Cultural Center,' and dad-blame it if the
Russkies or the Chinkos or the subverts—whoevers frugin dang
thang it is!—when they level the subways and bombflat your old
yankeebanks and Take Over, Dad— may he rest in peace—Blame
Me if they don't going to accept my little housy as their own
curseworthy Red New Yorky Cultural Center!"*

*"You get the idea, men?" Hartford's living voice now was
taking over again from his little machine, which lay smoldering
quietly, soothing its own batteries into lower play or automatic
something altogether different, if needed.*

*Mr. John spoke up the quickest. "Yes, of course. We build for
the commissars, you mean."*

*Tom Hoving was biting his fingernails up to the elbow and
rolling his eyes. "Architecture—!" was all he could say, when
someone kindly extricated his lower arm and stuck some ciga-
rettes in his mouth in its place. Sipping and sucking languorously
on the unlit cylinders of chopped leaf, the Museum director
added, softly: "Mother of the arts."*

Rockefeller was already on his wrist phone to Wallace Harrison, the man who'd been so good as to put buildings on the space John had given to the world or otherwise gotten rid of when it appeared the unwholesome oyster danger from the East River might actually reach a critical threshold in combination with the slums he'd been keeping on the same spot (someone'd had the bright idea of calling that project "the united nations," but honestly, now it seemed to John D 3 that Hartford's idea might be much more right on). "Walls, . . ." the oil heir was droning. "Walls. We're going to have to build that new opera house, after all. Big, solid, squarish. I'll tell you why later. Later, Walls! Ah, and oh yes—we're going to need some kind of prettied up hammer and sickle for over the stage. Tomorrow, Walls! Tomorrow at the earliest! Ears only."

Bob Moses was in a snit. "This is a victory for Labor!" he was shouting.

Whether or not the Culture Barons are archfiends in cahoots with the CIA and other assassins, playing reckless games with each other and plotting new wrinkles in the cold war all the time, who they are and how they think is important to the hundreds of thousands of artists in this country and the millions of patrons of the arts. Are their aesthetics the best ones possible? Or, as some critics suggest, are the businessmen who run the arts actually the archenemies of the artists? Who are the Culture Barons indeed? And what are their interests, presuming we can identify them; are they pernicious, puritanical, parochial? Who are the men or women who stand at the intersection of power, money, and art, the crossroads of commerce and culture?

The reading for the course includes everything from Mills's *The Power Elite* to Susann's *The Love Machine.* I spoke with persons at every level of the artocracy (in what I consider a statistically good sample of Culture Barony), and I have attempted to chart the astronomics of the constellations of the great and the systems of art that galaxy around them. One always hopes to psych out the powerful. Somehow, when the effort's successful, they seem to lose their jobs soon afterward. Why is this so? Is our culture, in all its baronage, corrupt? I cannot answer that ques-

tion. But I met the fellows who seemed—sometimes with protestations I disbelieved—to consider themselves, and to be considered
by others, as the Culture Barons. Their words, their biographies,
and a description of their surroundings are useful for the light they
shed both on power structures in the arts and on the ways in
which the specific powerful individuals themselves work.

☆   ☆   ☆

Naturally, among the intellectual elite, there is disagreement
over the definition of "culture." To oversimplify, let us agree that
the late T. S. Eliot, a guardian of class distinctions and "purity" in
all things, would have included grand opera in his definition of
the word, but not rock music. At the other extreme, Marshall
McLuhan, a proponent of health through cross-fertilization of
forms, includes rock, nylon stockings, and television commercials,
and excludes as moribund the traditional grand opera.

From my thirty-year-old point of view, "culture" in this society has often been spelled "Kulture," in order to identify it ironically with that highly placed Nazi who said, "When I hear the
word 'culture' [Kultur in German], I reach for my gun." I do not
sympathize with this dismissal. But I don't much like the hypocritical exaltation of culture on the other side, whereby the vicious
pay lip service to the virtuous and hide behind the form as if it
were the content.

Culture is all that is not strictly economics, in the Marxist or
anthropological sense. It is in this sense that I would most like to
pursue the identity and interests of the Culture Barons. For
strictly practical reasons, however, I have had to limit the scope of
this book. In manuscript it was already five hundred pages long,
and thus I have had to omit any discussion of radio or television,
most of the record industry, symphonic music, and the many facets
of literature—newspapers and periodicals, publishing houses and
the noncommercial poetry establishment. Having apologized in
advance for these and other glaring omissions, I look forward to
the work that others will do in delineating the power structures in
these areas.

What I am left with as a definition of the word "culture" is
very much conditioned by the Culture Barons themselves. Be-

cause of the heavy influence of the Rockefeller family on New York City's Lincoln Center as well as on its museums, and because of the pervasive influence of these structures on the contents of my book, I am subscribing, for the purposes of this work, to a Rockefellerian position on the meaning of "culture." I will consider as culture all the kinds of activities that go on at the official "palaces of culture": chiefly the museums and the "performing arts centers." This, then, would include both grand opera and rock music, that form of dance called "classical ballet," and film as well as live theater. Some of these activities also transpire in the halls of painting and sculpture just as a bit of painting and sculpture finds its way into the music and dance areas. The Rockefellers, it will be seen later, are not particularly adept at verbalizing their cultural commitment. However, they play a big part in determining the *status quo* in culture as in other areas. To accept prevailing norms for a definition of the arts is to fall within their camp.

WHAT IS A CULTURE BARON?

Which are the powerful institutions and who is at the head of those institutions?

—Philip Nobile,
*Intellectual Skywriting: Literary Politics &
the New York Review of Books*

What is the ideal political economy of art?

—Kathie Sarachild,
A Program for Feminist "Consciousness-Raising"

There's a big difference between money-power and other kinds of influence.

—Richard Kostelanetz,
The End of Intelligent Writing

It's all mathematics. There's a definite number of Colt 45's that make up Marlene Dietrich, and you can find that out if you want to.

—Bob Dylan,
The Saturday Evening Post, 1966.

ART seems to have begun in festivals and ceremonies that were either sexual or religious or both at once. So profuse was the imagery of the fertility goddess in the ancient Near East that the first patriarchs, in their Mosaic code, made a special point of listing all her artifacts that must not be produced.

One speaks of the flowering of Greece, because the arts there were well developed, perhaps to a higher point than they are today. Aristotle defined the origins of the drama: "Tragedy arose," he says in *The Poetics*, "as did comedy, from improvisation—as practiced respectively by choral leaders of the dithyramb [a wild and emotional Dionysian hymn] and of the phallic songs such as are still in vogue in many of our cities."

By this time there were already theatrical producers called *"choregos." Choregos* were men of wealth who voluntarily assumed responsibility for assembling and hiring a body of choristers, engaging a trainer to drill them, purchasing or renting costumes, employing dramatic characters, and providing shows of various kinds. The Broadway producers of ancient Greece thus displayed their wealth in a satisfying manner and curried favor with the populace.

The Romans perpetuated, in a less pure form, the arts of the Greeks. As befitting their greater interest in the military, they added brass instruments to the Greeks' musical reeds and strings.

During the long centuries after the downfall of Rome, the arts survived in Europe as decentralized folk expressions pertaining to Christianity or witchcraft, and high culture retreated to the monasteries. Spectacular cathedrals were built; no one today is quite clear who did them or how.

The word "baron" suggests the concentration of money, rule by the sword, and a system of feudal obligations which ran Europe for a thousand years. Long before the term "robber baron" became current, there was, in the Old World, a highly elaborated hierarchy ranging from pope, emperor, and king at the top (who sometimes fought for precedence) down through at least eight grades of nobility, each with its particular powers, rights, and even style of crown. A "pecking order" we have come to call what was in reality a life and death order.

Baron was the lowest rank of the baronetcy and therefore the most numerous. We can guess that the medieval barons were probably the most jealously defensive of their claim to nobility and to the money, power, and privileges that separated them from the freedmen just below.

And then: *Pow!* The Renaissance! Was it due to Copernicus putting the sun and earth in their places? The Crusades stirring up the economy? At any rate, things changed. Renaissance artists were as happy as monkeys. They had plenty of work and plenty of people to tell them what to do (sometimes a little roughly—for example, on pain of excommunication—but at least they cared), and these patrons were in every court and cathedral and bank in every little Italian town. Leonardo worked mainly for the Este nobility in the town of Ferrara. Michelangelo was supported by the Medicis, who gave him a big, expensive chunk of marble to work on when he was just fourteen years old.

Of course there was a seed of contradiction in the blissful Italian scene. Even at this moment, at the height of the ascendancy of the Italian aristocracy in 1500, the Spanish Dominican Torquemada was surreptitiously introducing his White Brothers into Sicily. Opposing the Bourbon kings and allying with the middle class and Freemasons, the White Brothers were to become the Mafia.

The high arts as they are now conceived are closer in overall character to the high arts of the Renaissance than to any other historical prototype.

But the American revolution had the effect of slicing the pearls right off the barons' crowns. Every schoolchild knows that the United States was conceived in fundamental opposition to the nobility system and the established churches of Europe. Thomas Jefferson wrote the Declaration of Independence and then, for good measure, saw to it that primogeniture was abolished in America so that no large hereditary land holdings could create a caste of barons here. George Washington and the other patriarchs of the Constitutional Convention worked out the specifics of a nonkingly governmental system.

Brilliant as the Founding Fathers were, however, they did not foresee all the economic changes that were to occur in the life of their republic, giving rise to wave after wave of plutocrats. First the Colonial landholders like Carroll, Livingston, and Schuyler were challenged in wealth by the Federal bankers like Biddle and Lenox. These men were upstaged by international bankers and real-estate speculators in the early part of the nineteenth century. Civil War profiteers in turn became fabulously wealthy on the strength of railroads, oil and steel trusts, banking and finance—using as raw material the plenitude of new immigrant labor—and they inspired the label "robber baron." Scarcely a century after that magnificently outlined democracy had gone into operation, journalists were calling men like John D. Rockefeller, Andrew Mellon, Andrew Carnegie, J. P. Morgan, and Henry Frick throwbacks to the class of European rulers who had taken their wealth by force.

Because of the abundance of journalistic investigations of monopolies and robber barons at the turn of the nineteenth century, measures were taken against them and their concentrations of personal power. An income tax was set up in 1914 with progressively weighted levies. Monopolies became illegal. When the bottom fell out of the economy in 1929 a massive Federal program of deficit spending set up a social security system and unemployment insurance (as well as emergency relief measures) to protect the majority of the population. But the money barons were not seriously hampered in their work of accumulation. Shortly before the income tax was passed, foundations had been established into which the rich could funnel their enormous funds tax free. Additional multimillionaires joined their ranks: Henry Ford and the other auto barons in the early 1900s, then the Texas and Oklahoma oil kings who got rich between 1930 and 1950. In the 1950s and 60s new wealth accrued from the computer and photocopier, new types of cameras, weapons systems, and contraceptives.

In the economy in general in the early '70s, new fortunes were made in orange juice, ice cream, pet food and fast food, cleansers, faucets, and tire treads, indicating perhaps a movement toward domestic leisure. But even as there was talk of using up our natural land resources by overexploitation, the great expanse of the American personality was being mined and interconnected by new technologies. Hollywood was still movie-maker to the world, but the newly invented LPs hooked up millions with their favorite dream and mixed up personal and public histories. Amplifiers and electronic music came on the scene. Ballpoints and paperbacks were our first exports even to underdeveloped countries; what matter if people were starving?—at least they could express themselves! More than half the homes in the United States had TV by 1955; then orbiting satellites made television not only an

American universal but a global presence. And the largest conglomerate in the entertainment field, Warner Communications,
was making a $50 million profit in a year—as much as the entire
publishing industry combined.

The superprofitability of the new arts, or the popular arts, was
not lost on the power elite, who nevertheless did not consider
these arts to be as legitimate as their own. Beginning in about the
mid-'50s, when the McCarthyite political sentiment reached its
nadir and was observed by half the families in America on their
TV sets, some socioeconomic trends began reversing. In 1955,
William Randolph Hearst returned from a trip to Moscow and announced to the National Press Club that the Soviets were competing with us on the cultural front and in the arena of youth, as well
as in military hardware. In 1957 the Ford Foundation, previously
involved primarily in international politics, set aside money for
the first time for the humanities and the arts. Nelson Rockefeller
had been involved with the arts all his life, of course, but when
L.B.J. established the National Foundation on the Arts and Humanities in 1965, the antes were raised locally. One imagines
Governor Rockefeller's men trying not to lose face before the cowboy in Washington as New York State's new arts subsidy program
jumped unexpectedly from $2 million to $20 million in one year
and from there to $34 million.

In effect, though, the state arts subsidy programs of the last
decade have been in competition not with the U.S.S.R. but with
our own American mass culture. All this flurry of culturizing is
the elite's reaction to the ability of the truly popular arts to pay its
talent and see profits in the millions of dollars.

Rubbing shoulders with the new mass-producible forms of exaltation and entertainment, the antique and aristocratic fine arts
slid ever more steadily into multimillion-dollar debt. Opera is having an identity crisis, trying to modernize; legitimate theater and
ballet are both experimenting with the nudity and explicit sexual-
ity of the popular pornographic-vaudeville, or "grind," theaters;
young musicians speak of the possibility of there being no orchestras in fifty years.

But there is still power and influence connected with the
older artistic institutions, if not as much money as with the newer,
and individual impresarios who arise to claim a piece of the ac-

tion. Indeed, a much smaller number of egos have situated themselves at the confluence of money, power, and art than is generally imagined. Like a crowd of ruffian chairmen of the House Ways and Means committee, they wield significant, if not determining, influence on what becomes the culture of the nation.

To understand culture—profitable and not so—we must inevitably deal with its barons, though their barony may seem slightly metaphorical. But it is detrimental to individual responsibility to take for granted either them or the arts they direct, or to dismiss them as facts of life. Their identities and portraits are at least as relevant to us as are those of such other pseudo-nobility as the "Cattle Barons," the "Energy Czar."

The point is that culture is not made by chance or through "natural" processes any more than are railroads or wars. There are individual men involved, with institutions shaping their options, and interests and personalities determining their decisions, and even with some rough stuff mixed in with the lofty matters.

The Culture Barons, unlike the robber barons before them, are men who materialize dreams, anxieties, and ideals in our name, who specify and shape the wellspring of collective emotion for the rest of us. Their goals and tastes determine the matrix culture, which in turn determines so much else and affects us in so many ways. Ordinarily they are responsible only to their boards of directors or a handful of patrons and, to a lesser degree, the critics writing in their field. So their power is broad and deep. It juridicates not over any single matter or municipality but over the life of the mind we all inhabit. At least this is the power they mean to wield. As Alvin Toffler says, "There is no question but that the culture barons and patrons have enormous influence over what is performed."

The Culture Barons are few in number, perhaps no more than two or three hundred around the country. They are individualists with an extreme of self-confidence, guts, and *chutzpah*. An average person can hardly begin to speak their language. To some extent they are vulnerable, to a well-aimed barb of criticism. But they are not at all like a highly select committee of the enlightened. They are almost the opposite—the front-row students in that mass of affectionate animals that comprises unconscious society. Their tastes are libelously lusty.

Many of them are guilty of the worst kinds of social blindness—sexism, racism, classism, ageism—but they are also, in some sense, the highest products of our individualistic society. They are individualized; they have magnified their personalities and given them external physical manifestations. They are keenly devoted to the success they have achieved. They are Dickensian caricatures of what they are, and they are fiercely inner-directed. They are the survivors in the rat race of free cultural enterprise.

Culture Barons typically are bad on marriages. With so much happening in their sphere of activities, they appropriate more than the average number of mates. Joe Papp ended a 21-year union with one of his early actresses in 1973, and married Gail Merrifield, his longtime administrative assistant, making her his fourth wife. George Balanchine has been wed to some five different ballerinas, each more exotically stage-named than the last. Indeed, one universal characteristic of Culture Barons—cutting across all other sociological lines—is that they tend to marry at least three times and have two to four children.

They are in a position to act out their political wishes: just as Bill Graham can temporarily be boss over a Beatle (whose success is unequaled in the music business), so Otto Preminger is in a position to cast Sir Laurence Olivier, head of Britain's national theater, or former mayor John Lindsay as a policeman or a senator in his own fictional adventures.

Power over millions of dollars, thousands of people, interesting real estate, and unlimited dreams does not always go hand in hand with a clear-cut sense of personal responsibility, however. Clive Davis, former head of Columbia Records, contends he offered crooner Neil Diamond the unbelievable sum of—was it?—$4 million only because he had to match a Warner Brothers offer. Dino De Laurentiis, a leading independent producer in the genre of violent movies, explains this away by saying that violence is also on television and in the newspapers. And then there's the classic rationalization: A representative of the subbaronial group of theater benefit agents, called "the Golden Dozen," remarks: "We merely reflect the taste of the public."

Some of the Culture Barons have been true to their posts for twenty years or even longer. George Balanchine has been the presiding genius of the School of American Ballet for forty-three

years and of the New York City Ballet for twenty-eight. Joe Papp
has been with the Shakespeare Festival for twenty-two years. Rudolf Bing had been with the Met for twenty-two years before his
1972 retirement. W. McNeil Lowry in January, 1975, retired
from the Ford Foundation, where he had been for twenty-two
years.

The background of a surprising number of the Culture Barons
is in the clothing industry. There is no discernible reason for this;
yet many of the old Hollywood moguls were haberdashers or fur-
riers. Sam Goldwyn was a glove salesman; Paramount's Bob
Evans, production chief for *Love Story, The Godfather,* and
Gatsby, first worked in New York with Evan-Picone tailored
sportswear. The hottest agent in California, Sue Mengers, is the
daughter of a dressmaker.

The Haberdashery Factor holds true outside the movies too.
Sidney Janis, gallery owner and representative of Jackson Pollock
and Willem de Kooning, previously netted himself a nice nest egg
with the production of two-pocket shirts. Lincoln Kirstein's wealth
(he is the angel of Balanchine's ballet) derives from his father's
managerial role in Filene's, Bloomingdale's, and Macy's. Another
ballet patron, Rebekah Harkness, was a saleslady in Mainbocher.
The Culture Baron's emblem, S. N. Behrman said, is a "mailed fist
in an ersatz Renaissance glove fashioned in a British factory."

One type of Culture Baron is the man now over seventy who
came from Europe to exercise a great individual talent here.
This would include the late Sol Hurok, David Sarnoff, Alfred
Hitchcock, Otto Preminger, Rudolf Bing, George Balanchine, Serge Semenenko, and Sam Spiegel. They came from Russia in 1900 or 1905 or 1924, or they came from Germany in the
1930s.

Producers for the stage tend to be slightly younger—in their
fifties or sixties now—and, with the exception of David Merrick,
who hails from St. Louis, to have been born in New York City.

On the boards of the big museums, we find an overlapping of
the culture establishment with the regular military-industrial
power elite. To a man they are over six feet tall, Episcopal (except
for the Rockefellers, who are Baptist, and a few Unitarians and
Congregationalists), graduates of private schools and Ivy League
universities, especially Harvard and Yale, and one-time military

officers, particularly lieutenants in the navy. They have mostly inherited their wealth.

Curiously, two of the best-known collectors of art, Joseph Hirshhorn and Samuel Newhouse, are almost the opposite in type from the museum administrators. Hirshhorn, five feet four inches, and Newhouse, five feet three, are both Jewish, the sons of factory workers who had to moonlight in the struggle to rise to wealth. Newhouse, recently elected to the board of the Museum of Modern Art, made his money acquiring upstate New York newspapers.

Many of the art barons, both tall and short, made their money in exploitation of the earth. The Rockefellers, who built the Museum of Modern Art, gave the lion's share of money needed for Lincoln Center and saw to it that New York State began funding the arts, derived their wealth originally from oil; later they went into railroads, nickel, chemicals, and rockets.

Hirshhorn, called the "Uranium King," also has holdings in silver, lead, zinc, oil, and copper. The Guggenheims' money is in copper; the newspaper mogul Hearsts' is in silver. C. Douglas Dillon is diversified into oil, gas, chemicals, and metals. The town of Pittsburgh, once considered "Steel City" because of the economic interests of its local art patrons, the Carnegies and Mellons, is now more correctly the city of Gulf Oil and its derivative chemicals.

Three youngish aristocrats are Schuyler Chapin, fifty-three, former general manager of the Metropolitan Opera and descended from Revolutionary War general and landowner Philip Schuyler; Harold Prince, forty-seven, producer of such Broadway smashes as *Fiddler on the Roof* and *Cabaret* and self-described as upper-middle lower-rich German Jewish; and Thomas Hoving, forty-three, director of the Metropolitan Museum and the son of the chairman of the board of Tiffany's.

In music there are many powerful blacks, especially Berry Gordy and Smokey Robinson, who started Motown Records in Detroit. Another black, Ken Harper, was the man behind the recent Broadway smash *The Wiz*. There are two black Culture Barons in the dance. Alvin Ailey was born in Texas and raised in California; Arthur Mitchell is a New Yorker who attended the High School of Performing Arts. Both have their own companies.

Another group of Culture Barons, mostly active in the theater,

Aspects of the Culture Baronies

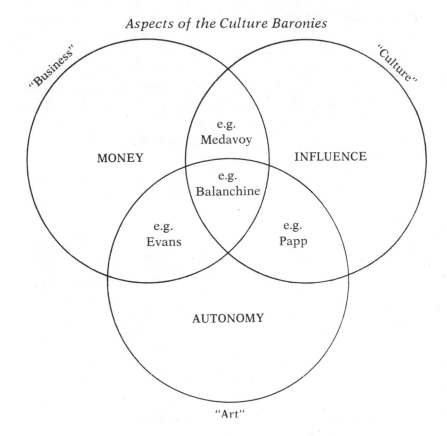

were all educated at New York University. These would include Harry Abrams, the art book publisher, a Briton; producer Kermit Bloomgarden, of Roumanian descent; producer Alexander Cohen; writer Neil Simon; and Simon's producer, Arnold Saint-Subber.

The Catholic Culture Barons are formal purists. George Balanchine phones Salvador Dali about his nightmares. Rudolf Bing likes being called "the last of the nineteenth-century dictators." Merce Cunningham (Irish and Slavic) and Andy Warhol (Czech) are two artists who command large masses of money by virtue of their daringly individualistic commitments to chance and to the mundane.

The Culture Barons of live rock and the movies are mostly men in their thirties; they came to power during the cultural revolution of the 1960s, building upon that, taking advantage of the commercial opportunities that opened up at that time. To the rock world, *Rolling Stone* is the Bible; to the movie world, *People* magazine.

Of the few Culture Barons who are women, most are not originally from New York City, though they live there now. These would include Cheryl Crawford, a founder of the Group Theater (from Akron); Martha Graham (from Pittsburgh); and Rebekah Harkness, ballet patron (from St. Louis.)

The Culture Barons are too odd a breed to classify. They run the gamut from Old World Roman Catholic through Colonial WASP to New World Jew (in several varieties). Only a token few are blacks or women. Politically, most center around the Liberal camp, though there are Conservatives, a Radical or two, and possibly some proto-Fascists. At the stage of their lives where they exercise Culture Baronhood, they are members of the gracious upper class—some by veneer rather than by wealth, others by both—but even so, many still carry with them the insecurities and the earnestness they used on the way up.

Before I begin to discuss the Culture Barons individually, I want to show them at their fighting best—in conflict, as they battle for control of Lincoln Center.

THE BATTLE FOR CONTROL OF LINCOLN CENTER

On any board of directors like Lincoln Center's, overwhelming sorrow came over finance committees at each manifestation of rising costs. . . . The affluent realtors, lawyers, brokers who charge themselves with the promulgation of art . . . naturally turn to efficiency experts to propose how costs can be cut. They crave the impervious wisdom of computers, time clocks, cost accountancy, and personal reformation. The efficiency experts are presumably hired because they have no knowledge of the special climate of the theatre and will be properly horrified by the looseness, changeability, fantasy and hysteria of professional behavior. . . . As for isolated personalities and their pretensions to unique service, isn't everyone replaceable and expendable?

—Lincoln Kirstein,
The New York City Ballet

It is no easier now that it was five years ago to think about Lincoln Center with any coherence, so irrelevant are its constituent parts to each other. The Metropolitan Opera, as a museum displaying mainly nineteenth-century valuables, exists in splendid isolation across the way from the New York City Ballet, most of whose repertoire has been created within the past twenty years, while the Repertory Theater, like an adolescent with a terrible case of *weltschmerz*, continues to struggle to find a personality and a definition of its own. The Center's only unity lies in its physical layout: a grouping on fourteen acres of various buildings, each of which was designed in a more or less varying style by a different architect.

—Robert Kotlowitz,
Harper's, 1967

The Battle for Control of Lincoln Center

DRAMATIS PERSONAE

The Prince   John D. Rockefeller 3rd
The City of New York   Robert Moses
The Dukes of New York
  Brigadier General   Charles Spofford
  Colonel   Joseph Hartfield
  Chairman of U.S. Steel   Irving Olds
  Publisher of *Fortune*   C. D. Jackson
  Chairman of Philharmonic, Met
    Museum, and IIE   Arthur Houghton
  Chairman of N.Y. Life   Devereux Josephs
  Chairman of Met Opera   Anthony Bliss
And a Few Others, Also Known as
  the Interlocking Directorates of the Opera
  and Philharmonic
Benefactors of Populism   The Ford Foundation
Beneficiaries of Populism   City Ballet (*i.e.*,
                     George Balanchine) and
                            City Opera

The State of New York   Nelson Rockefeller
The Baron of Juilliard   William Schuman
The Europeans   Sir Rudolf Bing
The American Aristocracy   Amyas Ames
The Old Left   Harold Clurman
                          Dore Schary
The New Left   Dick Gilman
The Citizen Emperor   Joseph Papp

URBAN DESIGN

The Broadway–Times Square area is like the principle of a cluster at the top. Like a chandelier in some second-rate costume shop upstairs from dirty books, a grouping of shining off-white/white/yellow bulbs with no more structure than a globule. The cluster at the top is friendly, reassuring. But Broadway is not only that. Broadway is also the harsh revolution of the police light atop "Playland," the yes vs. no principle, on and then off. This is the underside of all the beautiful love come-on—damnation, getting caught.

Psychoses rub up against each other upstage of these two principles, perfervid and needy, like gummy ghosts. Psychoses feed and grow on the Broadway–Times Square soil as on a life-support nutrient, for the Great White Way marks the spot where the very most cynical of the brilliant have put up their warring shingles.

Broadway–Times Square is meant to be destroyed, bombed bare, for sanitary purposes. That is some time away. But already its replacement has been built, and we are granted by the hidden personal powers all the time we need to salvage what we choose (and what do we choose?) from 42nd Street and cart it laboriously, or with temperament, up the G.W.W. to 64th.

Lincoln Center is like the principle of a snowflake. Like a perfection of centrifugal geometry with an absolute reference and source point. That thing: Is it hanging in the Metropolitan Opera? Was it donated by the Republic of Austria? Is it slowly gliding higher into the ceiling? And which verb takes precedence? And what deathlike perfections must we be ourselves to participate in the adoration of this radial God with our every vibrating footprint engaged in uncompromised Italian limestone?

We do not go to Lincoln Center to steal something there and sell it in the great marketplace below. No. The marketplace concerns itself now with exigencies and expediencies, communism made ugly with distortion, tendered to jaded and decadent tastes. Nuggets of the dark American psyche such as romp in the backrooms of the heartplace are not of interest to the ethereal dozen (or are they 15?) who flash briefly before our eye as they hail a cab to take them from here to a luncheon board meeting but who, at that boardly meal, shall discuss only the materialization and proportions of the noble and stoic. We come to Lincoln Center to bring there something of the crowd, some genius of the mob, to nourish it with ourself, and contemplate the deaths of these men, of ourselves, and eventually of Art itself.

This Lincoln Center, which has been taken as a model by one hundred cities, is it the piazza of our great central church? Its bigness is impressive. But why, to what end, are these shapes in bronze and glass and gold leaf so imposing? What are these hundred-year projections in travertine and marble telling us? What has the sweaty bleeding nerve-wracked fiercesome art of these days to do with these silent stylobates of cold exaltation beyond life?

The hulking sculpture in a shallow and dirty pool seems like a memorial to ruins or pollution.

Seymour Lipton's "Archangel" looks like a battered and hardened version of a stereo amplifier/speaker set, sort of a bronze apotheosis of a public address system. Is that what it's supposed to be? The opposite of Claes Oldenburg's soft telephone?

The five-ton copper alloy sculpture of "Apollo and Orpheus" in the Philharmonic suggests the magnificence of electricity with its copper wires, the instrument Orpheus might play in this age.

Henry Moore's sculpture is six tons of green, petrified, giant spit. The Calder piece is probably a gentle, herbivorous dinosaur.

Attendance at the cultural events of Lincoln Center has been solidly in the millions, with box-office receipts paying slightly more than half the expenses. But what is the quality of this cultural participation? Except for the diamond-studded opera crowd and the kids who pack the annual film festival, on a typical evening at Lincoln Center the folk drinking coffee and eating ice cream or just sitting among the lemon trees, waiting for a Cultural Event to begin, look quite a lot like the dispirited retirees you see outside the central all-purpose building in Kiev.

One of the essential components of the high arts is magnitude of scope, theme, action. The problem for us—so profound as to be almost unthinkable—is that since *War and Peace*, the only authentic literary theme of magnitude is the Communist revolution, and this we are structurally committed to gainsay. Our versions of the event itself are counterrevolutionary and preposterous (the movie *Nicholas and Alexandra*) or merely insipid (the movie *Dr. Zhivago*).

The hunger for magnitude can be seen on almost every level of the arts in America. The government and private wealth both support huge complexes of arts centers, clusters of palaces of culture. Even anti-establishment artists scratch marks in the earth or mountains on an immense scale.

In elementary school we study the Glory that was Greece and the Grandeur that was Rome, but we ignore the Lighthouse that was Egypt. Nevertheless, the motivations of the older culture are close to our own. The hippies are aware of this connection: they study the esoteric Egypt in Tarot cards, astrology, and the myth of Atlantis. Earthworks artist Walter de Maria planting a forest of lightning rods in the Arizona desert is in touch with the legend that the gold capstones atop the sacred tetrahedrons of Egypt were conductors of the electromagnetic energies of the atmospheric ion belts.

The pyramids were built by a culture that was highly advanced technologically, and possibly pessimistic. Their cultural-artistic energy was directed toward the preservation for the after-death future of samples of themselves. The mummy is the cultural antipode of the tragic Greek hero revealing himself in action.

Our culture now is similarly lighthouse-like, pharaonic, organized around a perception of absolute destructive power and therefore pessimistic. We are interested in a natural-scientific specimen portrayal of our own social subdivisions. Each impresario, each Culture Baron, each wealthy patron or foundation executive, seeks to immortalize his kind of art, about his kind of people, entailing his worldview. The main thrust of museum and cultural center construction, grand opera and some contemporary theater, can be seen as a mummification for posterity of individually curious substantive entities. In this way, rather than seeking to redeem themselves in each other's eyes—which would be an honorable motive—too many patrons of the arts try to erect a bulwark against their own deaths.

This is also how the American culture seeks to regain its forfeited magnitude. Lincoln Center is our Great Pyramid, our Chichén Itzá. At such awesome and somber gathering points we manifest our secret homage to the old beast-goddess of sacrifice, who inaugurated all the arts in the dawn of time, in pomp and magic and ritual and orgasm. What we call "culture" is really religion in the profoundest sense, for it could not have endured as mere diversion. The arts form an illusory façade over our own intimate and incomprehensible racial identity.

And this is why the pharaonic is a dangerous mode.

W. McNeil Lowry, head of the Humanities and Arts division of the Ford Foundation for two decades, denounces the maniacal building of museums and cultural centers as a "temple complex" and potentially disastrous. He blames the motivations towards elitism and power within the establishment.

One can imagine a culture with too many auditoriums and not enough to put in them—and a consequent regression to ritual circuses of the lowest sort.

The very first Metropolitan Opera production in the new opera temple at Lincoln Center actually had a 3,000-pound sphinx on its stage and the Egyptian army—hundreds of them—clambering over it, demonstrating displeasure with the Roman Antony; but the weight of darker Africa in the form of an elephant was too much for the literal situation, and shortly before the performance the revolving stage simply collapsed. With John D. Rockefeller 3rd in the audience, men in sneakers inside the monument had to run it along its golden floor.

John D. Rockefeller 3rd was the man who decided that the time had come for a cultural center in New York. Sir Rudolf Bing says so, and so do members of the Lincoln Center board. But the official histories are much more pluralistic. They tell us that Anthony Bliss kept files on a new opera house as far back as 1917; that NBC chief General David Sarnoff made a speech about the unsanitary and unsafe conditions in the old building; that Bing himself urged the construction of a new Met for twenty years. And of course there is the famous rumor that Carnegie Hall was about to be torn down, displacing the New York Philharmonic, which supposedly precipitated a decision.

From one perspective the curtain rises in the drama with the offer by New York City (that is, Robert Moses, "The Power Broker") of some land along Broadway to the Opera and the Philharmonic. He could get it for them wholesale—that is, with Federal Urban Renewal funds.

Three of the Met's board members, Brigadier General Charles Spofford, Colonel Joseph Hartfield, and Irving Olds (the chairman of U.S. Steel) traveled uptown with Moses and two of Rockefeller's architects, Wallace Harrison and Max Abramovitz (they'd built the United Nations on land he donated) to see what they might be getting. The spot was just a random place along Broadway, Route 9, the Great White Way, situated about a mile north of the glittery, tawdry theater district that had flourished in the earlier part of the century. In the 1950s this plot was a crowded Puerto Rican slum, wedged in between Fifty-ninth Street's Columbus Circle, with the Coliseum and its ever-changing industrial exhibitions, and Needle Park at Seventy-second Street, famous as an exchange point for junkies. "A hell of a neighborhood," commented one of the delegation. But they conferred with another Opera board member, C. D. Jackson, the publisher of *Fortune*, and decided to go ahead with it.

Meanwhile back on Fifth Avenue and Sixty-second Street, a certain dinner at the exclusive Knickerbocker Club had really kicked off the project. Spofford, Harrison, and Moses were the guests of member Arthur Houghton, the Corning Glass zillionaire and then chairman of the Philharmonic. He agreed to put some money in. It was thought that the Philharmonic would soon be needing a new home.

Spofford and Houghton approached John D. Rockefeller 3rd, to spearhead the money and land drive for the two organizations. Not only he, but also his father, gave their word they would put money into the project, and so there were three zillionaire backers.

At this stage, Spofford and Houghton were ready to put their opera and their symphony into one large hall together. Something like a Cinema 1 and Cinema 2. But Rockefeller's vision was grander. Not only would there be separate structures for the two arts organizations, but there would also be an educational facility on the premises. He stipulated that the Lincoln Center be an artistic entity, not just a landlord. And how was the Juilliard School selected for inclusion? David M. Keiser, chairman of that institution, recalls there was "no real opposition" to Rockefeller's decisions on such matters as the inclusion of an educational facility, to that facility's being Juilliard, to Juilliard's being asked to add a drama department financed by Lincoln Center, and to the inclusion of City Center.

At the opposite end of the telescope, Philharmonic conductor Leonard Bernstein says he believes that the inclusion of the Juilliard School in Lincoln Center was the ultimate reason for the Center's existence.

Before the Exploratory Committee for a Musical Arts Center was announced to the public in December 1955 (City Ballet mogul Lincoln Kirstein changed that to Performing Arts but then resigned from the committee because of a "philosophical" dispute), the "Dukes" of New York were already meeting with each other regularly to work out all their difficulties, hastening before public attention should enter and distort everything according to the Indeterminacy Principle.

The official guide to Lincoln Center postulates the existence of "a small group of anonymous Dukes of New York, who serve on most of the boards of most of the city's major public institutions. These Dukes are some of the busiest, most important men in New York, men who know how to move with each other, and, more importantly, how to make others move. They are the men who make time for what they believe in and know how to make that time mean something. What they do is not for the sake of public recognition, but for the challenge, the sense of inner satisfaction, the commitment to public service." Kirstein is less laudatory. He calls them simply "the interlocking directorates of the Opera and Philharmonic." Later the same men were to sit on the board of directors of the Lincoln Center Corporation.

John Rockefeller himself, a fragile, defensive man, has been quoted as endorsing a crony theory of public life. "It's a strange thing, but in all the many things I've seen happen there are always only a half dozen people who truly make it happen—no matter how big the thing is, it's often the same few people who make it happen." Having said which to Ralph Martin, author of *Lincoln Center*, he drafted for his committee yet another member of the Council on Foreign Relations, a clique that has been called more powerful diplomatically than the President of the United States.

"The men Rockefeller wanted," asserts the guidebook, "were the busy men with a record of success and a broad range of contacts."

The Dukes turned to their Prince to be chairman, says the

guidebook quaintly, for they knew John Rockefeller to be a man of "national stature, neutral views, and undisputed strength." Also he used his wealth adroitly, first putting in a half-million dollars as "seed money" and later coming through with tens of millions of dollars more from his family.

"The reports are—and I don't think I'm giving anything away here—that John Rockefeller and his family gave about $50 million. Which is not far from a third (of the total raised)," said Keiser, who, as well as being chairman of Juilliard, is a member of the Lincoln Center board, a former chairman of the Philharmonic, a member of the original New York State Council on the Arts, and the retired president of North American Sugar Industries.

These men met every other week at the Century Club or in Rockefeller's office to sip their soup noisily and masticate their roast beef and listen to John Rockefeller reporting his conclusions on the basis of conversations he'd had with people outside the meeting. "There was a great deal of advice sought by outside experts in the various fields, usually by the chairman," Keiser recalls. One such consultant was George Stoddard, chancellor of NYU, who had such a good idea for nonelitist educational programs that he became chairman of Lincoln Center's education committee.

Rockefeller is said, however, to have vetoed a suggestion by Clarence Francis that Lincoln Center be a national project.

In his office in the bleakly modern Juilliard School, David Keiser, the typical Lincoln Center Duke, is eminently a traditional man. On his walls hang the kind of portraits (of Mrs. Juilliard and Mr. Loeb, the school's patrons) one ordinarily sees only in an Ivy League dining room or men's club. He wears a sober three-piece suit of dark blue with matching blue socks, which he pulls at, in a frequent nervous gesture. And yet there are no antiques for his environment, which has been built in a Holiday Inn international style, and only a handful of books on a long shelf. (One of these, Waldemar Nielsen's *The Big Foundations*, Keiser's assistant Dick Porter only mentions to deplore.)

On hand at these early meetings were Chairman Rockefeller, Spofford, Jackson, and Olds for the Opera; Houghton, Keiser, and Floyd Blair for the Philharmonic; Kirstein for the ballet (till he quit); Harrison for architecture, Robert Blum as liaison to Robert

Moses; and Devereux Josephs and Anthony Bliss ex officio. City Center's Morton Baum served on the board for a few years but was reportedly kicked off for rudeness.

Ground was broken in the middle of the acreage in May 1959, with Eisenhower, Wagner, Hulan Jack, Moses, Rockefeller, and Keiser standing around the shovel, smiling for photographers.

Selected to design the buildings besides Harrison for the Metropolitan Opera and Abramovitz for the Philharmonic, were Philip Johnson for the State Theater (then called the Dance Theater), Eero Saarinen for the Repertory Theater, Gordon Bunshaft for the Library-Museum, Pietro Belluschi for Juilliard, and Jo Mielziner and Edward Matthews consulting. These men posed for the definitive architects' picture in *Look* magazine, standing and kneeling around a waist-high model of the buildings, and with John Rockefeller's pensive head and torso right in the central plaza where the fountain would later spurt. The Lincoln Center historian sees the beginning of the battle for control right here: " . . . several architects felt they were in a kind of tug-of-war," writes Martin, "each man subtly maneuvering for more space, each unconsciously determined to build a monument to himself."

But their battles were upstaged by the arrival of hundreds of construction workers who moved in to build five large theaters of Italian travertine limestone, basilican marble and glass, inlaid with real gold plate, red velvet, and bronze filigree and decorated with sculpture in stone and copper and "Monel Metal."

To pay for the gold-plating of the former slum, the Philadelphia engineering firm of Day and Zimmerman was hired. It worked out costs, estimating that the whole Center would require $75 million. Then a fund-raising apparatus swung into operation under the management of Kersting, Brown & Company, consisting of no less than five thousand fund raisers, easily enough to put a man into the White House.

It seemed like a preposterous sum. Previously, no collective fund-raising efforts for culture had collected even as much as $3 million at one time. But by the time it was complete, less than ten years later, $185 or $168 or $264 (depending on whom one asks) million had been raised from public and private sources. Nelson Rockefeller delivered $15 million of New York State money. And though some thousands of separate individuals and corporations contributed, only two dozen donors, whom Lincoln Center will not name, gave over a million dollars apiece, for a total of more than $100 million. The Rockefeller family may have given half of that, or considerably more than the total donation of all three branches of government. The Ford Foundation provided another $25 million. West Germany, Austria, Italy, and Japan gave gifts.

More than two thirds of all the money raised went into just three of the buildings, the Opera House, Juilliard, and the Philharmonic (now called Avery Fisher Hall), which ended up costing $47 million, $30 million, and $21 million respectively and were completely financed by private contributions. The State Theater and the Library-Museum were paid for almost entirely by public money and cost $19 million and $8 million. Eero Saarinen's Repertory Theater was privately financed at $10 million, and the parking garage and central plaza publicly built ($11 million). The land cost $9 million and was mostly paid for by private donations.

By some chicanery, possibly because of their being different kinds of structures than are usually built, building costs for Lincoln Center as it was being constructed rose only by 23 percent while elsewhere in the city they were going up 38 percent.

And the work transformed the neighborhood, by stimulating construction of more than $700 million worth of new buildings, allegedly increasing yearly tax revenue by $30 million in the surrounding blocks.

With the value of this modest section of slum real estate so vastly increased, the forces that swooped down to get their share included nothing less than all the biggest powers at work in the United States. The former chief of staff of the Armed Forces, General Maxwell D. Taylor, was brought in to mediate in the position of president.

But perhaps the most significant effect of the outlandishly successful fund-raising drive was that it made feasible the establishment of state arts agencies, also dealing in the realm of scores of millions of dollars.

The first power struggle that emerged from the gentlemanly luncheons every other Monday at the Century Club hinged upon the furious opposition of the Metropolitan Opera management to the inclusion in the Lincoln Center of the City Opera. Sir Rudolf Bing, an Austrian with a British knighthood, terribly dedicated to aristocratic manners, thought the opera company from the Masonic Temple on Fifty-fifth Street unbearably low. "We don't just conjure up kings and queens from a musical museum," the City Opera director had said. "We want to produce operas that democratize people." Its admission charges were only half of the Met's.

City Center is one of twenty-five New York City cultural institutions supported to a significant degree by the city government. From 1961 to 1965, City Center disputed the matter of control over the $19.3 million State Theater (built with funds allocated by Nelson Rockefeller's New York State administration) while Lincoln Center for the Performing Arts, Inc., was a privately supported institution.

City Center had originally been conceived in 1943 by Mayor Fiorello La Guardia, City Council president Newbold Morris, City Center finance chairman Judge Francis J. Bloustein, and tax expert Morton Baum, inspired by Roosevelt's Works Progress Administration, to provide "cultural entertainment for the masses at low prices." Properly speaking, it is a conglomerate of arts institutions, the oldest of its kind in the United States. In the 1940s, tickets cost no more than $2. Now the ceiling price is up to $10, but this is still lower than the other first-class theaters in town.

Bing argued with Morton Baum, City Center's president in 1961, that people would confuse the two opera companies and that there was nothing more important for an opera company than its distinct image.

But surely there was animosity involved, for New York's music critics had been of late pointing out that the musical level of the City Opera, the less expensive and pretentious operation, was actually higher than that of the Met. "City Opera plays a part in the cultural life of New York, the Met only in its social life," wrote Harold Schonberg. And one season Bing actually had to cancel his production of *Manon* because the City Opera's *Manon* was being hailed as "the best thing that's ever happened to opera in New York."

In the winter of 1964–65 this disagreement came to a head. William Schuman, president of Lincoln Center, wrote a statement officially offering the City Center thirty weeks of time in the State Theater. This was not acceptable to the late Morton Baum. For four months he conducted intensive negotiations with the Rockefeller brothers John and Nelson, with Mayor Robert Wagner, and with other officials. The papers reported that these talks sometimes erupted into acrimony and left feelings abraded. Baum was fighting for total control of the building for his group, for complete physical possession.

City Opera's Julius Rudel and City Ballet's George Balanchine, both supported by City Center, stayed aloof, though the choreographer's disposition was the key factor in the battle. In loyalty to City Center, Balanchine was reportedly ready to quit Lincoln Center entirely. This worried the Lincoln Center board. They wanted Balanchine's Ballet unquestionably, though not necessarily the City Opera; they were maneuvering for control of the New York State Theater with a two-headed City Center.

City Center's Baum and general manager Betty Cage fought tenaciously for a contract that would include their two organizations in Lincoln Center on favorable terms. Lincoln Kirstein says the attempts to contravene the rights of City Center were "highhanded" and "brutal." Bing remembers Baum as a man who knew what he wanted and how to get it. Keiser, a member of the Lincoln Center board, remembers that the whole City Center question was solved "in one long afternoon meeting, with all sorts of—I mean a lot of—people sitting around," but he doesn't remember what the haggling was about.

In January of 1965 it was announced that the four-year dispute over control of the State Theater had been settled in City Center's favor. And City Center, through its components the New York City Ballet and the New York City Opera, became a full constituent of Lincoln Center. In 1963 the Ford Foundation had put in its two cents—granting $3.1 million to City Center for expansion of its activities at Lincoln Center which was paid out only in 1965 when City Center secured a 50-year lease on the State Theater.

Everyone agrees that it was the Rockefeller brothers who settled the matter. Nelson had the clout of tens of millions of dollars of New York State money in use for the building of the Dance Theater for his personal favorite, George Balanchine. Kirstein, in a chronicle of the City Ballet, recalls that Nelson turned the theater over upon its completion with a cheerful "It's all yours, George!" In the official Lincoln Center guidebook "the decree" that City Ballet could not be let in and its sister company City Opera kept out is credited to "New York State." Rudolf Bing thinks it was John Rockefeller who squared off against him.

At any rate, City Center won, establishing for itself a unique condition of membership. Alone of the Lincoln Center theaters, the State Theater real estate is owned by New York City and rented to Lincoln Center, which then sublets it to City Center. (The city also owns the Library-Museum of the Performing Arts and maintains the plazas and garage. Lincoln Center, Incorporated, owns everything else and supplies its tenants with air conditioning, steam, water, electricity, and security forces.)

Morton Baum died soon afterward. And Bing admitted he had been wrong. "It hasn't seemed to have done any harm," he said recently. "The two operas are very cozy."

So that is how City Center won the first Battle for Control of Lincoln Center, sweeping north with its legions from Fifty-fifth Street and installing itself with pomp and abundant special privileges in the State Dance Theater. As with many battles, the territory itself was hardly worth it—Philip Johnson's building is not attractive in my opinion—but the real prize was the feather in the hat, the prestige of City Center's full membership in Lincoln Center. Further, no one can sneeze at the financial boon of receiving a second free home. The City Opera could now with impunity be a permanent thorn in the side of the Metropolitan Opera—though Bing, choking on the memory of his old animosity for Beverly Sills, recently "borrowed" for a performance by the Met, claims the two operas have gotten along nicely. And the City Center's policy of low-as-possible ticket prices can permanently rankle the big producers and promoters who want to wring more than that out of the Dance Theater. A victory for the long shadows, perhaps, of the Work Progress Administration and Fiorello La Guardia.

And so it turned out that the Rockefellers' *de facto* power was greater than that of the ex-chief of staff, in whose name City Center had first been given control over the New York State Theater. General Maxwell Taylor served as president of the Center for only a few months in 1961. His successor, William Schuman, the president of Juilliard and a classical composer, was accused in *The New Yorker* of conflict of interest because his own works were being produced at the State Theater by Richard Rodgers at higher admissions than the City Opera wanted to charge. He was not partial to City Center; he wanted the City Ballet out of the State Theater for five and a half months each year, and he brought in the expensive Royal Danish Ballet instead. Schuman finally gave up in 1968, three years after Baum's victory, realizing that he couldn't fight any more for control.

The new chairman of the Lincoln Center board, Amyas Ames, bent over backward to make City Center feel at home. Only three years later, when the Repertory Theater was having trouble supporting itself, he asked City Center's new head, Richard Clurman, if the Center wanted to remodel the Rep's operation also.

Amyas Ames is a vintage American colonial with the conviction that art is a political issue. He is the only man to serve as chairman of the board of Lincoln Center besides John D. Rockefeller 3rd, and he currently holds that post as well as the chairmanship of the New York Philharmonic.

Ames was born in 1906 and elected to the Signet Club while at Harvard. His forebears include a Governor of Massachusetts, the only Republican governor of Mississippi, and the head of the biology department at Harvard University. His wife, the former Evelyn Ingeborg Perkins, is the daughter of the head of the physics department at Trinity College. They have four children.

The Lincoln Center chairman lives on upper Park Avenue in the winter and on Martha's Vineyard in the summer, where he photographs wild flowers. He is six feet one inch, weighs about 185 pounds, and walks at least four miles five days a week. He was at one time a Republican National Committeeman from Long Island and calls himself an "interdenominationalist."

Formerly chairman of the executive committee of Kidder, Peabody and Company, Inc., Ames served two terms as a governor of the New York Stock Exchange. He has held high positions with the Carnegie Corporation, Harvard University, Rockefeller Center, the Environmental Defense Fund, the Joint Committee on Education, and the Investment Bankers Association of America.

As a founder of the lobbying group Concerned Citizens for the Arts, Ames was responsible for the New York Legislature's significant increase in the amount of its appropriation to the State Council on the Arts. He is also active in the Partnership for the Arts, which lobbies nationally. Describing his career, Ames has said, "I wanted to help tie the performing arts into political devel-

Amyas Ames, chairman of the board of directors, Lincoln Center for the Performing Arts (Michael C. Burke)

opments." On television recently, he contrasted "rectangular buildings, smog, war, and other difficult things" with "the human hunger" and reiterated that art is the political issue of this decade.

He has likened the development of Lincoln Center to a space project: "It requires an enormous thrust to get the rocket in orbit, and once it's there you have to worry about its direction." (Not, strictly speaking, astrophysically accurate.) His most felicitous achievement while president of the New York Philharmonic Society was the inauguration of concerts in New York City parks, an idea of Carlos Moseley's that Ames put into effect. It is estimated that 100,000 people turn out for these free Philharmonic concerts each summer.

Another big tumult in Lincoln Center arose over the Repertory Theater, which alone of the constituents has undergone three complete changes of management within a decade. Its first artistic directors, Alfred Whitehead and Elia Kazan, were veterans of the Group Theater and the old left of the 1930s. Kazan had named names to the House Un-American Activities Committee in 1952. So they had enemies on the right and on the left. Their first work for the Lincoln Center repertory, staged in a specially built Washington Square theater, was not well received. Critic Richard Gilman called them and their board "the cultural old guard," "businessmen," and "counterrevolutionaries." He blasted their "timidity and bad taste." Whitehead's friend, critic Harold Clurman, maintained that the aesthetic complaints were merely a smoke screen for political disagreement. He claimed that Whitehead had made enemies "because he had literally forced the board's hand in building the ANTA-Washington Square Theater, an action to which the most powerful member of the board was unalterably opposed." Clurman did not identify "the most powerful member of the (Rep Theater) board," but others have confirmed that this would most likely describe George Woods, then chairman of the theater board, who allegedly "lowered the boom" on Whitehead and forced him to resign. Probably Woods' power exceeded that of the late Mrs. Vivian Beaumont Allen, who contributed $3 million to the cost of the theater and specified that she didn't want any of Tennessee Williams' "dirty plays" put on there.

After Woods left to head the World Bank, the new Rep chairman, Robert Hoguet (another banker), invited two San Francisco theater rebels to be the artistic directors—Jules Irving and Herbert Blau—possibly describable as members of the new left. They came amid fanfare from Richard Gilman. From 1965 to 1967 they tried out in New York what had worked in California; but the critics hated it, the audiences didn't come, and their board grew increasingly unhappy. So Lincoln Center board member Hoguet and president William Schuman tried to steal one of Rudolf Bing's versatile minions, one Herman Krawitz, to come to the Rep Theater and salvage the situation. All hell broke loose. Bing, in Philadelphia, threatened to quit, calling it a "raid" (somehow Hoguet and Schuman had failed to notify him). Krawitz loyally declined the transfer.

In the summer of 1967 the tentacles of Broadway reached up to help, and the Rep Theater hosted the work of producers David Merrick and Arnold Saint-Subber, director Mike Nichols, playwright Lillian Hellman, and actor Peter Ustinov. Critics complained that the alternative idea of the Rep Theater was being undermined.

Ordinarily, Lincoln Center, Inc., runs a corporate fund drive each year and distributes money to its constituents according to the size of their buildings, thus perpetuating the balance among the different arts that was established at the Center's inception in the Knickerbocker and Century clubs. The Rep Theater, with only a $10 million building, was always the poor relation. But now, having gone through two sets of artistic managements and still having trouble accomplishing what its board wanted, the Rep Theater discovered, in 1969, that its share of the Lincoln Center Fund had been cut back even further. Board member David Keiser acknowledges this to be a degree of interference, adding coyly that *otherwise*, constituents are *not really* interfered with artistically or financially.

It was at this point that Amyas Ames stepped in, with an invitation to Richard Clurman's City Center (now snugly ensconced in the State Theater) to build a cinemathèque in the Rep Theater building, thus establishing a permanent film center in Lincoln Center and giving a home to the already existing Film Society.

Supporters of the Rep Theater took it hard. One Rooseveltian liberal, Dore Schary (author of *Sunrise at Campobello*), formed a Committee to Save Theater at Lincoln Center. Critic Stanley Kauffmann called Schary's group "knee jerk Culture defenders." Clive Barnes saw the whole situation as one of "fractious committees and feuding institutions."

The City Council failed to approve the scheme.

☆   ☆   ☆

After Morton Baum's death the leadership of City Center had fallen to Richard M. Clurman, chief of *Time-Life* correspondents, chairman of the board of *Time-Life* Broadcasting, best friends with *Newsweek* editor Osborne Elliott, and later to be Lindsay's Parks, Recreation and Cultural Affairs commissioner.

Kirstein describes Clurman as having "no special interest in opera or ballet; opera was something of a blank book; ballet, he might guess, was about dancing. He liked games, however—those performed publicly and others conducted otherwise." But despite collusion between Clurman and Amyas Ames, City Center failed to win the second major Battle for Control of Lincoln Center.

Richard M. Clurman, former president, City Center of Music and Drama; member of the board of trustees, Lincoln Center for the Performing Arts

Richard Clurman deserves attention. Though he no longer holds either the city office or the chairmanship of the arts conglomerate, his influence on the cultural affairs of New York has been sizable. He has been described as a "game player." Sitting in Clurman's office high above Fiftieth Street, I am surrounded by more examples of culture technology than I have previously encountered in the offices of Culture Barons: a television, two multiple push-button telephones, three auditorium-sized flags, an old *Time* cover of the Kennedys by Bernard Saffron, the Robert Indiana poster of City Center, a manual Royal typewriter, plus such oddments as an abacus and several wooden elephants. From here one has a view of the Hudson but a much clearer bead on the neon sign of the Hotel Taft.

Clurman is wearing a conservative three-piece navy suit and a supercomplicated wristwatch.

He tells me that his city office was an appointment of Mayor John Lindsay's and that he went out with the Lindsay Administration. However, he is very ticklish on the subject of his political affiliation. "I have been for most of my professional life, and though I no longer am, I still consider myself: a journalist. I regard journalism as a priesthood, and I considered myself a full-time professional spectator. So I have never enrolled in either the Democratic or the Republican party."

He concedes that in Presidential elections he has never voted for anyone but a Democrat. And that he is "generally considered to be a member of the Northeast Liberal Press Establishment—in the Spiro Agnew sense of the word." It seemed to me that he had the honesty of a journalist—many of whom are of course frustrated politicians.

How a journalist became involved in the cultural life of New York is a rather funny story. It was a "sheer accident and a bolt from nowhere." Clurman relates that he had friends from all over the political map, and that one day Mayor Lindsay just called him —at "that watershed event," the 1968 Democratic convention in Chicago—to say that he and the Ford Foundation were looking for a chairman for City Center.

At first Clurman thought he was being asked to recommend someone else; then he thought they'd meant to call his uncle, Harold Clurman, the theater critic, instead of him. Lindsay assured him he'd called the right Clurman.

It seemed that the Mayor and the Foundation were not looking for someone who could support the arts, or someone retired with a lot of time, but rather for someone "who is effective in his field and who could be interested in this subject."

Whereupon Clurman replied, "That is such a nutty idea that I will treat it with more respect than it deserves." And thus began Clurman's heavy involvement in culture. After becoming chairman of City Center in 1969, he soon found himself on the board of the School of American Ballet and president of the New York Foundation for the Arts. Previously, he says, he had "never even been in the P.T.A."

Clurman defines City Center for me as Mayor Lindsay defined it for him. City Center is not just an old building on West Fifty-fifth Street. The formal name of the organization is the City Center of Music and Drama, Inc. Actually, it's a performing arts conglomerate that has two theaters, he says: the State Theater at

Lincoln Center, where its two principal companies, the N.Y.C. Ballet and the N.Y.C. Opera, perform, and the old original City Center theater on Fifty-fifth. In addition to this, with a different relationship, there is the Alvin Ailey City Center Company, the City Center Joffrey Ballet, the City Center Acting Company, the City Center Children's Theater, and the City Center Cinemathèque. The N.Y.C. Ballet Company and the N.Y.C. Opera Company were started by City Center and are therefore wholly owned by City Center; the board of City Center is the board of those two companies. The Alvin Ailey Company was brought into City Center, but it has its own board and raises its own funds, though it is also subsidized by City Center. The Joffrey has the same relationship as the Ailey: they are, in business terms, "affiliated constituents."

While Clurman was chairman, from 1969 to 1975, City Center grew from an operation that had $6 million of expenses a year to one with $20 million a year. And it is, he contends, "by reckoning of people, company, and expenditures, the largest performing arts organization in the country."

When City Center floundered temporarily, Ford Foundation "came in and took over for us," Clurman said, referring to Ford's $6.2 million grant in 1974 (though Ford had been funding the City Ballet heavily since 1963 and the City Opera since 1957).

Clurman is proud that between 70 and 80 percent of City Center's income is earned at the box office, "which is an extremely high percentage for a performing arts interest." However, this still leaves them with about $5 million a year to be raised. They solicit help from individuals, foundations, and governments. City Center is the largest recipient of government funds of any performing arts organization in the country, Clurman reported, receiving even more than the Metropolitan Opera. The government funds are mainly from New York State and the Federal government. They receive from the city, for the maintenance of the State Theater, $300,000 a year. "This was in the legislation," Clurman hastens to point out. But the main way New York City supports City Center, as the city supports a number of other cultural institutions, is to let them use two major theaters rent-free.

Clurman declines to summarize "the long and bloody battle" that went on when the late Morton Baum set out to secure these special privileges for City Center. "I was in no way involved in it. I didn't even know Morton Baum as a matter of fact. . . ."

But in general, Clurman's view of the fracas between the former head of City Center and the Rockefellers and others representing Lincoln Center is as follows: "Lincoln Center in its original conception was to be a parent cultural organization, not just a collection of independent constituents and a real estate establishment. That is, there was a vision that Lincoln Center would be the cultural organization. And the argument revolved around whether the N.Y.C. Ballet . . . they wanted the N.Y.C. Ballet, they didn't want the Opera. Also they didn't want the New York—they didn't want City Center to have control of the theater. It involved a very ugly, long struggle, which Morton Baum finally won."

"How did Baum persuade the two Rockefellers?" I asked.

Clurman answers that Baum was able to entice Lincoln Center with the N.Y.C. Ballet. "Take us all," he said in effect, "or you won't get Balanchine."

"Was the N.Y.C. Ballet Company so loyal to City Center that they were really ready not to move to Lincoln Center? Or was that just a power maneuver?" I ask.

Clurman answers with a big smile, though speaking in a serious tone of voice: "No, they were not going to move to Lincoln Center on the terms that were originally suggested."

In response to a question he feels is overly tendentious, on the subject of the Rockefellers' role at Lincoln Center, Clurman (who was a member of the Lincoln Center board and of its executive committee for six years) describes the separate roles of the Rockefeller brothers at Lincoln Center.

"There is no doubt that the principal person responsible for the building of Lincoln Center is John D. Rockefeller," he says. "Without John D. Rockefeller, without his dedication to it, without his backing of it, without his sticking to it, Lincoln Center would not have been built. Any more than Rockefeller Center would have been built. So I would say he gets the principal credit, indisputably, for having built Lincoln Center.

"As for relations with City Center, or more specifically the N.Y.C. Ballet, that was Nelson Rockefeller. His New York State Administration built the State Theater. And he was very close to Lincoln Kirstein as well as to George Balanchine.

"The argument was not with Nelson, it was entirely with John.

"But it's over! And in fact when I became—and with many scars as a result of it—when I became chairman of the board of City Center I went to John Rockefeller and said, 'This argument has been over for two or three years. *I am brand new.* I was in no way involved in it. And I think all of us should now forget about that old battle, since it's been concluded, and get on with it.' And as a matter of fact, since then there has been an entirely collaborative relationship between City Center and Lincoln Center. Entirely. No strain at all."

Having completed which emotional recounting, Clurman briefly argued for city support of Lincoln Center, through public responsibility for guards, heating, and lighting.

Clurman—and the same will be so for the City Center chairman who will follow him—is involved in the artistic decisions of the constituent companies only as a voice, not in an official capacity. He cites a "rather unique" clause in the City Center bylaws which states that no member of the board of directors, including the chairman, may have any direct influence over the artistic decisions, other than the hiring and firing of artistic directors. "We can express our views. But our artistic directors are not required to take our views seriously." However, he admits it is a complex matter, since the board does hire and fire and does control the budget.

Though his predecessor Morton Baum ran City Center in true impresario style, Clurman does not consider himself in any way to be such a figure. He is simply chief executive officer—there is also a chief operating officer—and works in "a very close relationship, entirely collaborative" with Amyas Ames, the current chairman of Lincoln Center.

The hottest issue in his six-year tenure with City Center was the controversy over the cinemathèque in the Rep Theater in 1971, for which Clurman says, "I was responsible."

"One of the things that I felt that Lincoln Center and the city and City Center as well were missing was that film had not really been considered an art. That is, there was no provision for it at Lincoln Center. City Center, which had a lot of activities, didn't have any film ingredient. So we were looking around for a film ingredient. We'd started, and we'd got in touch with Henri Langlois—of the original Cinemathèque in Paris—and Langlois and we had entered into a partnership to create an American cinemathèque, drawing on his films. We'd actually started to build it in the basement of our old Fifty-fifth Street house. And we had raised about half a million dollars to do that. At that time by sheer coincidence—ever since Lincoln Center had opened they'd had great trouble with the Rep Theater, and there was great trouble with it then. The Repertory Company was failing, and the Theater was about to go dark. And we were building a film theater in our own basement.

"Being aware of that, City Center was invited to take a look at the Rep Theater, since we needed more theatrical space, and see if there was any way in which we could take responsibility for it. We looked at it, looked at it very carefully, and decided that there was no way economically to—for that building, although it was the most beautiful building exterior at Lincoln Center—there was no way economically—that it was the most expensive theater per seat to maintain in the world. And it had cavernous empty spaces in it. There's a backstage area that's about one hundred yards long! So at our expense and with the complete endorsement of Lincoln Center, we retained architects to redesign the inside of the theater, leaving the eleven-hundred-seat Beaumont part of it intact, and building a cinemathèque, a film theater, in it, and moving the Forum, which was not used at all then by the way, to another part of the building. And also adding on top office space and whatnot.

"This scheme would have cost six million dollars. And in fact the city was prepared to have the Rep Theater—Lincoln Center was going to turn the Rep Theater over to the city, the city in turn was going to lease it back to City Center for a dollar a year and give us six million dollars to reconstruct the theater and have it be a drama and film center at Lincoln Center.

"A great uproar developed over that. The uproar in my view was preposterous, because it involved suddenly a love affair with 'what a wonderful theater it was,' and—"

Was that Dore Schary's Committee to Save Theater at Lincoln Center?

"Right. And also there was a great deal of animus against having films. Having all those dirty people smoking marijuana watching films! It got to be a very noisy battle. And I made a great mistake: I would call it the 'Liberal Fallacy.' The mistake was that the scheme was so patently good and in the public interest that I couldn't see any way for a kind of empty hysteria to defeat it. So it went along splendidly; it was about to be passed, it was about to be done—"

Passed by whom?

"By the City Council. They were about to appropriate— It had already gone through the whole mechanism; in fact, this is unheard of in city procedures. The final *pro forma* vote before the City Council. I organized no claque, because it seemed to me such a good scheme that everyone was for it except this noisy opposition to it.

"At the very last minute, literally when the City Council was about to vote it—the premise was that the theater was going to go dark and it had to be saved—at the very last minute the people from the Repertory Theater company stood up and said 'Nonsense! We are a sound organization. Why are you taking our theater away from us?' Now, that was a total turnabout, and alas, to speak plainly, it was just a lie. That is, they were about to go out of business; they did, some months later, go out of business, but because they said it was a grab on our part to take the theater away from them, rather than the fact that they were going to go out of business, we had to say 'What? We're not reaching for anything,' and it never happened."

Was Jules Irving the artistic director of the Repertory Theater at that point?

"Yes, and Robert Hoguet was chairman. And other people had come in. But what happened at the final meeting was that those people stood up, without telling either Lincoln Center or City Center, and said, 'We're perfectly healthy.' So the city councilmen said, 'Well, we have no right to take the theater away from you, and why should we put city money into it if you can keep it going.' Some months later it went out of business, as you know. A very bad piece of work.

"I hold myself responsible for having made that mistake, because if I hadn't committed the Liberal Fallacy and I'd known then more about how politics work (which I know a bit more about now), I would have organized for it."

You say it had gone through the whole procedure already. What steps had it gone through?

"First of all, Lincoln Center had to want us to do it; Lincoln

Center wanted us to do it. Secondly, we had to draw up preliminary plans; we drew up preliminary plans. Thirdly, we had to get
the endorsement of the Mayor, to invest the six million; we had
the endorsement of the Mayor. Fourthly, it had to go before the
City Planning Commission; the City Planning Commission passed
it. Most consequentially, it had to be passed by the Board of Estimate; it was passed by the Board of Estimate. In the city procedure, when something has gone that far, the City Council, I don't
think ever since LaGuardia's day, has ever turned down anything
that's gone that far. But because of the strange circumstances at
the meeting I describe to you, it was aborted."

☆   ☆   ☆

Richard Clurman is a good guy, the kind of man who drips
journalism and lights up when he reminisces about a college
newspaper. He was one of the people who fought to bring WNCN
back to New York as a classical music station, and succeeded.
Always bipartisan, he worked for the Republican Lindsay in the
city government and then Democrat Carey in the state as chairman of a task force on arts and culture which completed its work
in April 1975.

His favorite philosophical homily comes from an unnamed
Greek: "Happiness is the exercise of vital powers along lines of
excellence, giving them scope." He adds, though by this time it
isn't necessary: "I work a lot."

☆   ☆   ☆

But the battles of Lincoln Center are not yet over. Even as
this book was being written, a new skirmish was shaping up over
Avery Fisher Hall, which was being entirely remodeled. Furthermore, the parent body, Lincoln Center, was "helping" younger
brother City Center reorganize its management. Beneath such apparent harmonious intermingling, what subtle power ploys?

OPERA:
A Legacy to the Met

. . . and he was just so boring and persistent she agreed to marry him. . . .

—A clubman

WHO is the enemy? (as the Chinese say). Tom Wolfe identified the enemy correctly when he cited them as blue-jowled, wearing rep tie, belonging to Brook Club, having Junker sentiments (they were the reactionary political party of Prussian aristocracy fighting to maintain their privileges), members of the Grand Jury Association, with incomes around $35,000, worth around $300,000, living on the Upper East Side of New York City in a Park Avenue co-op. These are the hard core.

The soft core enemy would then be (to paraphrase Wolfe again): the women with Miss Porter face and Mary Astor voice, Junior Leaguers who graduate to the Ungaro Boutique—and the men with Eaton Square combed-back hair, who eat dinner at the New Haven lawn club and went to Yale.

☆   ☆   ☆

Opera emerged as a distinct form shortly before 1600 in the Médicis' Florence. A group of noblemen called *"Camerata"* began meeting for the purpose of reviving Greek tragedy. The father of the scientist Galileo was among them. He made a case for

43

the simplicity of sound as against the earlier polyphony. This became known as the New Music movement and spread to Rome and to the Republic of Venice, where the first public opera was established in 1637. Private opera existed for kings and princes and their guests by that time also in Vienna, Munich, and Paris. Claudio Monteverdi's *La Favola d'Orfea* was the first opera in the modern sense of the word, financed by the Duke of Mantua, in whose court Monteverdi was a diplomat. Later, Naples came to dominate European opera. Sopranos took the melody lead away from tenors by way of the Huguenot Reformation in sixteenth-century France, but the Italians counter-reformed by putting *castrati* in as leads.

In seventeenth-century France, Corneille and Racine wrote tragedies and Molière wrote comedies, and all were patronized by the absolutist king Louis XIV because they wrote pleasantly rather than with difficult social messages.

Musical changes symbolized social changes. With the coming of the age of modern democracy at the end of the eighteenth century, claviers, the predecessors of the piano, began to be tuned to equidistant notes for the first time. Perhaps the addition of valves to the brass instruments in the nineteenth century heralded the division of imperialism into nationalities. Opera of the nineteenth century on the whole became folky, mystical, and nationalistic.

Opera has survived since then in the West without overwhelming popular support. In the 1880s, Brazilian rubber barons built an opera house deep in the Amazon and imported the finest European stars to sing for a handful of people. Since the dawning of the bourgeois age some hundred years ago, opera has been a plaything of the upper and upper middle classes, a counter in their wars for status and prestige.

The first Metropolitan Opera House was built in the United States on Fourteenth Street (the present Academy of Music) by such families as Lorillard, Traverse, Belmont, Stebbins, Gandy, and Barlow, all of whom got together in the Union League Club. But the families who had acquired their wealth during the Civil War and were therefore the "newly" rich—Vanderbilt, Astor, Morgan, Roosevelt, Goelet, Iselin, Huntington, Gould—were jealous of the social privileges the others had at the opera, and so they built, twenty-five blocks farther uptown, a new Metropolitan

Opera House on Thirty-ninth Street. This was done, legend has it, on the strength of an insult. Then for some decades the wealthiest people in the country supported it: Otto Kahn, affiliated with the banking house of Kuhn Loeb, did the job almost single-handedly in the 1930s. Then Texaco came in, and Eastern Airlines; also *Readers Digest*'s De Witt Wallace; Corning Glass's Houghton; Belmont, Sloan, and of course Rockefeller.

Now Lincoln Center has been built exactly the same number of blocks farther uptown, at Sixty-fourth Street. Some see the private tax-exempt culture corporation as a move by the third generation of Rockefellers to take culture control away from the previous dynasties of the American ruling class, with the new Opera House symbolizing the era of Vietnam War wealth.

Ah, the opera! (Or in Italy, the oh-pay-*rrhha!*) So lovely, and so . . . anachronistic. To contemplate a knighted Austrian presiding over the fortunes of one thousand folk all housed in one great palace, and to consider his importation of selected, highly evolved specimens of European culture for the delectation of the metropolis no less than the junior leagues of the New World hinterlands, and to remember that some of America's most wonderfully Right Wing millionaires support all this endeavoring—is to recall, by the mystique, that loose confederation that bound together the lords and lieges of central Europe throughout those many misty Catholic centuries, and made a culture out of Catholic ceremony, united in spiritual dominion and affinity where mere secular interests raged in war below. Sir Rudolf Bing forgot one time that opera was not really the same thing as Catholicism, when he suggested a High Mass kick off the culture festival in Protestant Edinburgh. But the Methodists have had their revenge: they started Chautauqua and *Playboy* magazine.

Sir Rudolf Bing was the soul of a degenerate grand opera, an opera whose performers cheated the United States on their income tax, an opera that nostalgically venerated the eighteenth and nineteenth centuries in Italy and Germany to the exclusion of all other culture, an opera that was the social currency of the very rich.

Sir Rudolf Bing, former general manager, Metropolitan Opera Association

Now that Bing has been ousted—to the delight of his enemies—his memory still lingers over the Metropolitan like a
twenty-year ghost that won't give up. His legacy seems to have
been artistic uncertainty, managerial tumult, financial crisis. And
the real man, Bing himself, can still be heard calling from a dis-
tance at his successors, still sure he knows how to do it best.

I look at the pale burnt-orange brick structure with its elegant
slices of columns and sets of round-arched windows, its lacy fire
escape in a graceful slope. Carnegie Hall has a perceptible romantic mystique, and clustered around it, a permanent world's fair:
the Nippon Club, the Zen Oriental Book Store, the China Pavil-
ion, the Russian Tea Room.

Across the street from this building, in the Columbia Artists
Management building, built of parody-brick, we now find Sir Ru-

dolf Bing, for more than two decades the reigning demon of the Metropolitan Opera, now just another tragi-comic has-been.

The most striking thing about Sir Rudolf Bing (he pronounces his name quickly, but with more attention to the vowels than they are usually given in English, something like "Seerh Ryeuedowlph Beeenque") is his instinctive dedication to the aristocratic values: the stately, the classical, the graceful, the elegant, the dignified.

(During Bing's first season at the Met, Alfred Lunt, in eighteenth-century costume, lit candles under a monogrammed false proscenium for Mozart's *Cosi Fan Tutti,* and in his memoirs Bing recalled that Lunt's "grace and carriage and understanding of courtly style set the mood for the entire performance to come" and made *Cosi* the hit of the season.)

Bing was the son of the head of an Austro-Hungarian steel and iron trust that went down with the monarchy, a frequenter of the Viennese intellectual salons of the 1910s, and an opera worker for forty-eight years. Recalling his twenty-two years as general manager of the Metropolitan Opera, Sir Rudolf remarks that his relations with everyone "have always been correct."

He also admits to running the Opera as "a militant democracy, in which one man ruled." His mere presence in the boxes at the start of an opera was enough to tighten the performance, so he came every night. Observers say the house "ticked like an intricate Swiss watch" under Bing's tyrannical management.

(Another time, also in his first season, Robert Merrill left the Met for a part in a Hollywood movie. Bing refused to let the singer return without a formal written apology. Nor did he try to justify his attitude, calling it merely "a principle without which there could be no hope of first-class opera productions ever.")

The Met's press chief, Francis Robinson, acknowledges Bing's achievements: he quadrupled the Opera's subscription list, doubled the season, and gave many great shows. But Robinson adds a kicker: "Bing hated people." Robinson overstates the case, but Bing's autocratic methods were well known.

Bing in his prime was a pointed and beautiful man, tall and thin and centered like some kind of sylvan faerie. In photos next to plump sopranos or stolidly opaque bankers, he looks imposingly fragile. Only occasionally, standing by John V. Lindsay, or seated across from the Earl of Harewood, cousin to Queen Eliza-

beth and administrator of the grand opera of London and Edinburgh, did he seem to have found his true society. In a photo next
to Jacqueline Kennedy Onassis, his presence seems only tempo-
rary; one imagines him off on the nonce to Hamburg or Vienna,
Milan or Paris, cocking an elfin ear at the relative perfection of
voices there, to steal the divinest for offering up to the ultimate
audience in New York City.

One of Bing's controversial imports was Herbert von Karajan,
of Salzburg, Austria, whom he invited here to conduct Wagner's
Siegfried. Karajan was attacked in the United States for having had
Nazi sympathies; the designer he brought with him spoke only
German; Bing was accused of "trying to establish an American-
Austrian axis." Bing steadfastly maintained that his stars' politics
were as irrelevant as their sex lives; however, his retirement occurred shortly after the Karajan brouhaha. On several levels there
seemed to be something funny going on. Eastern Airlines, whose
head is known for right-wing political sympathies, was the sole
backer of the Wagnerian "Ring Cycle" of which *Siegfried* is a part.
One of the characters in that work is Wotan, the god of wisdom,
poetry, war, valor, and death, and to whom the ancient Teutons offered human sacrifices. ("Who's Wotan?" asked the man in the
lighting booth during a rehearsal as Karajan was trying to increase
the wattage on him.)

Emblematic of Karajan's shenanigans or of grand opera itself:
When the Austrian conductor came to the Met, he caused them to
install several thousand dollars' worth of more powerful bulbs
than are ordinarily used in the United States; then he projected
the light through almost opaque slides, smothering it "for a more
complex effect." Even Bing thought that was crazy.

In the course of his career as general manager, Bing fired
thirty-nine singers and hounded Maria Callas about her weight
until she lost fifty pounds. New York critic Clive Barnes called
him "adept at handling patrons and subscribers, but not a conductor nor has he a marked music sensibility. He is a public relations
man and a businessman, with an unquestionable profound interest
in music."

Bing handled public relations with the finesse of a courtier.
Abstractions about conduct mattered less to him than the eccen-
tricities of the people he dealt with. One star had to travel with his
dog, so Bing negotiated with the owner of Eastern Airlines about

the dog's air-passage. A second star feigned illness; he called the malingerer's bluff. Maria Callas refused to work because of something a rival singer had said about her. With a touch of self-mockery, Bing describes how he placated her with a contract and "my very best version of the kiss-the-hand routine." Later he fired her because she refused to go on tour.

And still another time, Bing offered to take a second-act aria in *The Magic Flute* down a whole tone for Callas—even though, as a youth, it had shocked and disgusted him when he thought people were trying to improve on Beethoven or Dostoevski.

He tried so hard to please his European talent that nearly all of them had their tax returns prepared for years by an accountant who subsequently went to prison for violating tax laws. They would call their wives managers, their poodles secretaries, Bing a dependent (this may have been a joke); and would show a loss after a ten-week season in which they'd taken in $100,000.

Though he hired and fired everyone on the Metropolitan's thousand-person staff, chose the work and the cast, and made sure that realization of an average of five productions a year was possible, Bing was also concerned with the unnecessary discomfort of an elevator man (so he ordered a stool). He recalls that he pioneered in the breaking of the traditional color bar.

The former general manager's taste in aesthetic matters was resoundingly conservative though his politics was liberal all his life, he says. An Austrian Catholic with a British citizenship and knighthood and a preference for Russian novels, he favored Italian opera. Second after that, he produced German works, with an occasional French and a very rare English or American.

People don't want to go to modern opera, he frequently claimed, because "we love what we know. We go to *Traviata, La Boheme,* over and over again. There are not too many masterpieces of modern opera. . . ." Asked for some, he mentions *Wozzeck, Peter Grimes, Rake's Progress,* which he personally dislikes though praising Stravinsky, and possibly Sam Barber. "But mainly people want to see Mozart, Richard Strauss, Puccini, Verdi, of course Wagner." Another time he suggests essentially the same list: "Wagner, Mozart, Verdi, Puccini, Bizet." "Genius is the only thing that survives in this rare art," he declared. And he argued that the important soloists would not perform modern opera.

"You can't get a Tebaldi or a Callas or a Nilsson or a Corelli or a Tucker to sing contemporary opera," he asserted. And to a composer he wrote that, given the recurrent financial crisis of the house, "it would be utterly mad and indeed unjustified if the management was contemplating spending a great deal of money on the production of an opera which, however good or interesting, will most likely not be a box office success."

Bing frequently mentioned Hamburg, where, with state support and press acclaim, modern operas are performed—to an empty house.

He was most roundly criticized for this total avoidance of modern opera. Writing in *The New Yorker*, David Hamilton excoriated the Met's audience as fifty years behind the times, "because Americans are not unrealistic enough to write grand opera, and the Met is not performing modern Europeans. [The Met's public is] roughly where the Philharmonic's public was twenty-five years ago, before Mitropoulos, Bernstein, and Boulez began the modernizing effort that is finally beginning to bear fruit at Avery Fisher Hall. Could a similar effort be effective on the Metropolitan front?"

Having offered his substantive arguments against modern opera, *i.e.*, "the job of the Met is to put old masterpieces into new frames," Bing makes a joke about having critics beaten up.

When the Ford Foundation first started giving money to the arts, in 1958, their very first grant, of $100,000, went to the New York City Opera. Humanities and Arts head Lowry explained that this was done to give American composers encouragement to write in that important art form, to give them a right to fail "like Puccini and Verdi had." Ford wanted to test whether there was an audience for modern American opera. And it turned out there wasn't, Lowry admitted sadly. The Met had done only Barber; then they did Levy. Chicago had none; then they did Giannini. San Francisco had done none; then they did Dello Joio. But only the New York City Opera is continuing, Lowry declared. One thinks of Ginestra, the Argentine composer.

The subscription system at the Met, which now fills ninety-four to one hundred percent of the seats, was promulgated by Ford on many other operas.

Other aspects of Bing's aesthetic legacy include a reduction in the size of the women, who dwindled on the average from size 20 to size 14 during his administration (still heavier than film stars, but a noticeable change). He also tried to upgrade the quality of Met productions, specifically by insisting on more imaginative and better-rehearsed staging, and improved scenery, costumes, and overall spectacle. *Time* magazine hailed these changes enthusiastically, saying Bing had helped the art of opera achieve "the Wagnerian ideal of *Gesamkunstwerk*, the amalgamation of drama, singing, acting and dancing into total theater." (Musician and author Robert Craft, on the other hand, an intimate of Stravinsky, found costumes, set, and casting all poor.)

In the matter of Lincoln Center, Bing was out of his element. Some of his board wanted the *gestalt* of the new opera house to be big and democratic—seating 5,000 and eliminating the boxes for elite customers. And they wanted to invite the City Opera next door, since Nelson Rockefeller was contributing state money to the neighboring theater on condition that George Balanchine's low-cost, high-quality City Ballet be performing there—and the two were sister organizations. Bing hated City Opera, but he failed to keep them out—probably because his reasoning was so patently illogical: he was afraid the uneducated would confuse the two opera companies, and worse yet, choose to attend the cheaper. But Bing fought for opera's traditional accoutrements at the Met and won some of them. Boxes were retained instead of more democratic tiers. And because Mozart had been composed for a certain size audience, as he maintained, he kept the seating capacity down to 3,800, a mere 100 more than there had been in the old Met.

Most unsuccessful was Bing's legacy in the matter of design of the new house—ostentatiously baroque fixtures in a big, hulking, Stalinist box of a building. Because Bing didn't want the Met "to look old-fashioned and cheap next to the new theaters of Europe and Russia," architect Wallace Harrison installed fruity flower-petal slabs of gold all over the ceiling, gaudy retractable chandeliers donated by the government of Austria, and Chagall's worst work to emblazon the glass front of the structure. Some have noted that the marble in the lobby is hidden under the red carpet, while the concrete is clearly visible. The ornament directly over the proscenium arch resembles—wonder of wonders!—a modernistic hammer and sickle, in the dark.

Robert Craft remarked that the place looked as though it had been unloaded on the capitalists by some sharp People's Republic Minister of Culture *apparatchik*. "Graceless façade and awkward interior" was the verdict of Lincoln Kirstein, chief patron and entrepreneur of the neighboring City Ballet.

By virtue of function and pre-eminence, however, the Metropolitan Opera is a grand spot, one of the only three places in America where large-scale operatic productions are mounted. (The others are San Francisco and Chicago.) When performers look beggarly, their rags are actually made of raw silk, painstakingly abused. There are three invisible back and side stages nearly as large as the one the audience sees. Those flower petals on the ceiling are a million square yards of twenty-three-carat gold. "It was built to last 100 years," says the guidebook.

And *Fortune* magazine says it is "the world's most advanced factory of fantasy," because of thousands of backstage switches automatically controlling the scenery and lighting. Next door at the New York State Theater, where the City Opera and City Ballet perform, all sets must be moved manually.

The Met is the world's largest opera house (as long as a forty-seven-story building is high), and the most expensive centerpiece ($47 million to build, $24 million a year to run) in the world's largest cultural center. With eighty-seven years of touring and forty-five years of radio broadcasts, the company is often called the national music institution. And whatever the architectural or decorative problems at the house, conductors feel that "performing at the Metropolitan is something akin to reaching the Holy Land."

The Met gets an immense share of public and foundation money for the arts since it is, with symphony and museums, the most prestigious form of culture on the shadowy hierarchy of taste. Today interest in ballet, opera, and the symphony, theoretically open to everyone, amounts to a definition of the upper class.

As a sacred cow of class status, the Met inspires some meaty *ad hominem* criticism. R. Meltzer, writing in *The Village Voice*, called the people at an opera he attended "the gotrocks clan," "manic moneybagsers," "hoarders of wealth," and "bejeweled seahags," and the soprano "just another shallow insipid variation on the whole Kate Smith–Joan Baez bellow scene." The affair was "worthless tedious dull dead crap," and the reason people came to see it instead of just watching gold being mined, was that it was the most culturally sanctioned form of noise (and everybody likes noise), it was dead as opera-fans themselves were, and it was quicker than a trip to Europe.

A slightly milder expression of basically the same view was made by Robert Craft, who saw at the Met "corporation presidents and their blue-rinse spouses applauding each ill-conceived and worse executed stage trick as if the music did not exist."

Barnes described the Metropolitan opera goers as "the Social Register's overachievers." And a spokesman for the Ford Foundation, which funds the Met generously if ironically, declared there are in the Met's audience more physicians than any other occupational group.

Presumably the Social Register's overachievers and the physicians come to the Metropolitan Opera for occasional glimpses of the magnitude of the human spirit (if not the impressive costumes) or to seek an exalting spectacle of total theater. Political sovereigns have shown up in significant numbers, such as Golda Meir, John Lindsay, Nelson Rockefeller. As have near-sovereigns, like John D. Rockefeller 3d, Arthur Goldberg, and Jacqueline Kennedy Onassis.

☆   ☆   ☆

History of the Arts at a Glance

PRIMAL SOURCE	OLD HIGH ART	MASS ART
Animal sacrifice ⟶	Opera, Theater ⟶	Television
Parade ⟶	Dance ⟶	Sports
Incantation ⟶	Music, Poetry ⟶	Radio
Costume ⟶	Sculpture ⟶	Film
Notation ⟶	Painting, Writing ⟶	Cartoon, Computer
History ⟶	Prose ⟶	Phonograph

☆   ☆   ☆

A security guard named Emilio escorts me into the opulence of the Met from the stage door underground at Sixty-fourth Street, across long transverse passageways and finally onto the famous red carpet and up an elevator. Upstairs along the south wall of the

Schuyler Chapin, former general manager, Metropolitan Opera Association (J. Heffernan)

Met, just a little above street level, is the office that was built for Sir Rudolf Bing when he was general manager and was then currently occupied by Schuyler Chapin. The room is medium-sized but lush, like a drawing room of an indefinable period antique. Red carpet flecked with black lies deep on the floor. Beside an inviting brown velvet sofa there is a large cut-crystal ice bowl, suggesting conferences with board members or the wooing of sopranos and patrons. I am offered a wing chair. Photos of the stars, of the Opera House, of the general manager's family, cover the walls and spill over onto the desk.

Looming on Chapin's west wall, over the spot where Rudolf Bing's desk formerly stood, was a giant photolike painting called "Washington and His Generals," who stand in relaxed military formation to confer on strategies. The pose is exquisitely inspiring. It is done in documentary-like tints. One imagines nothing less than a world conference of presidents meeting in the shadow of that tableau.

The painting, of course, belonged to Schuyler Chapin, whose

great-great-great-grandfather, General Philip Schuyler, was up there on the wall with Washington.

Entirely appropriately, Chapin had a wonderfully apocalyptic bicentennial sense of things. In the forepart of his brain, he feared what the executive committee of the Metropolitan Opera's board of directors might do to his opera. He worried that they would "blow the whistle" on it, that they would make irreparable changes, such as closing the House. And if something should happen to the Met, "it would have a domino effect on all the other cultural institutions in the performing arts," he said. "If the doors were to be closed, it would change the situation in government and for private patrons; people would say, 'Without the Met, is there really any reason for supporting lesser organizations?' "

The Metropolitan Opera was of course in the most pressing financial straits in its history, even though eighty percent of its income came in at the box office. That still left a whopping $9 million deficit annually, to which the state and Federal governments contributed $1 million apiece. "Nowhere near enough," as Chapin said. "And we have been steadily spending our capital funds over the past decade." To make matters even worse, the inflation of recent years had caused a drying up of private patronage sources. Whereas an Otto Kahn could almost single-handedly support opera at one time, now there was less private money available for the ever-growing deficit.

"We are looking for a clearer ability to obtain government aid," Chapin said. "We want to remix the proportions." For example, instead of the two governments' paying $2 million out of the $9 million deficit, he thought the three branches of government should pay $7 million.

What Chapin meant in more concrete terms is that he would like the people of the United States to put up the $6 or $7 million now being fronted by Texaco, Eastern Airlines, and Ford. Yes, he conceded, this would imply that government pay a great deal more to all the arts, since the grants to the Metropolitan Opera currently stand as one of the largest among them.

But because of his hobby of reading history and his identification with his Revolutionary forebears, Chapin was optimistic. He recalled the enormous financial distress suffered by the Colonies after the War of Independence, under the Articles of Confederation, when it seemed to be impossible to force the new states to pay their taxes. "The Constitution would never have gotten written if America hadn't hit bottom," he pointed out, acknowledging this was not the standard academic view of the period. "Intellectuals would hoot me out of the room," he said, with a smile.

He saw the current period of economic distress, particularly for the arts, as an opportunity to reorder priorities and withdraw public money from expensive weaponry. He believed that if the quality of life was to be considered in the next few decades, then the increased governmental support for the arts which he favored must come. "It's time that the U.S. decides what priority the arts have in our national scheme of things."

How much public support should be given to opera, which, after all, has never been a popular art form in America?

"Opera, like contemporary painting and literature," Chapin replied, "is not to every taste. But that doesn't mean it shouldn't be available for the many that do like it."

Chapin, who is related on his mother's side to the Burdens, who sit on the board of the Museum of Modern Art and co-own *The Village Voice,* is married to Elizabeth Steinway, of the piano-manufacturing family. Martin Mayer, writing in *Esquire,* made the point that Chapin was "dangerously at home in fashionable and intellectual New York."

Of himself, Chapin said, "I guess I'm a perfect example of someone brought up with an upper-class background," meaning that he knew his nurses, governesses, and servants better than he knew his parents. He attended the Allen-Stevenson School and then Millbrook, which he quit before receiving a diploma. A certain amount of time was then spent in Cambridge, Massachusetts, attending Harvard as an unmatriculated special student, and the Longy Music School.

Chapin went to work at NBC, beginning as a page boy, at fifteen dollars a week. During the Second World War he was a pilot in the Burma-China-India theater and flew more than two thousand hours. Upon his return he sold television time; he broadcast in English to the Arabs; and he was general manager of the "Tex and Jinx" radio and TV programs.

During the mid-'50s Chapin worked as an artists' booking agent for Columbia Artists Management in the Midwest. From there he came back to Columbia Records in New York, supervising the Masterworks program and becoming vice president. From this post, which he held only a year, he was appointed programming vice president for Lincoln Center by Center president William Schuman. He planned the summer festivals at Lincoln Center for two years running and then moved on to the Met to assist newly appointed general manager Goeran Gentele. When Gentele died in a car accident only months after assuming the post, Chapin became "acting general manager" and, a year later, full general manager.

One of the first administrative changes Chapin made was a general retrenchment. His new productions for the 1973–74 season came in, with one exception, between $100,000 and $250,000, which was significantly less than costs under Bing.

Chapin's departures from the legacy of Rudolf Bing included several other kinds of modernization. On Sundays the Opera House was leasing space to rock impresario Ron Delsener, who, at the time of this writing, had presented contemporary musical acts including The Who, Melanie, Labelle, and Blood, Sweat and Tears. "Mainly this provides additional income," Chapin explained—$10,000 per Sunday, with the house otherwise empty on that day. He claimed that the contemporary acts "have to be the best in their field." The determination of the quality of the rock acts, as he described it, was apparently an informal procedure, involving Chapin's colleagues in the record business (he was formerly employed by Goddard Lieberson, who was then head of Columbia Records), knowledgeable persons on the Met staff, and discussions with the impresario-promoter. "There's been no opposition so far," Chapin said, adding, "We think it is appropriate for the Met to be involved in the contemporary scene."

Another facet of Chapin's modernization involved the occasional use of fashionable all black and white sets on traditional operas. "I believe that opera is total theater and that I must try as far as possible to address opera problems in such a way as takes in contemporary theatrical mores," Chapin declared.

Chapin told reporters that he wanted to bring in new blood to the Met, such as Mike Nichols, George Balanchine, Jerome Robbins, Bob Fosse, A. J. Antoon, John Schlesinger, Peter Hall, and Lindsay Anderson. He wanted to take the Met to Los Angeles for a month in midwinter. And he saw some possibilities in televised opera (Bing had specifically dismissed such talk as "mass communications gimmickry").

("I don't suppose grand opera will retain much of its majesty on that little screen," I suggested.

"I suppose it won't," agreed a member of the Lincoln Center board, David M. Keiser. "But you may have to settle for that. If you had to charge fifty dollars a seat, very few people could go. It might very well be a solution. Just like using TV in schools, I'm sure you sacrifice something.")

Chapin felt that the televised opera would be worth its defects because of the number of people it would introduce to the art form. "I'm evangelical," he said, "about getting as many people as possible involved in the arts."

An article in that day's *New York Times* discussed "the elitism" of the Met's ruling board. Chapin commented almost angrily, "Of course there's a need for more community participation on the board—and no one knows that more than Mr. [William] Rockefeller." But he saw that problem as less pressing than the extraordinary economic situation with which the presently constituted board was trying to deal.

As the *Times* pointed out, Chapin, as general manager, was responsible to a board of directors who represent the very cream of the city's social elite. Lawyers, oilmen, manufacturers, brokers, and bankers, the Met board members are among the less than one percent of Americans who attended private preparatory schools; and almost to a man they went to only the best of these—Choate, St. Paul's, Exeter—and then on to Harvard, Yale, or Princeton. About half of the fifty-one are listed in the Social Register; the others are past and present heads of such corporations as General Motors, General Electric, Readers Digest, and Texaco. They belong to New York's unobtrusive all-male clubs: Links, Knickerbocker, Century, Pilgrims, etc.

Chapin's view of "the legacy of Sir Rudolf Bing" (who served as general manager of the Met through the 1950s and 1960s) was that it was a legacy of autocratism, to be rejected as no longer workable. This was mainly true, he said, because of the craft unions, of which there are fourteen involved in the Met and which have "gone beyond their original function."

In 1961, labor disputes provoked Bing to close down the House rather than accede to union demands, and to refuse an offer from then-President Kennedy to send his Secretary of Labor, Arthur Goldberg, to arbitrate. Some Metropolitan officials, such as press chief Francis Robinson, date "the dropping of Bing's stock" from that incident.

Chapin would indicate only that in the '60s Bing stopped making "enormous contributions" to the Met and "went for five years into neutral gear." He called his last five years in office "actually a deficit" and said that the decision to replace Bing came not from the general manager himself but from the Met board.

Strong emotions were obviously still raging between past and present opera administrations, though all hesitated to talk for the record. But the epithets they traded were potent: the ousted one is called "furious" "jealous," "an old man who won't let go"; while the current power structure is called "mad" and "tricky."

"Opera as an artistic form, as total theater," commented Chapin, taking the long view, "is always controversial. A lot of this stems from the curiosity and fascination of people in the press about affairs in this house. Last year, for instance, there was a little to-do over our Isolde, Katarina Ligenza: it was broadcast as the greatest crisis in our ninety-year history. The conductor was not the most retiring soul in the world. The journalist wanted to keep the words flying. Suddenly there was a big *chazerai!*

"The Met is highly visible. It is our only national music institution. And I hope I know, when I move out of this highly visible spot, just to step aside and let my predecessor—I mean my successor—handle it."

In addition to rearranging the artistic organization, Chapin's administration called for an across-the-board salary cut of ten percent for everyone earning over $10,000. This was in the process of being discussed by the unions when I interviewed Chapin, and the unions were, of course, unhappy with the plan. The purpose of the salary cut, Chapin said, was "to buy time, to approach a balanced budget starting with a total savings of $2 million, to look for a clearer ability to obtain government aid."

Chapin, who had an Oriental bronze Fu dog on his desk, described himself as "Unitarian, but evangelical about the arts." His tastes in reading, he said, were catholic, though he favors mid-

William Rockefeller, president, Metropolitan Opera Association

nineteenth- to twentieth-century history. "I find it reassuring to
see that the human race keeps making the same mistakes." He
sympathized with the nervous pressure on his singers, and valued
most in artists "the artists' ability to develop their talent with a
feeling of responsibility toward it."

He bade me good-by in a friendly way, with the phrase re-
maining in my mind: ". . . that this great house continue to exist."

☆　　☆　　☆

The Metropolitan Opera was currently being run by general
manager Schuyler Chapin, by chairman of the board George
Moore, by president of the Met association William Rockefeller,
and by executive director Anthony Bliss.

William Rockefeller's great-grandfather was a brother to the
first John D. Rockefeller, making him a second cousin once re-

George S. Moore,
chairman of the board,
Metropolitan Opera
Association

moved to Nelson Rockefeller. His father, William A. Rockefeller, managed his own investments (*i.e.*, was idly rich), and his mother, the former Florence Lincoln, was divorced and remarried to George A. Sloan, president of the Metropolitan Opera from 1940 to 1946. The current president of the Met took the office in June 1974, when George Moore moved over to the chairmanship. Born in 1918, Rockefeller has a diploma from Yale and a law degree from Columbia and is married to the former Mary Gillett.

George Moore comes from a humbler background. Raised in St. Louis as the son of a railroad claims inspector, he won a scholarship to Yale and was hired to his first bank job because he was the student who had saved most money putting himself through college ($7,000 in 1927). From there he worked his way up to president and chairman of the First National City Bank, joining a few clubs on the way: Yale, River, University, Links, and others in St. Louis, New Canaan, Chicago, and Mexico City.

A tale is told in some of those club dining rooms about Moore's youth: It is said that as a self-made Yalie, with a nasal, upper-class accent and a pushy manner, he pursued a languid Mexican woman aristocrat around from bathing spots to watering

Anthony A. Bliss,
executive director,
Metropolitan Opera
Association
(Christian Steiner)

holes; and was just so boring and persistent, she agreed to marry him. Moore later divorced Beatriz Braniff y Bermajillo, the daughter of the Marquis de Mohernando, who had handled protocol for King Alfonso XIII of Spain, and married Charon Crosson.

Though retired from FNCB since 1970, Moore has also held directorships in Borg-Warner, Federal Insurance, W. R. Grace, Mercantile Stores, United Aircraft, Union Pacific R.R., and U.S. Steel. He has been on the executive committee of the Inter-American Council of Commerce and Production and was vice chairman of the Council for Latin America and is a member of the advisory committee of the Organization of American States. It would be correct to call him a domestic and international monetary policy adviser. He is a Republican and a Roman Catholic.

Anthony Addison Bliss became executive director of the Met shortly before Chapin was let go in 1975. He has his B.A. from Harvard and his LL.B. from the University of Virginia; he has been married three times and has six children from these marriages. He too served a term as president of the Met, from 1956 to 1967, and now, in addition to running the Met, serves on the dance panel for the National Endowment, as chairman of the board of the Foundation for American Dance (which runs the Joffrey Ballet), and is a partner of Milbank, Tweed, Hadley, and McCloy. He is sixty-three years old and lives in Oyster Bay, Long Island.

☆　☆　☆

At the age of seventy-four, Rudolf Bing is in decline, like a European nobleman. Retired, he stays mornings in a shabby little office across the street from Carnegie Hall and hasn't gone to the opera in two years ("except one, last week, because MacNeil was kind enough to invite me"), although he used to attend four and five times a week, entertaining in his box. "Alan Rich says that I am the last of the nineteenth-century dictators," he tells me upon my entry into his office. "I rather like that. It means I should get special protection; I am an endangered species!"

Just outside his door, men are busy working in tiny cubicles piled high with papers. But his office is a spacious afterthought, a hiatus in time.

He wears a silky brown suit, a tight collar, a black tie. He is still bald and sinewy like the captain of a spaceship, six feet tall and less than 140 pounds. But now there are sudden lights of pain in his brown eyes, strains of bitterness in what he says, a sense of rejection by colleagues that colors his deep affection and nostalgia for the vehicle he has lost.

The man who once had final say over the most glamorous grand opera in the world, who hired and fired the world's prima donnas, now musters all the dignity he can (and it has always been his long suit) amid nondescript office furniture, with a mostly empty calendar on the desk before him, and says he doesn't want to talk about the Metropolitan Opera.

He explains why: "I don't want to appear critical about the present Met management, and there's very little else I can be."

Bing feels concern for the crisis the Met is now in, deep affection for the institution that was his life for so long, and a glimmering of frustrated responsibility—"not the right word," he says, because the new management is not asking for his advice. (Not long before, the new executive director, Anthony Bliss, told *The New York Times* he was going to call upon Bing as a consultant. But that was merely *pro forma*.) "I had lunch with Mr. Bliss once, six weeks ago. That's all. I wish Mr. Bliss well, but that's as far as it goes." Bing mentions how long he's known Bliss, calls him an old friend, is still careful not to appear critical.

But it is hard for him to keep silent on the subject. A few morsels fall: "When I see what's going on now, I feel well rid of it. Many of my managerial innovations have been forgotten, ignored, or taken for granted. For example, the breaking of the color bar; people take it for granted, but it was very difficult then. The pension system. When I took over, the choristers had to sell ties in Macy's half the year. But I instituted the full-year opera season, which is how it is in every civilized country." By "civilized country," Bing explains, he means wherever opera is subsidized, and he quotes statistics in today's newspaper indicating that the Vienna and Paris operas are very well subsidized indeed. "Now they're cutting back the year again! I worked to lengthen it.

"And their deficit—I don't know how they did it. I left the Met economically as well as artistically sound. There was an endowment of $7 million, the downtown house was worth $9 million, there was $2 million left over from the Ford grant: total assets were $20 million. And in the next two years they raised $10 million. Now they have a deficit of $10 million. They went through $40 million in two years!"

Having sworn so many disclaimers and promised repeatedly not to say anything, Bing finally reveals that he has a hard time understanding the power structure, which at that time had a general manager and an executive director with overlapping areas of responsibility ("and neither knowing very much about opera!"). "Either you have a general manager or you don't," he says. And shortly afterward, Chapin as general manager was superseded in power by Anthony Bliss, Bing's old office being abolished altogether.

"But I can't deny I miss it," Bing went on.

His life is uncompromisingly stark. As was always his wont, he still does not attend movies at all or own a television set or (except rarely) listen to opera on the radio or go to cocktail parties or dinner parties. It's been a long time since he's been to the ballet or theater. What does he do? He reads—Tolstoi, Dostoevski, Theodore Dreiser—and talks to his friends. His life has focused down sharply onto the few blocks from Central Park South where he lives with his wife of many years and dines in hotel restaurants along the street, and Fifty-seventh Street, where he works at Columbia Artists Management, Inc., for two hours every morning.

At CAMI, Bing does occasional special projects involving opera singers in concerts—a Tucker gala, a series of twelve stars at Carnegie Hall. He receives a retirement pension of $47,000.

He is also teaching "The Art of Management" to twenty undergraduates at Brooklyn College and fifteen graduates at the City University who come to his class, says Bing, "to see the man who fired Callas." When he is describing what he teaches to these students, namely the ethics of management, with examples drawn from his experience, he says "relationships with inferiors, er, I mean subordinates." He thinks the ethics of management remain a constant, though power structures may change, from one corporation or cultural institution to another. But he declines to make any comments on the power structures of any other of the great cultural institutions. "I was so spun into the Met," he demurs, "like a web. I don't know how any of the others ran, even though they were so close. What went on at the Met was so totally absorbing, I had no private life."

No, Bing had not read the book on the new Met that had been recently published. The only books in his office were three copies of an Italian edition of his Memoirs: *5000 Nights at the Opera*. He is happy about that. He says it sold sixty thousand copies in English and thirty thousand in German. And that they are translating it into French, which he thinks is a bad idea.

I suggest to Sir Rudolf that he represents the passing of a courtly and aristocratic style, that the changes going on at the Met are being done in the name of "modernization." And that the new Met's ethic values the survival of the institution over the survival of the individuals involved.

"I do value, even today, manners," he says. "And I valued talent and quality, as I saw it, though that gets us into the insoluble matter of different tastes. It was not so much aristocratic as people I thought were talented." He mentions a few names, to indicate a range: Beverly Webster, Franco Zeffirelli, Marc Chagall.

"On artistic matters, everyone is entitled to his own judgment," says Sir Rudolf Bing. "But I brought contemporary stagecraft to the Met. Among the one hundred or so productions that we did, there were a great number of distinguished performances. *Die Frau Ohne Schotten,* that last *Otello, Peter Grimes.* And there were hardly any distinguished conductors who did not work for me."

He recalls that he argued for a new Met for twenty years and that it finally went up on the scare that Carnegie Hall would be torn down. Bing points a finger out his window at Andrew Carnegie's Music Hall, still standing, all graceful Romanesque windows and faded burnt ocher brick and lacy ironwork staircase, as if in some way its continued existence perhaps vindicates him. As if to say: They didn't really need Lincoln Center, and all that that wrought.

But he speaks well of Lincoln Center: ". . . a respectable enterprise. Praiseworthy. One of the jewels of New York City, after the United Nations and what's that big building? The Empire State Building.

"Mr. John D. Rockefeller had the idea that he wanted a cultural center," says Sir Rudolf Bing, cutting through a significant amount of periphrasis in the official version of how Lincoln Center got established. "His brother Mr. Nelson Rockefeller was governor of New York, as you know. So the combination was pretty powerful."

Even in the definitive work on Lincoln Center by Ralph G. Martin, Nelson Rockefeller is generally euphemized as "New York State." And while John D. is acknowledged "the prince" of the operation, the leading role is given to "the Dukes of New York" who brought the idea to him.

What went on between the Met and Lincoln Center proper during those years when the new buildings were first opening up, 1964, '65, '66, '67? Bing recalls only subcommittees of the big Lincoln Center board, some of which met in the Philharmonic building, others in Mr. Rockefeller's office, where "the paid employees, like me and Mr. Julius Rudel, would be called in, asked to speak our mind, and then ignored." And he recalls that when Vivian Beaumont gave $3 million for the Repertory Theater, Bing suggested to a subcommittee they call it The Old Viv.

Dutifully, he asserts that the constituents of Lincoln Center are totally independent, each with its own board and not told what to do. On a matter affecting all Lincoln Center — the question of whether to let in City Opera as well as City Ballet —Bing faced off the Lincoln Center board and lost. Why? Because of John D. Rockefeller, who was chairman, he says. City Opera was invited in. Bing had feared that two opera companies within the one complex would undermine both their identities. "I was wrong about that," Bing now says. "It hasn't harmed us or them."

Bing is not sentimental about the source of the Rockefellers' influence. "Money talks fairly loudly in this world," he says drily.

He doesn't suppose the new chairman of Lincoln Center, Amyas Ames, has all the muscle chairman Rockefeller had. But he praises the man warmly: Ames has "knowledge, cultural background, sincerity, and ability."

Bing politely calls George Balanchine "one of the great choreographers of our day," appending the fact that Lincoln Kirstein "pays for most of the expenses" of Balanchine's New York City Ballet, according to his information. And when asked whether Balanchine's ballet company is as much the national company as the Metropolitan is the national opera, Bing replies that no, N.Y.C. Ballet and the American Ballet are the national companies.

(Is there anything more than coincidence in the fact that the ABT is headquartered only a stone's throw, hardly fifty yards, from the very spot where Bing is now sitting? I am a great proponent of the Ruling Geographical Metaphor.)

A few blocks away elsewhere is City Center, sometime home of the City Opera and City Ballet and formerly headed by Morton Baum. Bing's praise for Baum is tinged with enmity. He says, "Baum was an excellent man. He knew exactly what he wanted and how to get it. He was more of a Culture Baron than I was; he had the power to manipulate. I only hired and fired people, like any manager of any store."

But Bing has grown unduly modest, for it is undeniable that in his two decades at the Metropolitan he exerted a significant artistic influence and combined the two different kinds of power, artistic and financial, more than any other contemporary figure in the fields of music and dance.

Or can it be that the discussion of the new Met and the old Met and Lincoln Center and the new world at CAMI ("I have to see what goes, how the public reacts, how the press react") has depressed him and that, like so many men, he is hating his retirement and wishing it hadn't happened and dreaming far back to a time before all this Met had even begun for him: during the Second World War when he managed a store in London; and now he is speaking of store management and admitting that he "enjoyed London."

So, precisely on the stroke of the hour he asks if he has answered enough questions for me and apologizes for some vague defect and gently as a tissue cut-out of a prince helps me put my coat on.

"Thank you for coming to see me," says Sir Rudolf Bing.

BALLET:
The Monopoly

Balanchine the Russian dancer had the Warner Brothers mixed up with the Ritz Brothers. He didn't know which ones he was training and which ones he was working for. He used to go around saying, "I cannot train these Warner Brothers to dance."
—F. Scott Fitzgerald,
The Last Tycoon

G EORGE BALANCHINE dominates the dance world in America. Of all our Culture Barons, the award for most interesting childhood must go to George Balanchine, who danced for the Czar and for the Bolsheviks, and paid the price of tuberculosis and pleurisy and pneumonia and near starvation for the chance both to see the Russian Revolution firsthand and to abandon it, in favor of the international bohemia of the Riviera. And for this priceless quality of interestingness, we Americans are paying him well.

☆   ☆   ☆

Classical ballet dates from the Italian, Spanish, and French courts of the fifteenth and sixteenth centuries, though other forms of dance go back even further. The first getting up on toes is supposed to have occurred on the terraced gardens of Louis XIV's palace at Versailles, and the king took his nickname *"Le Roi Soleil"* from a ballet written for him, in which he appeared in person as

69

the Sun in allegorical dress. Toe dancing was then exported to Russia under the patronage of Empress Anna, where it became particularly resplendent in the nineteenth century in combination with the music of Tchaikovsky.

Partly because the Czars, right on through the last one, Nicholas II, were pleased with the ballet, and their grand dukes fond of courting the ballerinas, ballet in Russia came to be pre-eminent in the world. At the Maryinski Theater in St. Petersburg, effects were achieved with costumes and scenery comparable to the splendor and magnificence of the later Hollywood epic movies.

One of the adolescents at the Imperial School studying ballet under the Czars' aegis was little George Balanchivadze, who adored the life of court theater. When the Communists overturned the old order (and Lenin, addressing the people from the balcony of the prima ballerina's apartments, seemed like a lunatic to the thirteen-year-old boy), the ballet school and theater continued as before, with less food and less heat, he recalls. Balanchine remained to dance for the Soviet state; but at the age of twenty he emigrated, on the pretense of a dance tour, with three others of his company. The company of the exiled Russian Sergei Diaghilev, he felt, was more creative than anything that was happening in St. Petersburg.

Now George Balanchine is seventy-two. Streams of reporters have come to his School of American Ballet over the last forty-two years to watch rehearsals and pay homage to the man with the gurgly Russian accent, wearing the expensively tailored cowboy clothes, who is responsible for transplanting a dance tradition to American soil. His salary has been quoted as low as $200 a week, even though the multimillion dollar State Theater at Lincoln Center was designed with him in mind and built for him and his dancers by his special patron, Nelson Rockefeller. Similarly, the Ford Foundation has also supplied his school with several millions of dollars for scholarships and talent hunts (even though the New York City Ballet cannot accommodate all the talented young dancers), and has funded heavily six other ballet companies around the country (Pennsylvania, Utah, Houston, Washington, D.C., San Francisco, and Boston), four of which share Balanchine's aesthetic.

Balanchine in person has a cool, zen charisma and doesn't like

to talk. His female ballet pupils worship him like a god. He is unquestionably top man in the most rapidly expanding of the performing arts in the United States, ballet master absolute in the city
that is the dance capital of the world. Though the Soviet Union
still claims to be the home of the classical ballet, Balanchine disputes that; "Russia is the home of romantic ballet," he said in
Moscow in 1962. "The home of classic ballet is now America."

The elements of Balanchine's classicism include clean-cut sil-
houettes with no wasted movements, musical scores by Mozart,
Bach, Bizet, Stravinsky, etc., plain backgrounds rather than elaborate sets, and the abandonment of traditional ballet plots. His aesthetic is the opposite of "the method" used in the theater, though
some writers claim he was influenced by Stanislavski in the direction of artistic reform. He himself says he is most indebted to the
musician Stravinsky, who taught him to simplify. Some writers
feel he takes his inspiration directly from his dancers' stretching,
jumping, and turning, with the result that his choreography tends
to be acrobatic and gymnastic. He himself says that his dancers
"don't have time" to learn interpretation and communication, because the techniques are hard enough. One often hears Balanchine's dancers praised for the rigorousness of their technique,
and the choreographer himself for having "taste."

On the other hand, Balanchine's work has been dismissed as
unemotional, computerized, and rigid. Recently his "lack of feeling" has been berated by the critics; in the '60s it was more fashionable to deride his "emphasis on youth" and to speak of the
ballerinas he had dismissed at age twenty-nine. Perhaps the
harshest words have come from Alan Rich in New York magazine:
"As much as I am bored by the mechanisms and empty precisions
of Balanchine's company on a typical night, I am bored most of all
by the contrived, pasted-on facial masks of its dancers."

Balanchine creates the quintessentially classical alongside the
satirical and modern and topical and is generally criticized for the
latter, rarely the former. A spoof ballet set to the tune of an airline
commercial jingle, "Pan Am Makes the Going Great," was called
disastrous; a woman writing in The Nation pointed out his signal
failure in another piece to build upon Gershwin or to recreate the
idiom of jazz.

Balanchine had joined the impresario Diaghilev in Paris in

1925, leaving Russia as part of a tiny dance troupe of four persons within the year after the Maryinski directors forbade their dance pupils to appear in his ballets. It was not that the climate in Soviet Russia in the 1920s was hostile to the arts; on the contrary—the Czar's box in the theater, after the revolution, was assigned for the use of opera and ballet performers; the arts were generally uncensored; such great talents as Mayakovski, Pasternak, Kandinsky, Prokofiev, Eisenstein, and Malevich (the first abstract expressionist) all flourished.

However, Balanchine, as he was soon renamed by Diaghilev, was "a profound and strenuous anti-Communist" in his politics and his orientation, and so he left. He is to this day a devout communicant of the Orthodox Church, whose Byzantine ritual and music appeal to the mystic in him. And to his theatrical sense: Balanchine in his youth dressed in black clothes, wore long hair, and even put a dab of greasepaint under his eyes.

In Europe, Diaghilev's company enjoyed the patronage and attention of the most glittery of intellectual high society. Shortly after Diaghilev's death in 1929, Balanchine succumbed to a delayed effect, perhaps, of the Revolution years: pneumonia, pleurisy, and tuberculosis. Back from the sanitarium, he worked, in a very few years, in France, Denmark, Italy, Monte Carlo (Monaco), Argentina, and England.

In 1933, in London, Romola Nijinsky introduced Balanchine to a young American from Harvard: the American, Lincoln Kirstein, had dreamed about an American ballet company for years, and he had the money to buy one and Balanchine was accessible. . . .

The two came to America and started the School of American Ballet straightaway, though the dance company didn't get off the ground without a few false starts. Balanchine had an unsuccessful three years choreographing the ballet at the Metropolitan Opera and a decade of constricted choreography for Broadway and the movies. During these years critical approval of his work was slowly warming from an initial distrust of his "decadent Riviera aesthetics."

He lived a kind of Riviera high life though, driving an MG, drinking champagne, courting a ballerina with jewels. He was such a lover of the beauty of the ephemeral that he would go out of his way not to run into a beautiful dancer he knew from the past, in order that her present appearance not spoil his cherished memory.

When Balanchine saw that he was the only choreographer of note in Europe or America who was not asked to work for the newly organized Ballet Theater in 1939, a collective venture, he came to grips with his commanding Georgian personality. For the next ten years Lucia Chase's Ballet Theater monopolized the ballet scene in America. But in 1948, on the invitation of City Center's Morton Baum and with funds raised by Lincoln Kirstein (whose personal income was $60,000 a year) and help from Nelson Rockefeller, Mrs. W. K. Vanderbilt, and Edward M. M. Warburg, Balanchine's performing group officially became the New York City Ballet, a public institution. As one newsmagazine summarized it: "Lincoln Kirstein's faith and money saw the N.Y.C. Ballet through its infancy." But Balanchine's biographer, Bernard Taper, credits City Center's Morton Baum: ". . . for all the City Center's disadvantages, having the place as a home it could call its own has been probably the decisive factor in the New York City Ballet's survival."

Today the original positions of Chase's Ballet Theater and Balanchine's N.Y.C. Ballet are reversed. Though they did not covet the City Center stage, where Balanchine's dancers served their sixteen-year apprenticeship, Oliver Smith, codirector of the Ballet Theater, lately bemoaned the fact that now they were the ones without a permanent home. Couldn't Ballet Theater and New York City Ballet share the State Theater? Smith wanted to know.

Observers of the ballet scene say that Lincoln Kirstein is the power at City Ballet, that he runs the company. Balanchine, by contrast, is only a maker, a craftsman, who declines even the label "artist." Kirstein is a large and irascible fellow, a type it is now fashionable to call "abrasive." Even before ground was broken at Lincoln Center he had quit its board of directors over a philosophical disagreement; he has spelled out in detail his hostility to the architecture and sociodynamics of all the Lincoln Center buildings other than his own, ominously hinting that future ages are going to get them for it. He has called the Museum of Modern Art "the greatest promulgator of trash in history."

But the official guide to Lincoln Center got its licks in, too, quoting what *The London Times* had said about the man: "Lincoln

Kirstein, Balanchine's lieutenant, is ubiquitous and so unreliable . . . that an exact estimation of his position is difficult. Well-off, erratic, with a public manner so prickly that his chief talent seems to be for making enemies and alienating people, it might seem that, after so long a time, he could afford to relax."

On December 15, 1963, the Ford Foundation announced $8 million worth of grants to ballet. Of this amount, about $5 million went to Balanchine's School of American Ballet and the New York City Ballet Company, a part of which was administered at the school but spent on local scholarships. No other dance troupes in New York City were awarded funds, and only six other companies from all around the country.

Dance critic for the N.Y. *Herald Tribune,* Lillian Moore, was among those who deplored the grant, which, she maintained, "since almost every one of these companies is strongly influenced by the New York City Ballet, represents an endorsement of an artistic dictatorship." She named the other classical ballet companies that should have been funded: the Joffrey (ineligible then, they were funded a year later) and particularly the Ballet Theater, which had discovered and fostered new choreographers, unlike Balanchine's company; and the modern dance companies—Martha Graham's, Jose Limon's, Paul Taylor's. "The Ford grant propagates the fame of someone who is already firmly established," she said on the radio. Brunetta de Matteo, dance critic for *Show Business* magazine, added that Balanchine's expenses are not great, since he pays only a token rent. Harold Garton, dance critic for *Backstage,* went on in the same vein, deploring both Balanchine's monopoly and some of his specific practices.

Kirstein referred to the criticism of the grant as "waspish, idiosyncratic, and virulent."

W. McNeil Lowry, for the Ford Foundation, explains that Ford could not give a grant to the Ballet Theater because that company had asked for a carte blanche underwriting of $5 million in unexplained deficits. And that they did not fund Martha Graham or any modern troupes in 1963 when they made their ballet grants, but they did some years later.

Balanchine defends himself. He doesn't charge royalties for the use of his ballets, he says. Shaking a finger, he fumes, "I personally added to Ford. You see, education for education's sake means nothing. After dancers have learned what they can learn, they have to have ballets to dance. So I give anybody in America who asks, small schools, big schools, whatever—I give them my ballets free. The critics accuse me of taking Ford's millions, but they never mention this thing I do. No one else gives their ballets free. If I wanted to charge for the rights to my ballets, I could be a millionaire."

In the years since Ford's first big grant to ballet, Balanchine has enjoyed an almost uncontested hegemony. The *Information Please Almanac* describes his company as "virtually the national ballet company," though admitting to a degree of controversiality in that statement. *Newsweek*'s Hubert Saal calls the N.Y.C. Ballet "the nation's most important cultural institution" and Balanchine himself "the supreme figure in the history of dance." Clive Barnes describes Balanchine as a genius, who has "produced dozens of works that are likely to survive." (He has created about 150 ballets altogether.)

Some speak of the big three ballet companies in the world as the Bolshoi, the Royal Ballet (of England), and Balanchine's. Others prefer to refer to the three most important ballet companies "in the West," which they define as the Royal Ballet, Balanchine's N.Y.C. Ballet, and the American Ballet Theater.

New York's Alan Rich decries the influence Balanchine has over dance at Lincoln Center, writing that he has "effectively suppressed the possibility of much of significance [happening] in the way of opposing views of the dance," and that he has "set his heavy hand on decisions concerning dance at Lincoln Center."

The power structure within Balanchine's school and ballet company has been called by the *Times*'s John Corry "as democratic as the court of Czar Nicholas II." Balanchine's closest friend, Lincoln Kirstein, says of Balanchine: "He has authority to the nth degree." Surrounded by hundreds of young girls and a few dozen boys, Balanchine enjoys unlimited adulation which he does not discourage, being known even to give advice on where his students should live. ("Not downtown"; that is, not in the Village.)

Like the chief of a harem, he picks out the girls he wishes to favor for their long legs, their "bird bones," their small heads, their strong backs. Once he said, possibly in jest, that he also likes his dancers to have big feet.

But he is not interested in promoting stars. He bills his dancers alphabetically, which *Show* magazine has called "ego-levelling." Some years ago he told a reporter that when a dancer gets too interested in her own career, such as by looking for independent bookings, he has no further use for her.

One of his prima ballerinas, Suzanne Farrell, not long ago aroused his wrath by marrying another dancer. Suddenly she felt she and her husband were not being given good roles any more; then the two stopped working for Balanchine altogether. She danced a while with Béjart's Twentieth Century Ballet in Europe. Then she finally returned to the New York City Ballet "less coltish," as *Saturday Review* said.

Balanchine clearly has a Pygmalion complex. Some of his leading dancers, like Patricia McBride, have been under his tutelage since they were fourteen years old. Five times in his life he has actually wed one of his ballerinas—always the very young and very beautiful, even as he himself aged.

It might be said that Balanchine's dancers are underpaid. A dancer in the *corps de ballet* makes $150 a week. By contrast, the resident principals in any of the major ballet companies get about $750 a week. And guest fees for international stars at the A.B.T. range anywhere from $1,000 to $10,000 for one performance.

Balanchine lived with his most recent wife, a ballerina who was paralyzed by polio, in a little house in the Connecticut woods until their divorce. Now he lives in Manhattan alone. He votes Republican and considers himself a mystic. He is also a Georgian patriot, happy to entertain some of his fellow Georgian musicians visiting America with lavish food and drink and reminiscences of the state that produced Stalin. He expects to live to age 135, on the strength of his Georgian lineage. He has all sorts of enthusiasms, though his cooking, which once ran to things like partridge in sour cream, now consists of more simple items like lentil soup. Some interviewers conclude he likes science fiction, others that he watches Westerns on TV, still others that he likes and recommends to his dancers Tolstoy or Pushkin or popular science or the Bible. A collection of all his enthusiasms has a scrapbook quality: from Braque to Jack Benny, from French sauces to ice cream. At some point in his life he has indulged in baton twirling.

☆   ☆   ☆

Modern ballet begins with the Russian impresario Diaghilev and Igor Stravinsky's *Firebird* of 1910. What is called "modern dance" may also have originated around the turn of the century with the topless performance of Isadora Duncan, an internationally known radical. Under the name of "expressionism," it manifested itself in Weimar Germany as a reaction against the grind of ballet schools. An unsympathetic critic described it as "barefoot dancers . . . a maximum of effect with a minimum of technique. The bizarre and the exotic alternated with the puerile. There were also rare individual creations of artistic and musical integrity. Fake orientalism became the vogue."

Scarcely a decade after Duncan's 1922 performance in Boston, the first performance of the School of American Ballet headed up by George Balanchine ushered in an era of pre-eminence for Balanchine's style of classical academicism. Now *Newsweek* calls Balanchine and Martha Graham (a follower of Duncan's) "twin ministers" of dance in the United States.

At a Martha Graham recital it is possible to see some of the better-known celebrity liberals such as Woody Allen, Paul Newman, Joanne Woodward, Robert Redford.

☆   ☆   ☆

According to a criticism in the avant-garde publication *The New York Smith,* Arthur Mitchell's all-black Dance Theater of Harlem has been given all the funds it has asked for from public sources and even more, while the multiracial Alvin Ailey company has had to go begging. *The Smith* acknowledges that Mitchell's company is one of the leading exponents of ballet and jazz forms, but it holds that the Ailey company is the more polished professionally—and is training fifteen hundred underprivileged kids.

Clive Barnes thinks the Ailey group, though it has power and punch, nevertheless erodes the distinction between classical and modern dance forms, which he does not believe is a good thing.

☆   ☆   ☆

Two Views of Rudolf Nureyev:

1. *That he has been the biggest influence on Western ballet since Diaghilev. More influential than Balanchine, Fokine, Ashton, Tudor, Robbins, or Fonteyn. That he is the counterpart of Martha Graham.*

Nureyev did for ballet what Tarzan did for jungles, i.e., popularized it. His virtuosity and intensity set an example for other male dancers. He staged previously unknown works. He made the Australian and Canadian ballets into international companies. He helped many partners, many companies.

—Clive Barnes,
The New York Times

2. *[Deploring the sensibility of the Royal Ballet] "An exhibition of Nureyev's . . . muscle-bound buttocks and steel-thewed thighs is in contrast to the concealing of the charms of Juliet and her attendant goslings by floor-length skirts."*

—Robert Craft,
Stravinsky

☆   ☆   ☆

The Harkness Ballet is said by Clive Barnes to have "set new standards in bad taste." *The New Yorker* comments more discreetly on the expensiveness of the costumes. From snapshots, Harkness' ballets appear to be lewdly decadent and caricaturized, rather like the surreal nudes painted on the walls of its theater.

The patron of the Harkness Ballet has been compared with Catherine de Médici, the sixteenth-century queen of France, who underwrote the world's first ballet (and killed a lot of Protestants). Born Rebekah Semple West, Rebekah Harkness married an heir of Standard Oil and is now worth an estimated quarter or half billion dollars. Tall and with a girlish figure at the age of sixty-one, she takes daily music and ballet lessons and does yoga to control her abdomen. She is called hard-faced, deep-voiced, and fast-moving, and has been married three times.

Harkness lives in a New York City penthouse, a Hudson River estate, a mansion in the Bahamas, and a Swiss chalet.

Her prize possession is a gold, gem-encrusted Salvador Dali chalice kept behind burglarproof glass and under guard at 4 East

Seventy-fifth Street (formerly the town house of the president of IBM). The chalice rotates by electric current as golden caterpillars on a gold and lapis lazuli tree open into butterflies with wings of jewels. Laughingly she says that when she dies, "The pearly gates are not for me. My ashes are going into that chalice, and I'll pirouette forever."

Speaking of her philosophy and work, Rebekah Harkness says, ". . . the arts all came out of palaces—there's no reason why America shouldn't have something like the old court theaters of Europe." And again: "When the smoke blows over and the war is over, you'll still have Michelangelo and Bach."

Somehow her balletic productions have not inspired quite such lofty comparisons. A Broadway star commented that the filmy apricot curtain in the new Harkness Theater at Broadway and Sixty-second was "just like a boudoir scene from a Norma Shearer movie."

"You know I don't have to spend my money on ballet," she retorts, "I could buy some yachts instead."

Agnes de Mille, a good and strong woman who choreographed *Rodeo, Oklahoma,* and *Carousel* for Broadway and the movies, among other hits, is the niece of cine-legend Cecil B. de Mille. She is also the daughter of a playwright and the granddaughter of Henry George, who was a crusader for the "single-tax." She thinks The All-Time Greats are Euripides, Michelangelo, Shakespeare, Bernard Shaw, and Martha Graham.

She also thinks there should be a General Strike in all the arts and entertainment.

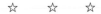

In his sixty-three-year career, the late Sol Hurok represented more than four thousand performers, including Anna Pavlova, Isadora Duncan, Andrés Segovia, Margot Fonteyn and the Sadler's Wells Ballet, Artur Rubinstein, Efrem Zimbalist, Jan Peerce, Marian Anderson, Stanislavski's Moscow Art Players, the Bolshoi Ballet, the Moiseyev Dancers, and other operatic, musical, and ballet groups and individuals from around the world.

Hurok, a Jew, did not leave his native Russia till the age of sixteen. In about 1911, at the age of twenty-three, he began his first ventures as an impresario, arranging concerts for labor organizations and workers' clubs. He had the idealistic notion—spelled out in his autobiography *Impresario*—of "bringing music to the masses." *The New York Times* wrote on its editorial page that Hurok had "done more for music in America than the invention of the phonograph."

In 1972 the Jewish Defense League bombed Hurok's midtown Manhattan offices for obscure political reasons, injuring a secretary. Hurok, whose claim to the title "impresario" is almost unequaled in the world, died the following year, in transit between a meeting with the guitarist Segovia and one with banker David Rockefeller.

☆   ☆   ☆

To understand who Oliver Smith is, for someone who knows nothing about ballet, is to know that the ballet scene is dominated by two large organizations in New York City: George Balanchine's School of American Ballet and New York City Ballet on the one hand—also known as "the wise guys" for their snappy, put-on style of aesthetic—and Oliver Smith and Lucia Chase's American Ballet Theater, known in the trade for its conservative, "safe guy" image.

In interviewing the conservative Smith, I discovered him to be an intriguingly pleasant, overgrown little boy with a slightly longish white Sluggo crew cut. He was also rather delightfully late for our appointment, his plump amanuensis Charles Franz bustling about for nearly an hour papering me with conflicting excuses. (Franz euphemized the delay as "lunch at the Plaza"; Smith himself spoke more bluntly of a "bar somewhere.") I gathered this made him a bit more of an artist than a Culture Baron.

He was wearing a black and blue large-plaid suit, a striped shirt, and a red tie with thieves' knots on it. Besides directing the Ballet Theater this is the man who designed the sets on most of my favorite childhood stage and screen productions: *Brigadoon, Oklahoma, Auntie Mame, Guys and Dolls*, etc. At any rate, Smith sits at a confluence of art, power, and money.

Oliver Smith, codirector, American Ballet Theater

A.B.T. headquarters is in a fifty-story glass tower just across the street from Carnegie Hall and called the Arlen Building. On the fourth floor of this building with A.B.T. are also Allied Artists, Universal Attractions (Our Latin Thing, Inca Records, etc.), Red Mogen David, Emanuel Celler, the *County Eagle News*, Arthur and Bertha Kahn, the International Council on the Psychological Dangers to World Peace, L & M Scientific Research and Development Corporation, the Office of Nonmilitary Strategy, *The Sullivan Letter*, and Xerox machines.

His codirector, Lucia Chase's, office, where we are, has a cozy Harvardiana decor: crimson carpets, leather and upholstered armchairs in that Colonial style favored by the college, and real bookcases. But overlaying this are some surprisingly drippy artifacts,

Lucia Chase, codirector and patron, American Ballet Theater

such as one finds, say, in the drawing room of a provincial maharajah. Papier-mâché ballerina dolls. A hand-lettered and ugly scroll from the Greenwich Country Day School dating from 1956. Flimsy, tentative, and fussy watercolors hung in geometric patterns—Smith's work.

He lights up a Carlton and rests it against his cheek as he sits, legs crossed, to talk to me.

Both Clive Barnes and Alan Rich, dance critics, love Smith's A.B.T. immoderately. Barnes calls its repertory classic, and the company eclectic, ecumenical, and national, "undoubtedly the classic established company of American dance" and, after the Met, "probably the oldest continuous theatrical institution in the U.S." Rich is equally laudatory, though in different terms. He praises the Ballet Theater's romantic incandescence, the exhilaration and drama of interaction, the personal passion, the fact that the dancers react to each other with their full physique.

Choreographer Agnes de Mille was discovered by the Ballet

Theater, as were Leonard Bernstein, Jerome Robbins, and Eliot Feld.

The key political issue in the life of Smith's dance group in 1975 when I spoke to him was the lack of a permanent home. The Ballet Theater at that time danced only ten or twelve weeks in the year in New York City, about half of that in City Center at Christmas, and a few weeks in Lincoln Center in the dog days of summer. Officially called "the resident dance company of the JFK Center for the Performing Arts" in Washington, D.C., this only meant that the company danced there for a few extra weeks.

According to dance and theater critic Barnes, the time they spent in New York was "not enough for a major New York performing arts institution. [The A.B.T.] needs a theater it can share all year round with the Joffrey and some of the larger modern dance companies. That theater should have the facilities and the desirabilities of either the Met or the State Theater."

In Smith's words: "We play at the JFK Center in Washington longer than we play anywhere else. Ballet Theater is the only world-renowned company which is nomadic. It does not have a permanent home. This is a very unjust situation. We should be able to play the N.Y.S. Theater an equal length of time with the N.Y.C. Ballet, which I consider the other great dance company in the U.S. And we should share that together. I don't know why Mr. Rudel has to be in there all this time, but that's something elsc. It was built as a Dance Theater and paid to be that by the taxpayers of New York State. And I would like that to be shared by Ballet Theater, Joffrey Ballet, all the great dance companies in the U.S., and let Mr. Rudel go perform his operas in the City Center. While there's this great tug of war, we're just drifting around."

I asked who was the arbiter in that tug of war. Smith said he would "rather not get into the political machinations of that. But, I would think it'd be the board of Lincoln Center. Because it's their real estate. [Laughs] Rather than a public trust, I say."

What are the problems with performing in City Center?

"It's inadequate in every sense. First of all, architecturally, it's one of the most hideous rooms in America. It has a very small stage, smaller than most Broadway houses. It also has an orchestra which is not properly raked, so that if you sit in the first third of the house, the dancers' feet are cut off by about eighteen inches. It has a very small orchestra pit. It has the most hideous show curtain in America, which has just been installed there—a plaid shower curtain!"

A few months after our interview, the Ballet Theater, along with the Joffrey and Ailey dance troupes, signed a contract to buy the Manhattan Center Theater on Thirty-fourth Street in New York for $10 million. *Variety* described the project as having been initiated by Oliver Smith and negotiated by volunteer consultant William Zeckendorf, Jr. The building purchased was built in 1902 as the Manhattan Opera House by theatrical entrepreneur Oscar Hammerstein, who hoped to go into competition with the Metropolitan Opera but did not succeed.

Q: What is the cultural significance of the A.B.T.?

A: Well, first of all, we've presented work by more American choreographers than any other company. Second, we have developed more American dancers into international status. I admire the other companies considerably, but many of the stars in the other companies got their start in Ballet Theater. Ballet Theater is what I would call the matrix company.

Q: What do you think about avant-garde in ballet?

A: There's no such thing as avant-garde. Certain artists when they are at the beginning of their careers, at a certain stage of development, do interpret past vocabularies in an individual way. And that's what's considered—to the degree of that individualism—that's what makes it avant-garde. For example, Martha Graham, who was one of the very great forces in dance history, observed very closely the works of Wigman, the German choreographer. And she was very influenced by Oriental dance. And out of her own poetic, creative soul, she moved dance a whole dimension ahead. She's a particular genius. Merce Cunningham is actually today quite *démodé;* he interpreted in choreography what Duchamp was doing in art in the 1920s. Béjart is awfully old hat today.

The best of the contemporary choreographers are still Balanchine, and Anthony Tudor [of the A.B.T.] and Jerome Robbins. And they're still more avant-garde than the so-called avant-garde.

Q: What do you think about the Ford Foundation's projected deficits for the arts in the neighborhood of three hundred million dollars?

A: Yes, I've read those reports. Yes, they project an enormous deficit. If one read those reports one would just stop. I think the United States is rich enough that they could do with a little less terrible television; I'm not talking about public television. We could do without three bombers. And they could do with one less concrete intersection on the road program. I feel it's up to the American public to decide what they want. We're living in the middle of a revolution. The people are becoming a great deal more aware of their government. They wanted Nixon out of office; our whole political system is being—is going to be—reorganized. They don't want Mr. Mills deciding how money is going to be spent. And if they don't take on the responsibility, they won't have any art. I'm getting a little grim.

Q: What is the financial structure of Ballet Theater?

A: Lucia Chase has been a generous contributor, but she's by no means the major contributor. We have a very active board of directors which pays about a fourth of our expenses; another forty-five percent comes in at box office admissions; the New York State Council gives about a fourth. Some money also comes from the U.S. Endowment, the Rockefeller, Ford, and Duke foundations, and from small contributions.

In total it's a four and a half million dollar operation.

Q: Is there any institutional or family connection between Miss Chase and the Chase Manhattan Bank?

A: None that I know of. I think that's one of those ill-researched legends.

Q: I know your work had the original goal of a fusion of ballet and theater. What do you think of Jerome Robbins' attempt to build a new musical theater? And of Joseph Papp's attempt to construct a national theater?

A: The goals are very identified with the drives and the talents of the individuals involved. Both are very talented people. I think Robbins, one might say, very carefully and reflectively, is a creative genius. I don't consider Joe Papp a genius for one second. I think he's a very active and very fine producer and certainly has directed very well and is a remarkable person in our theater. I'm very grateful he exists. I think Robbins' contribution is infinitely more lasting in our theater. But I don't like to get into comparisons.

One of Joe's problems is that he's got that shrine up at Lincoln Center and he doesn't know what to do with it. [Laughs]

Q: Whom of your colleagues do you admire?

A: I think I admire Robbins most of all. I admire Lenny Bernstein very deeply but in a different way. On the international level, I admire Peter Brook. It's a limited number.

Q: Can you tell me something about *Oklahoma,* which you designed?

A: It's very interesting to think about *Oklahoma,* because it's when America sort of fell in love with itself. Today it seems quite naïve. But the good things still come out: I mean, there's a marvelous score. The form of it is very well constructed. And of course the marvelous dances of Agnes de Mille, who was the first choreographer to recognize my talents and to use them. It was stylistically an outgrowth of Agnes de Mille's *Rodeo.* I think that without Agnes it would have perhaps been a fine show but never a historic show.

Q: What's the essence of a great Broadway musical?

A: Great musicals get written only when a composer sits down and writes lovely tunes. All the rest is pure window dressing.

Q: What did you think of the new musical *Sgt. Pepper's Lonely Hearts Club Band on the Road?*

A: I think it was just godawful. But it was just a vulgarization, not a musical. That's like what I call an old Fancho-Marco revue. Or a television spectacular!

Q: How many Culture Barons do you think there are in the United States?

A: Not a great many. Well, combining opera, music, the visual arts, writing—it must run into the thousands. And that breaks down, relatively, to about twenty-five people. [Laughs] What I mean is, there are twenty-five people and then a lot of cousins and nephews and nieces. There are really very few families. In art, it's the Mellons, most of all, and the Rockefellers and

Carnegie and Frick. And in the world of ballet, Lucia Chase and Lincoln Kirstein are the two great patrons. But it comes out of a passion, you know; it just doesn't involve money— that's very important. It involves a personal passion, a dedication of time, and an interest in artistic collaboration—that is to say, a fascination with other artists.

Q: So it's the opposite of the desire to starve in a garret?

A: Yes, that's true; it's to provide a home for that expression. In other words, it's a very humane thing. When you say "baron," it's not like a robber baron, it's not like the so-called robber barons, whose only interest was in building vulgar large big houses, or living it up, as they say, and buying a *box* at the opera. But there was an Otto Kahn who contributed a vast amount of his fortune to make the Metropolitan Opera possible. It's in the tradition of the Médicis and the Svartzes and the great popes and Queen Elizabeth I. (Svartz was the rival banker to the Médici, like Morgan and the Rockefeller-Chase National. And Kahn's bank was Kuhn Loeb—but we all know that!)

They want to spend their money on human beings instead of things. The barons of culture are interested in people who are alive. In living human beings creating in their time. The pope who made Michelangelo paint the Sistine Chapel was a madman: you either did it or you got excommunicated! But by God he painted that thing!

Q: How did you get the commission to do de Mille's *Rodeo* at the age of twenty-four?

A: I was introduced to her by Aaron Copland, who I would say was just an acquaintance, not a friend. But he was familiar with my work, and so he suggested an interview with her. She looked at my portfolio, she liked it, she took a chance.

Q: How do you select works for Ballet Theater to produce?

A: It's something that Lucia and Mr. Tudor and I select; not one of us selects anything—it's a collaborative effort. Our work would fall into two categories. One is a long-range viewpoint of classics, which we continually want to feed into our repertoire. We feel that that's one of the functions of Ballet Theater. And then we do contemporary work as we can find it.

Today, for example, there are very few choreographers. I mean, there are a lot of them, but there are not very many good ones. Choreography is not at a very high level—I'm excluding the giants, the well-known Establishment. But that comes in waves. Choreographic productivity comes in waves, just like painting. You have this great explosion of twentieth-century painting in France, and then it came to the United States; but it was followed by Pop Art, which is ghastly! I mean terrible! If you think of choreography, you've got the great epoch of Petipa, which was a whole creation of dance forms, and then you'd have to skip a whole ways; you might pick it up again with Massine and the whole Diaghilev bit, but except for Massine and Nijinska it wasn't in all that great shape. And today we don't think very much of their choreography really. We think a lot of Petipa. And then you get into Tudor, Robbins, Balanchine, Graham, Ashton—Robbins got into that class simply by his [unintelligible]—and then you have Macmillan, and we had Cranko, and Neumeier. And then you go on to others. But when you get down to the bottom—there it's pretty pathetic.

I don't mean that as snobbish as it sounds. That's a very arrogant thing to say. I don't mean it that way. It's just that, if you're a painter today running around with your portfolio trying to get in to the galleries, you're working in a league with Picasso, Miró, Braque, perhaps Roualt, Soutine, De Kooning, and that whole period of abstract expressionism.

The young choreographers, working all around the country today. They all have some talent. It's just that there's such a tremendous awareness of dance. . . .

☆   ☆   ☆

So we see two different ballet companies, two different opera companies, run by venerable, mostly older men with different characters and backgrounds, fighting for territory and for money. They are unlike in their aesthetics, but they are also like each other; they are competitors in the tradition of Coca-Cola and Pepsi-Cola. Some argue that this is the beauty of America, that we have here no Minister of Culture to proclaim once and for all that Coke (or Pepsi) shall be universal and Pepsi (or Coke) re-educated. But on the other hand, some argue that America has a dearth of Culture Barons and a dearth of culture. Perhaps lurking in the structural warring of the City Opera and the Met, the City Ballet and the American Ballet Theater, there is a clue to why we do not have more opera companies and ballet companies.

In the theater, we find a slightly different pattern.

THEATER:
Broadway's Heroes
and Hoaxers

Eighty-five percent of everything done in the theater is ninety-nine percent determined by six or seven men. Those are the exact figures.
—Tom Jones,
Broadway and television actor

Within five years, I submit to you, the entire Broadway theater may vanish.
—member of the audience
Labor Relations in the Performing
Arts Panel, Lincoln Center,
December 1974

The theater is like beads. Some people are into it, and some aren't; but it has no relation to the real world. Joe Papp thinks it has, though. He thinks theater affects all of our lives. Joe Papp is a great man.
—Wallace Shawn, playwright
(*Our Late Night*)

T HEATER goes back at least 2,500 years, and what happens on stage has always been politically significant. For some reason American Communists favor Greek and Shakespearian tragedy over Restoration comedy, and they fill the high-up, cheap seats of the opera.

In the fourth century B.C. Aristotle defended the tragedies of

Aeschuylus, Sophocles, and Euripides as the highest of the arts—even though these plays were popular. His opponents argued that epic poetry was superior because it was harder to understand. Something of the same kind of disagreement is still going on today.

Under Elizabeth I of England, theater flourished alongside maritime exploration. William Shakespeare had his own repertory company, which performed in a theater large even by today's standards: the Globe accommodated 3,000. Friends of Joseph Papp maintain that the Globe repertory was the most democratic institution in Elizabethan England. Friends of Broadway point out that a Shakespeare play recovered its production costs in two weeks, whereas today it takes nine months. At about the same time, the great French playwrights also had their own repertory companies.

In 1789 an antitheater act was repealed in France, which perhaps ushered in the Revolution.

In New York City at the turn of the twentieth century, somewhere between 250 and 300 theaters were built for the legitimate play. The Palace! The Tivoli! The Bijou! The Roxy! Theaters given nicknames and initials and named after Squares. And no movies! Theater production and attendance reached a peak at the time of the First World War. Just then the three Shubert brothers, Sam, who died fairly soon, and Lee, and J.J., bought more than half of these many theaters. At the moment that people call "the peak" of theater in America (1905 or 1926, according to different sources), the Shuberts owned about 150 legitimate houses in New York and another 750 across the country. They were the modern Theater Barons.

But movies usurped the place of live plays, and gradually the houses were converted. The number of establishments in New York City showing live plays declined from 285 at the beginning of the century to 63 at present. Of these The Shubert Organization still has 17 in New York City.

Though "the Shuberts" are no longer producing plays, as in the old days when they had a reputation for hard-nosed rapacity, they are investing heavily in a number of Broadway shows. According to some Broadway producers, the biggest trend in theater power today is that theater owners are participating in the production of new work. Besides the Shubert executives, such owners include Roger Stevens, Conrad Matthaei, Lester Osterman, and James M. Nederlander. But these people don't really get involved in the artistic side of the work, according to producer David Black, and are therefore responsible, he contends, for the fact that no new American straight play has made money since *Who's Afraid of Virginia Woolf?* (1962). One critic calls them "strange characters"; another says they are "good guys."

Gerald Schoenfeld, chairman of the Shubert board, attorney with the firm of Schoenfeld and Jacobs and a frequent spokesman for the theater owners' trade association, the League of New York Theaters and Producers, is the very picture of a baron. His head is concise in gold-rimmed glasses, white-haired around the sides and bald on top. He dresses conservatively in a gray suit, dark socks, and a solid dark tie, he is tightly chubby around the middle and through the neck, and his feet are small and his trousers just an iota too short.

He outlines the specific history of a labor dispute between the theaters and the musicians which in his view had been correctly solved, as of early 1975, under optimum circumstances:

"Now, when we had to negotiate the last Broadway contract, we had a problem of dealing with outmoded minimums of men, and outmoded seating capacities that determined the number of musicians that had to be employed in any particular theater. Basically, if you had more than one hundred seats, you had to employ twenty-five musicians. Now, the economics of the theater business had evolved to such a degree that the application of that rule no longer made any sense. So you start off a negotiation with a major revolutionary change that you wish to effect.

"You try to advance that to a large committee: that is not the administration of the union; this is the rank and file committee. And you're right away talking in terms of reducing the number of jobs, of establishing a lesser minimum. Ideally what we were trying to do was to establish what we thought was a realistic minimum for each particular theater by name. We did not achieve the millennium with this negotiation, but we did make a major stride towards it.

"Now, the problem we had at that negotiation was first of all dealing with the leadership of the union, to whom this kind of

change represents a large problem, but also with a theater com-
mittee, to whom jobs are the most important thing, just like the
leadership. It takes, in a negotiation of this kind, in my experi-
ence, a couple of months of negotiating, in order to establish an
attitude, if you will, or a climate, conducive to a receptivity of
this kind of a fundamental change. You can't accomplish it in ne-
gotiations of a week or two weeks; it has to be a long, drawn-out
discussion with examples and background and history. And basi-
cally you have to evince a position that makes economic sense.
And also a belief on the part of the people you're negotiating with
that what you say, they can believe. Now we were able to achieve
this; each theater now has a particular minimum. There has been
an evolution of a smaller musical show as a consequence of this,
which is now being presented in theaters which heretofore were
dramatic theaters, which never played musical shows, which has
created more employment opportunities for musicians, which has
resulted perhaps in a change of the art form of a musical show.
And it is perhaps economic necessity that has resulted in change,
where the union has gone along and has not necessarily suffered
as a consequence.

"And this is true, also I can state in respect to Local 1, the
Stagehands Union, in respect to problems dealing with the au-
tomation of scenery, where the union has cooperated and been
sensitive to the technological changes that have gone on."

There are now only about three important Broadway producers and a dozen more who do an occasional play. Play selection is to some extent influenced by twelve nice Jewish ladies
who form a loose association of theater benefit agents, and who
sell one fifth of all tickets sold on Broadway.

Comparing the present to the period of the flourishing of theater earlier in this century, to the flowering of American playwrights in the days of Eugene O'Neill and Clifford Odets, there is
common agreement that the theater is in a slump. Multimillion-
dollar producer Hal Prince heartily endorses *The New York Times*
epithet, "a fabulous invalid." But explanations vary.

Agnes de Mille calls theater today "a chaos and a shambles."
Miss de Mille ascribes it to a lack of enlightened patronage.

The official view is that there is a "cost disease" inherent to
all mass-producible art. First propounded by Alvin Toffler in *The*

Culture Consumers in 1964 and then written up by Princeton economists William and Hilda Baumol for *The New York Times* and the Ford Foundation, this hypothesis is that the arts, being necessarily limited by the human factor in their productivity, inevitably suffer from the rising costs of materials. In some form or other this thesis was repeated by nearly every Culture Baron I interviewed, in every one of the arts and in the subsidy agencies.

The suburban explanation blames the deterioration of the Times Square neighborhood under the mayoralty of John V. Lindsay, which theoretically discourages people from having "a night on the town" such as used to be possible, and which is still possible in London's West End. This view is taken by former theatergoers who have moved out of the city coincident with the influx of blacks and Puerto Ricans to city schools.

The radical explanation for the invalidity of the theater was expressed in a letter to the *Times* by *Second City* producer Bernard Sahlins. He held that landlord, public relations, and union costs are all much higher for Broadway theaters than for theaters in other cities and even for off-Broadway theaters in New York. Other producers admitted unreasonably high landlord costs were a big factor but felt the position too radical to take for the record.

Owners of theaters may of course argue in reply that they feed money back through their charitable foundations to the creative side of the theatrical world. In 1974–75 the Shubert Foundation gave 108 grants to theatrical interests, totaling $1.2 million. This included $145,000 to the New York Shakespeare Festival, $125,000 to Town Hall, $50,000 to the Phoenix Repertory Theater, $37,000 to the Roundabout Theater, $35,000 to the J.F.K. Center in Washington, and $30,000 to the Yale Drama School.

☆   ☆   ☆

Producer David Black, who claims that he was at one time the largest Broadway producer after David Merrick and Harold Prince, makes an impassioned case for government intervention in the theater to offset the corruption of private influence.

Sitting in a dark East Side apartment surrounded by extraordinary dark, hulking furniture from the set of his production of *The Aspern Papers,* he ran down the real power wielded by the producers (not much) and other groups. All the producer *per se* really does, he said, was to pick a play or get an idea for one and commission it. Subsequently his powers are all negative; he can stop the money flow, rip up the contracts, fire people (at the price of the royalties), or close the show out of town.

Financially speaking, said Black, the producer is not in a particularly strong position. The theater owner got a million dollars, in one case, and the author a quarter of a million, before the backers had been repaid and therefore before the producer got any profit over his couple of hundred a week in salary. Author Susan Slade, for her script *Ready When You Are, C.B.!* got a whopping sixty percent of the subsidiary rights.

David Black came on in our interview more like a member of the frantic acting community than like a producer, much less a Culture Baron. He was eager to talk, eager to share with a reporter a thesis he'd written on the situation of the theatrical producer (". . . and do you think you might be able to help me get it printed?"), full of angry castigations, statistics, anecdotes, and well-documented gripes. He seemed younger than his years, and still idealistic.

The producer has no real muscle, Black concluded.

The Theater Development Fund? Never helped save a dying show.

The League of New York Theaters and Producers? Never more than fourteen people at a meeting.

The Rockefeller Fund under Stephen Benedict? Not enough money. No significant work. Should be subsidizing playwrights, not tickets.

The New York State Council on the Arts? A farce, a disaster.

The Theater District? Not nearly as nice as London's, where they serve cookies and tea in the aisles. But then again, it's important to remember that America is dipolar, the culture divided between New York and Los Angeles. And the architects' models of all those new theater buildings between Forty-first and Fifty-fourth streets looked much better—landscaped and with outdoor cafés—than the actual finished buildings. In sum, it's Mayor Lindsay's fault that people don't want to come to the neighborhood. And the Netherlands' Queen Juliana, who is the largest foreign owner of American real estate.

Regional theater? Better for authors, since The Disillusionment of the last six or seven years.

The Federal Government scene? In America, responds Black, we spend more than $40 million a year on the arts, enough to pave merely two miles of a four-lane highway and an amount that could easily be absorbed by orchestras alone. In fact, orchestras do get a lot of it, for mystical reasons having to do with the superiority of Bach's Masses over the rock masses. The reason for the allocation of funds as it now works has to do with the fact that a very small number of people are in control and that they are power mad. They move from arts councils to other organizations and institutions. Their reasons for involvement in the arts are not good ones, and so the powerful cliques fail to improve the quality of life, merely hopping between power structures.

State subsidy in general? Better off with government than private. Playwrights should get the money—not all of them and not all at once. Power should not be a part of these things.

As his personal solution, Black quit the theater and spent a few months in real estate.

☆   ☆   ☆

The sensibilities on Broadway are absurdist, psychoanalytical, intellectual, nostalgic, camp, hayseed, hoax, and heroic. David Merrick is an example of hayseed, along with those dozen theater benefit agent ladies, who are friendly and wholesome and do volunteer hospital work. Hal Prince is master of hoax, or pizzazz, with which he superficially decorates his basically meaningless productions.

The imports from Britain mostly belong in the intellectual category, though some are absurdist, some psychoanalytical, some camp. The leading proponent of the British theatrical import is producer Alexander Cohen.

Kermit Bloomgarden works in the area of the intellectual. Various producers take turns at the nostalgic. There is a lot of camp emanating from the TV studios. None of these forms have any lasting value except Papp's heroic.

Joe Papp is many things in New York, the least of which is superstar. Almost single-handedly he has created a whole new type of theater, which is both popular and classic, as if tapping a previously unexplored vein of the city's artistic life. His rivals in the provinces—Pittsburgh, for instance—fear he means to swallow them up, to make of his already large enterprise a "national theater," with all manuscripts submitted to New York for approval and the chosen ones farmed out to the hinterlands for performance. Papp denies this. He claims a national theater wouldn't serve his purposes at all.

Papp is committed to the idea that the theater has an impact on social life. He does not present work that is absurdist or nostalgic or camp; he is not interested in the pretentiously intellectual, the psychoanalytical, or the British-for-its-own-sake. His plays invariably relate to New York City life, whether they be an all black *Bedtime Story* or a Puerto Rican *Hamlet* or a shocking little work by a woman about mastectomy. He has created a theater of relevance. And so he has supporters and enemies at every rank in society.

Papp is indignant about the negative reception often given his work by the critics. He accuses them of shirking their duty to inform and educate the public whom they represent, and—even worse—of being too old, entrenched in jobs that are effectively not open to women, and sexually and emotionally maladjusted. In short, he sees the critical establishment as itself irrelevant to modern social life.

With respect to those he has taken under his wing—playwrights, directors, actors—Papp is like a supernice college dean ("Everything in life is a school," he says), complete with pipe and patched-elbow tweed jackets. One hears of numerous examples of unknown and struggling young writers and other talent to whom he has given unofficial grants of money. His policy is to perform the second play of a playwright he has produced, regardless of the merit of that work, simply as an expression of his loyalty to the writers as people, and his commitment to their artistic development. For such favors they swear undying loyalty in return.

"One night we had a three-and-a-half-hour discussion about the unfocusedness of the second act," says Thom Babe, author of *Kid Champion,* a 1975 production. "It was a very fruitful conversation. It sharpened the act. Papp is not biased but relevant, with re-

Left to right: playwrights Thomas Babe, Miguel Pinero, Dennis J. Reardon, Michael Weller, and John Ford Noonan, with producer Joe Papp (Sy Friedman)

spect to content. It's not just a question of craft."

Myrna Lamb, author of *Mod Donna*, produced in 1970, says, "I was really in love with him. I probably still am."

"Papp inspires sycophantic support and jealous bad-mouthing," said another playwright, Michael Weller, author of *Moonchildren*. "He has something akin to taste—I don't know if it's the real item. Some of his works are terrible; I wouldn't do them in a million years. But his commitment to me is absolute; whatever I write will be done."

☆   ☆   ☆

Joseph Papp is everyone's lovable junior high school social studies and English teacher, miraculously risen to power. Almost uniquely in New York, he is doing something to foster the development of new playwrights.

In his youth he played the mad prince Hamlet on stage and the wandering minstrel prince Nanki-Poo and Scrooge, Dickens' repentant miser. As an adult, Papp was staging *Hamlet* as a Puerto Rican selling peanuts and balloons. British critic Clive Barnes hated it. Papp threw peanuts at him.

In the media capital of America the founder of the Shakespeare Festival and the Public Theater is a young prince, a hero of the muses, an heir apparent, like the Hamlet and Nanki-Poo he played in his youth. His admirers actually compare him to Shakespeare. Says Akrim Medany, dean of the Carnegie-Mellon University School of Fine Arts: "This is not an age for playwrights. Papp is Shakespeare as Shakespeare would be if he were alive today." Other compliments Papp has received include: "New York's premier cultural politician" (*The New York Times*); "golden boy of good theater" (*The Village Voice*); "the maximum director" (*West Side Literary Review*); "the most dynamic force in contemporary American theater" (Barnes, *Viva*). His detractors scowl at his closed-shop domination of the theater-of-relevance scene in New York and his seemingly still unsatisfied ambition to be head of an American national theater; they call him, ironically, "Napoleon" (*Time*) or "Caesar" (*Newsweek*) or "Don Quixote" (*Cue*).

For twenty years now, Papp has been mounting one Shakespeare play after another, free to the people of New York. First in a ramshackle Lower East Side church, then in Central Park, and for the last three years on the lovely stages of the Lincoln Center Repertory Theater designed by Eero Saarinen. By last year he had gone through Shakespeare's complete works: seventy-nine different productions of all the tragedies, comedies, and histories. And since the opening of the Public Theater in 1967, he has been also doing other plays by young writers—a total of fifty-five shows at small admissions charges.

One of his original purposes, Papp recalls, was to show plays for free. And another was to produce Shakespeare in an unpompous, un-British way.

Statistically, he is already the national theater. He is funded by the three largest foundations and the three levels of government. Papp's organization is by far the largest acting combine outside of Hollywood, and the largest employer of live actors anywhere in the country. Despite an occasional complaint from an unemployed actor that his casting office is hard to penetrate, the Public Theater has a generally good reputation in New York's huge acting community. That is understandable, because it provides jobs, at Equity wages, for approximately 350 actors a year, and another 75 in $100-a-week training workshops. This is half as many actors as are employed everywhere else on the stages of New York; 838 actors were employed on Broadway and off-Broadway in the 1968 season, 583 in 1969 according to *Business Week*. Papp has employed approximately 5,600 actors since he began producing here twenty years ago.

Seated in his huge neorealistic downtown office in front of a four-foot-tall illustrated volume of Shakespeare dating from 1852 and worth perhaps $40,000 ("Some guy died and left it to me"), Joseph Papp now oversees fully a dozen separate theaters, most of which curl cozily around one another in one renovated antique building.

A pundit has compared Papp's Public Theater domain, hard by the Bowery and the Lower East Side, with the Quirinal in Rome, "ferociously grand in its palatial poverty, capitol of a penniless land."

Another has called the complex of theaters a chambered Nautilus: a self-contained, internally referential, infinitely spiraling mollusk world. But that is a pun, for "Nautilus" is also the name of an atomic submarine. And upstairs last season the Public Theater hosted a little group calling itself "the Manhattan Project," another pun on atomic power. The fierceness of the metaphor is probably not accidental.

Papp's crew of writers and directors and blacks and aristocratic women who militantly refer to themselves as "actors" and electricians and stage managers and lighting designers and secretarial girls and all the young men artists and administrators run a tight, loyal ship. Their feeling for their captain shades into the autocratic; sometimes it frightens or disgusts outsiders by its embarrassing gushiness, its explicitly Freudian content. Most of the time it is a terribly efficient theatrical delivery machine, running on an energy that is at the least idealistic, and at its height, more properly speaking, messianic.

The operation has a distinct interface with the Yale Drama

School, where Papp taught in 1966. Directors A. J. Antoon, Jeff Bleckner, Barnett Kelman, and Ted Cornell all come from Yale. So do playwrights David Rabe (actually, the New Haven *Register*) and Robert Montgomery and actor Stacy Keach (New Haven's Long Wharf Theater).

One of Papp's most ardent admirers does accuse Papp of an artistic fault peculiar to megalomania. That is, she says, he loses sight of personal boundaries and starts thinking that everything in a play emanates from himself. As a consequence, this woman saw a staging idea of hers used in another person's play "before it had lived yet in my own production." The experience was terrible, painful, "a live butchery," she relates. But she also trembles in fear that Papp will recognize her complaint and be angry with her.

The captain admits he is autocratic about artistic decisions. "I make the major artistic decision, which is choosing the play," he says. "Nobody else makes that decision, but people can talk to me if they want to."

Some have reported that what Papp looks for in an actor is "class," a sense of self-value and character, which may manifest itself in something as simple as posture erectness. What he likes in a director is that he or she be radical, mature, and have a sense of humor. And all that he will say about how he chooses plays, at first, is that he must have "a feeling about it, in terms of its content and its structure." To a more sympathetic reporter he elaborates slightly: he likes "plays that will make an impact on society, that will reach great numbers of people, that are simple and direct like David Rabe's."

With as many as twelve productions humming at one time, Papp receives between thirty and fifty unsolicited play scripts each week, far more than any other New York producer. He has a full-time staff of twelve to read each of the manuscripts more than once, headed by Meir Zvi Ribalow, a young Princeton poet who got the job by stumbling bravely into Papp's office.

Papp's taste in plays reflects first of all a distaste for the school of the absurd, the experimental-for-its-own-sake, and the improvisational. Neither does he like what he terms "flag waving." The middle ground between the so-called avant-garde in art and the so-called vanguard in politics, which is nevertheless at the forefront of feeling, powerful, complicated, and authentic, is the area he has staked out for his work. "I have no goals; the work is all," he claims. And yet that work reeks like so much raw hamburger. Rockstars and superwomen stalk his stages. Psychotic amazons going mad from the loss of their breast. Wised-up black and Puerto Ricans inside a prison who murder and learn a lesson from it. The agonies of racial and sexual justice and retribution for the Asian war. These are the kinds of thing he sponsors.

"I like complexity," he told me. "Whenever the black realizes that he's as fucked up as anybody else, then I say, 'Okay, I'll do the play.' Same thing with the women's lib thing. There has to be some recognition of what the total truth is. Though you can still say what's wrong and what's right within that situation."

When I talked with him he seemed intuitively to be valuing warmth, youth, populism, and mixing, though he never used these words. "What I value is mainly good character," he said. "Someone, people who relate to other people in a whole way. Society encourages the opposite—to ignore, to conceal, or to make your way over somebody's dead body. I like people who don't do that. Who find a way to make a life not at somebody else's expense, or your own . . ."

He is a pleasant-looking man, with classic character in his face, modestly dressed in brown among the beiges and greens of his surroundings. He looks softer and gentler than one would expect from his reputation. And also better-looking than in his photos—possibly because he is conscious, to the point of stiltedness, of not making any misleading gestures in front of a camera.

"But I am not a Culture Baron," Papp protests. "That doesn't describe what I do or what I am. 'Baron' is a German word—it implies inheritance, property, nobility, great sums of money, and power that relates to money. I don't have any of that. The barons of the theater were the Shuberts at one point, who owned all the real estate—more than half the theaters on Broadway plus a far-flung empire of theaters all over the country.

"I work from the inside out. Not for any external reasons. My work begins with my ideas and feelings about the theater." He concedes that others may describe him differently.

Although numerous Opera and Theater Barons (such as Schuyler Chapin and Amyas Ames and Harold Prince) have publicly spoken in favor of city and state support of their arts, Joseph

Papp, one of the public's major beneficiaries, seems to take a teasingly different view. "Opera could be supported by one person. Yet more and more, by default, support is going into the hands of the city. I prefer the old way," said Papp. "I like the idea of the rich patron. There's a certain elitism that's essential in the arts. Democracy would kill it. Naturally you want taste. If painting were dependent upon popular acceptance, art would be dead. It would be all realism. Or 'new realism.' You wouldn't have had the chateaux of France.

"Of course the rich people who dominate the Met are retrogressive. The development of new work might take fifty years. Otherwise, when these people die out, you'll have nothing."

When asked about colleagues in the theater whom he admires, Papp mentioned Kermit Bloomgarden—concerning whom there was a *Times* clipping on his desk. And also Zelda Fichandler of the Arena in Washington, D.C., Gordon Davidson in California, and Michael Langham in Minneapolis' Guthrie Theater. He called the Broadway producers, "with one exception, family men, dullards." But then he praised their "businessman's orientation," the way they "nurture, and husband, and are meticulous" about their productions. "I wish I were a better businessman," he remarked.

Egged on to comment on David Merrick and to defend himself against the charge of frequently firing directors, Papp retorted heartily if a bit disjointedly: "Merrick has replaced directors and actors many more times than I. I've done it maybe twice. [Alice] Childress thanked me for it—that was the only time I did it to a writer.

"As for *Boom Boom Room*—[Papp was accused of male chauvinism in the firing of director Julie Bovasso in *Boom Boom Room*, by Patricia Bosworth in *The New York Times*, Nov. 25, 1973], I stepped in just to save [Bovasso's] life; she was absolutely bewildered. The *Boom Boom Room* article was totally inaccurate. It makes good copy to attack the boss all the time. How many plays do I produce compared with Merrick's one or two a year? I produce eighteen or twenty. Replacing a director is a thankless task, only for extreme emergencies. I don't think I'll do it anymore."

And as if presenting his final defense, Papp concluded, "I

always do a writer's second play, sight unseen, even if the play isn't good."

Papp's early years are lost to the legend. Aside from the identity of his parents, the locale of birth, and the fact that he played Hamlet, Nanki-Poo, and Scrooge in childhood productions, we know nothing about the young Papp until we see him producing vaudeville and broad burlesque atop a flattop in the Pacific. Home from the Navy, he went to California, where he swept and mopped the floors at Actors' Lab before graduating from the institution in 1948, at the age of twenty-seven. Making this point, Papp turns to a Vermeeresque new-realist painting hanging behind his desk, which shows three women mopping up the floor of a library.

Another painting, on the opposite wall, shows a black girl and a white girl playing on a city street. Also new realist.

In Hollywood, he says, he observed the futility of an artists' board trying to find salvation through collective management. He felt the decisions of a theatrical organization, like those on an individual work of art, should be made by one person. He returned to New York City.

His first attempt to "find a place" in theater in New York seemed disastrous. He did *Bedtime Story,* by the then living Sean O'Casey, off-Broadway, using black actors. The *Times* critic commented, "whoever that guy is, he should get out of the theater." Papp recounts that he took the criticism seriously and went and sat, depressed, in a muddy place in Central Park for five days. But then the play earned a best-of-the-year award, and he was on his way.

He was asked to direct in a Presbyterian church on East Sixth Street; his first budget, in 1954, was $25 for the season. Actors contributed their unemployment insurance. He and they did a lot of physical labor, like putting up the lights. They stole equipment from a Bronx theater. The next production, in the East River Amphitheater, had a budget of $750. But then something snapped again, and money started coming in from the outside. "We had to work very hard, on a shoestring, for the first five years," Papp says.

A hurdle was crossed, strangely enough, when Papp was fired from a stage manager's job at CBS-TV for political reasons and, simultaneously, attacked by Parks Commissioner Robert Moses, in

1958. Though unsuccessful in his initial attempt to get $40,000 from New York City at this time, he was supported by the *Times* and the *Post* and consequently reinstated at CBS—and the first flurry of private contributions started coming in, one notably from Rodgers and Hammerstein. Only three years later, Mayor Wagner's Board of Estimate awarded him $60,000; and subsequent city governments increased the figure a little every year till it reached an annual level of $500,000. Mayor Lindsay even raised $27,000 privately in 1966, just to make the grant a round figure.

Another money crisis occurred in the summer and fall of 1970. Roger Stevens chaired an emergency committee to save the N.Y. Shakespeare Festival and Public Theater and sent Governor Rockefeller a telegram. As a result, Papp's outfit received $100,000 from the National Endowment every year for the next several years. And late in 1971, New York City bought the Astor Library for a cool $2.6 million and donated it to Papp.

Paradoxically, the very idea of free theater, even Shakespeare, made it hard for Papp to get support from the largest arts-granting institution, the Ford Foundation. Longtime Arts and Humanities division chief W. McNeil Lowry explained that Ford is not interested in funding organizations "that do not have at least a gamble at survival." Ford feels that artists should be in touch with what the community is willing to pay for. This position held in Papp's disfavor for several years, until 1973, when Ford developed its Cash Reserve Program, for which the Public Theater and the Lincoln Center Repertory Theater are both eligible. Papp jokes that Ford owes him "$5 million in reparations."

The Shakespeare in the Park performances continue to be free. Still, the Lincoln Center and Public Theater portions of his operation bring in at their box offices thirty-five percent of the gross income for the whole outfit. Papp charges approximately five dollars for a seat, less than any other of the high cultural events like opera, ballet, or legitimate theater, about as much as an expensive movie.

Last year the National Endowment for the Arts gave Papp's organization a quarter of a million dollars, the N.Y.S. Council on the Arts gave three quarters of a million, and the N.Y.C. Parks, Recreation, and Cultural Affairs Administration gave $650,000. Of all the governmental bodies, the city has been the largest donor, with a total gift of $5 million over the last thirteen years.

Foundations, including Ford, Rockefeller, and Mellon, gave $1,300,000 last year. Individuals gave about $275,000. Nineteen thousand subscribers, at $40 per person, contributed for the privilege of getting a seat.

Among Papp's "benefactors" (those who have given $5,000 or more at any time since the founding of the Festival) are Actors Equity, AFL-CIO, Rebekah Harkness, the Rockefeller Brothers, the Shubert Foundation, WCBS, and sixty-four other individuals, family foundations, and businesses.

Twenty-three persons or companies are listed by Papp as "donors," which means they contributed $1,000 in the previous year. The list includes Consolidated Edison, Morgan Guaranty Trust, the Rodgers and Hammerstein Foundation, and most of the members of Papp's board of trustees.

Half that contribution qualifies a person for the list of "founders." This list includes Helen Hayes, Jerome Robbins, two or three garment workers' unions, and several local drama institutions, for a total of thirty-nine listees.

The longest list is that of "patrons" for the current year. American Airlines, Bloomingdale's, the Capezio Foundation, Gulf and Western Foundation, a hospital employees' union, another garment workers' union, and three hundred people and other organizations gave $100 last year to Papp's Shakespeare Festival.

One influential donor who bestowed power on Papp along with money was Mrs. Russel Crouse, head of the Theatre Development Fund and widow of the playwright. According to her daughter Lindsay, who acts and choreographs for Papp, it was Anna Crouse who engineered Lincoln Center's offer of the Rep Theater to Papp.

Perhaps at the root of the envy or dislike some other theater people feel for Joseph Papp is his astounding record in obtaining money for his projects.

When questioned about this, Papp is modest and reserved. His relations with the current mayor are formal, he reports; and no, he doesn't know how city budget cuts are going to affect him. His relations with John D. Rockefeller require a telephone call. But he admits to feeling put out at the Rockefeller Brothers Fund, which cut back on a grant he thought would be $350,000 and forced him to cancel two plays last year.

Asked about his past, Papp is the kind of highly successful man who is romantic and patriotic about his own life story. He caresses certain chapters lovingly and obliterates others.

Because his work first changed markedly in 1967—when he acquired the downtown theater and began to do modernized versions of Shakespeare and new plays—I asked Papp what had happened to him generally, in the '60s. He seemed to like the question and kept returning to it in other contexts.

"Every sensitive person was affected by the sixties," he said. "From those who were actively a part of it to those who were on the outside . . ."

He said his son Michael had asked him to speak at Vassar in connection with a demonstration of Transcendental Meditation. He went, Papp said, just for his son's sake but rebutted the claims of T.M. in the name of the artistic process. "This idea of relaxation," he said, with emotion, "it's false, anarchistic, fascistic. Anything that applies to everybody, to eliminate tensions . . . even if there were such a thing I wouldn't want it."

He showed me a letter a girl at Vassar had written to him, in appreciation of his speech, on the subject of the artistic process. And then he waxed eloquent about the agonies of creation. "Good writers operate from their blood. There's a wound. They are representatives of everybody, but they've found a way to articulate it. Most people don't.

"The main thing that adults could do in the sixties was to protect the young. They were being slaughtered! That was everybody's obligation. They're still being destroyed!"

Papp told me about a theater group from Texas that had lived in the Public Theater for a while, calling themselves "Stomp." "The kids were sick, the girls were pregnant, their teeth were rotting. I watched that thing disintegrate. It was an amazing show, a brilliant director, both beautiful and terrible."

Papp saw the events of the '60s as "all one thing—from leading the radical movement to lying stoned on the doorstep, smoking your life away—it was all one thing." Since then, he sees increasing Puritanism, conservatism, depression, even possibly counterrevolution—though these dismal events are dangerous to talk about. "Unless the labor movement turns totally around . . ."

"When we were fighting over *Sticks & Bones,* CBS claimed the blue collar workers didn't want to see it," he told me, in reference to David Rabe's play about a Vietnam veteran. "But even if they voted for Nixon doesn't mean they all think alike, doesn't mean what they are," he argued. "Now they've lost jobs. Even a conservative can turn into a raving radical to survive." Rabe's play about a returning veteran had been scheduled for airing on television literally the same day the war officially ended and the return of POWs was announced.

Another brilliant irony of Papp's timing had also occurred in 1969–70, in connection with the nascent women's liberation movement. Papp had recognized a *fait accompli* and the good character of a little delegation that came to him calling itself the New Feminist Repertory Theater and headed by Myrna Lamb, though the women's movement was not yet much spoken of, and one of Lamb's troupe was only later to become president of the National Organization for Women.

Though encouraged by Papp's own in-house repertory workshop (the Free Living Open Theater Group) to do a feminist musical, the eight or ten of them from the New Feminist Repertory Theater had hesitated before coming to see the legendary producer.

Papp himself was a myth, and Lamb was a product of the Newark slums. She stared at his phone number for three days before calling to ask to see him. His secretary, Gail Merrifield, put her off. This aroused Lamb's suspicions, but Merrifield reassured her with protestations of sincerity.

But Lamb's play *Mod Donna* was an authentic work of art, a freewheeling original format encompassing the unbearable materialism of the social structure and psychic-religious roots of sex. Though she already had a grown daughter (an actress), Lamb was fighting with the energy of a woman in her early twenties to make up for the time it had cost her to get out of all the traps. And Papp recognized her vigor and the vigor of her group, for it was the same vigor that the aristocracy recognized in him and made them want to be near him, to give him money.

He produced *Mod Donna,* "a Space Age musical soap opera with breaks for commercials." And directed it himself, which, as he said, brought out the feminine side of his personality—his better self.

The feminist satire/passion play opened at the Public Theater the day of the Kent State shootings, May 1, 1970. Later that week Cambodia was invaded.

The audience, even the actors in the play itself, reacted violently. "What right—?" people screamed, have you to worry about these things when people are dying? Myrna Lamb stood up at the end of the play to defend feminism. Papp's own people attacked him for being too feminist.

Meanwhile the Shakespeare Festival was in an economic crisis. Papp had $2,000 cash in hand; his payroll was $19,000. He was laying out $4,000 or $5,000 a week for Mod Donna. Lamb claims "he was almost in jail" for debt. They locked him out of his theater building. John O'Connor on Channel 13 said the Public Theater should be closed for producing Mod Donna.

With all this, Papp closed Mod Donna on June 7. Betty Friedan had turned down an offer from the Times to review the play, fearing it would be bad and therefore embarrassing.

Barely weeks later, that August 26, some 25,000 to 50,000 women participated in the first big March Down Fifth Avenue for women's liberation. If the play had only been kept open through the summer, Lamb muses, it might have plugged into that suddenly visible grass-roots phenomenon.

But her future was assured. By 1972 she had recommendations from Papp, from Schuyler Chapin, and from the Rockefeller Foundation's Howard Klein, and so she began to receive grants averaging $7,000 a year from Rockefeller, Guggenheim, and the National Endowment—each year being the only woman in her category to win.

And in 1974–75 Papp was working on another of Lamb's productions, tentatively titled Apple Pie and dealing with the situation of a Jewish girl in love with a black man. His loyalty evokes a profound emotion in her, makes an oasis in her life.

Papp in New York City is like the black statue atop the Victoria Memorial in Calcutta—a bit surprising perhaps but totally in his element. In a city with 10,000 would-be actors, ninety-four percent unemployed, he can be master boss, with a full time staff of talent scouts out looking for actors with training and innate

Joseph Papp, producer-director of the New York Shakespeare Festival and the Public Theater

class. In a city that often bemoans the death of its theater, he can make a bid for guru: his plays are numerous and full of political commitment. He was born and raised in the Orthodox Jewish sector of Brooklyn to Ukrainian and Lithuanian immigrants named Papirofsky and was affected strongly in his youth by a mature and humorous radicalism. He was schooled in the Navy and in California, but he came back again to New York because he had concluded that "with the exception of the Hollywood film, New York has about seventy-five percent of the culture of America, in terms of standards, quality, audiences' alertness, knowledgeability, and sophistication."

Papp actually seems to revel in the peculiarities of New York

life. He has tales of talking down psychotic actors (finally calling
the police on them), of getting revenge on a Puerto Rican typewriter thief and on Harlem knife-wielders, of storming out of a
certain machine Democrat's office when the politician demanded
ten percent of the city's funding as a kickback, of refusing the
Mafia's invitation to direct a dirty movie. He smokes a Meer-
schaum pipe and lights it with A & P kitchen matches. He boasts
about the fast driving he does throughout the city in the early
hours of the morning. He lives in an unfashionable and racially
mixed part of town.

When he leaves The City, however, for instance to speak to
Pittsburgh's wealthiest culture patrons and steel and chemical and
Gulf Oil millionaires, Joseph Papp seems to be the very embodi-
ment of a national theater. He stands resplendent in a cobalt velvet suit; he drily insults the town he is visiting. Directors of the
local ballet and opera companies eye him with suspicion and tell
one another that his goal is to control everything that gets produced in their provincial playhouses from one central clearing office in New York City. Aging actresses in long dresses from the
Pittsburgh Players fail altogether to understand the import of the
speech he makes, in which he blames his negative reviews on
critics who are too old, too male, too hung up sexually. The rich
western Pennsylvania regionalists seem to wish he'd get more to
the point and explain clearly what he wants from them and what
he intends to do to them.

Perhaps Papp feels it goes without saying—or perhaps he is
tired of saying it or feels it has been spelled out elsewhere—but
he never mentions his overall goals to the older Pittsburghers. If
he had defined them, he might have mentioned setting up a strong
platform for living writers, new work, and the presentation of real
social issues, or overcoming the terrible economic weaknesses of
Broadway with an efficient, even formidable, delivery system—
"an apparatus with the power to thrust that good play onto American stages and then into the mass media of television and film."

☆   ☆   ☆

CULTURE BARON IN PROVINCES RAPS
MALE DRAMA CRITICS AS OLD, SEXIST

Speaking before a crowd of civic leaders recently stuffed with chocolate mousse by the Duquesne Club and Gulf Oil, as well as to earnest U Pitt students with poignant geographical inferiority complexes, in the Carnegie Institute's splendiferously marbled Music Hall, Joseph Papp of the New York Shakespeare Festival and Public Theater managed to offend virtually everyone in his audience. He called for the assumption of major newspaper and magazine drama criticism responsibilities by persons of different gender, age, and emotionality than those currently holding the positions.

After listening to many excerpts from critical pieces, both favorable and negative, of Papp's own work and in reference to modern classics like Beckett, some students vigorously applauded their drama chairman Favorini's accusation that Papp was "obsessed" with the critics.

But the N.Y.C. Culture Baron maintained that critics are legitimately representatives of an audience who are as "corrupt" as they are, and whom they have the responsibility to educate. Papp seemed to imply that his own much-praised twenty-year promulgation of Shakespeare has been in some measure a "priesthood" conferred upon him by others, and that given the opportunity he in fact prefers to mount new theatrical works. Specifically, he likes to actualize young writers "on their way" and to probe the themes of these young voices—even when it reveals "murder in their hearts."

Papp deplored the fact that there are effectively no women drama critics, that *The New York Times* has no explanation for this, that *New York Times'* unqualified praise is a prerequisite for a play's commercial success, that the only favorable review in New York City for his recent play *Mert and Phil*—written by Anne Burr and concerning the destruction of a woman—was done (in *Cue*) by the only woman to review it.

In answer to a question, Papp outlined what he sees as qualifications for the post of drama critic. His comments—"that he or she not be uptight or sexually frustrated or ambivalent about his masculinity or her femininity"—drew a restrained gasp from the well-heeled arts bigwigs, long used to dealing circuitously with the ubiquitous homosexuals of opera, ballet, and theater. Papp buttressed his recommendations with the explanation that these are necessary factors in being able to feel and understand the best dramatic work being produced today. (He also mentioned, as a qualification, the rather more traditional academic familiarity with theater.)

Many from the Gulf crowd felt, to their irritation, that Papp was apologizing for his recent work. But to other observers Papp's motivation for a sometimes Lenny Bruce-like speech was nobler, possibly even an ambition to martyrdom. He laboriously revealed many of the terrible things that have been said about the new plays he has done recently, without attempting to refute the criticism or justify the plays. From his point of view he was establishing the inability of both critics and audience to grasp what he believes at least 98 percent of the time quite firmly to be seriously good work, important, and very likely great. He was ostensibly less interested in debating the merits of his record than in noting the processes of materialization and change between director and actor, writer and producer, play and critic.

In a closing sentence, Papp noted that there had been a time when Broadway plays were not alienated from their audiences and critics. Summing up his separate arguments as to why present-day critics are failing to lead audiences wisely and educate tastes, one came away with the generally disturbing conviction that it is because they are too old to get up the theater steps, let alone understand politics after the 1930s, that they are too neurotic and Puritanical to be able to hear certain words, let alone absorb sexually complicated dramatic situations, and, in short (though Papp hesitated on the word, and put it in quotes, so as not to be too uncharming), that they are too sexist to understand why a woman would neglect her kids to write a play in the first place.

The very next day after talking over the heads of the fairly hostile Pittsburgh industrialists and bankers and lawyers, Papp rolls up his sleeves for a more spontaneous get-together with the drama students of Carnegie-Mellon University. A well-endowed and modern institution, its drama students are nevertheless in hippy uniform: mostly blue jeans and drab sweaters and shirts—with an occasional brilliantly colored serape or plastic red star—many carrying army knapsacks, with a sprinkling of sketchbooks among their other paperware. Papp is happy to be with the students. He boyishly sits down on a table on the stage, his knees dangling, looking something like a Good Humor man in his beige suit, white bucks, and bowtie.

The kids listen to him with respectful pin-drop silence. Then they ask questions. What about "the future of musical comedy?" (His verdict: "A lot of musical comedy has gotten too serious. I mean pretentious, pseudo. Take *Pippin*—that was a boring, boring show!" The kids laugh heartily.) Another question: "How do you find new plays to do, and are they already produced?" ("No, ninety-nine percent of what I do starts from scratch.") A young black says, "What do you think of the television program 'All in the Family'?" (Papp gulps. Then says he thinks it's worthless but admits he laughs.) Another asks, "What do you think of the VFA?" apparently the degree they are working for. "What's a VFA?" Papp replies. The student accepts that as a perfectly good answer, but Papp apologizes for his own deficient education. It has been written elsewhere that Papp cares nothing for degrees, qualifications, credentials.

Joseph Papp earns $25,000 a year, much less than commercial producers like Harold Prince, David Merrick, or Otto Preminger, but he clearly has more influence than they—to encourage or discourage theatrical work according to his lights and to affect existing cultural tastes. In his sphere, power relations depart entirely from standard capitalist conventions. His eminence is charismatic. He inspires love—total, overwhelming, mushy love—from his writers and directors, whom he treats with unconventional loyalty apart from pecuniary success. Around him has developed a quasi-political institution by virtue of the strength of his personality, his vigor, his power to make people want to work for and receive approval from him.

I loved Papp for that speech on the need for young, heterosexual, female critics ("Papp in Stix Raps Sex Bias of Foes"). It seemed as though it had been addressed straight to me. I loved him for liking the kids he talked to better than the rich people. He reminded me of a wonderful social studies and English teacher I had, way back in junior high school, who was rumored to be a Communist because he criticized things. And I was ready to go to work for him even while he was clearly not inviting me to his sexy little Pittsburgh soirées.

Papp is the star of his own drama.

"Success can kill you, but don't worry about that now," he told the kids.

☆   ☆   ☆

David Merrick is one of the big three of New York theater, with Joseph Papp and Hal Prince. With Papp handling the behemoth off-Broadway Shakespeare Festival and Public Theater operation, Merrick and Prince split between them the plurality of Broadway profits.

Merrick is said by informed sources to be "sort of artistic," "sort of interested in the arts." "He wants to make a million on shlock but go to heaven anyway; he's Jewish in his mind." "His major skill is in creating the fluff and furor after the show's opened."

Merrick apparently runs a tight org, with all his staff directly answerable to him. Crafty, he terrifies his underlings by use of his mythic personality, his legendary blasts at mistakes or incompetence. But when he is not in full flower he seems like just another pleasant, bland, carpet salesman.

The difference between Papp and Merrick, said one young playwright who knows them both, is that Merrick is going for dough with art on the side, whereas Papp is nurturing people and earning money on the side. "Merrick would be paralyzed if he had tons of dough," added the playwright, "but Papp would heave a big sigh of relief and get to work."

☆   ☆   ☆

Asked to name a philosopher he likes, Hal Prince responded "Nietzsche." I chuckled. So he amended it to Santayana.

Hal Prince is the critics' darling, the favorite of the Establishment symbolized by the buildings so near his office: Warner Communications, RCA, the United Press. The Establishment itself, drama division (i.e., Clive Barnes of The New York Times), calls him brilliant, certifies his taste as impeccable, confers upon him the ultimate accolade of nobility: "class."

As producer and director of shows on Broadway for the last twenty-eight years, Prince has averaged slightly less than one new play each season. Among these was the blockbuster Fiddler on the Roof, which ran for eight years, a superprofitable musical about Jews in Russia being tyrannized by their neighbors and tyrannizing their own daughters. He has also mounted the work of Stephen Sondheim, Leonard Bernstein, Bob Fosse, Jerome Robbins, James and William Goldman, Boris Aronson, and other currently fashionable artists, in a series of successful shows that might be considered the vanguard of the conventional.

Harold Prince, producer of *Fiddler on the Roof* and other Broadway plays

In his autobiographical *Contradictions: Notes on Twenty-Six Years in the Theatre,* Prince speaks extensively of his collaborations with these men (and an occasional woman, such as his associate producer, Ruth Mitchell; his assistant, Annette Meyer; and the costume designer for *Candide,* Franne Lee). He gave Bob Fosse his first break on the strength of a recommendation from Jerome Robbins. He found Stephen Sondheim a pupil of Oscar Hammerstein's and apparently made him into a collaborator of Leonard Bernstein's. A few names dominate the index of the book (which could have been called "Collaborations" at least as easily as *Contradictions*) like overlong lists of extracurricular activities in a high school yearbook.

Prince defends his friends as "stimulating" to be with. And he even defines the formula for a successful show as "professional behavior in collaboration," to be continued until its stimulatingness wears off.

Fiddler on the Roof made $11 million. Hal Prince got thirty-five percent of that. That's $4 million on one good guess, on a gamble that people would go to see a song and dance about the persecution of the Jews. The situation was satirized in Mel Brooks's *The Producers,* a movie about producing a show called *Springtime for Hitler.* Both *Fiddler* and *Springtime* starred actor Zero Mostel. Was it Zero Hal Prince was gambling on?

He has a number of contradictory things to say about the caricature of Russian Jewry that ran for eight years on Broadway and was then sold to United Artists. It was realistic and abstract, he says, ethnic but possibly universal, fascinating but alien. He opted for Zero Mostel to star; he pushed for scenery as similar to Chagall's dream scenes as possible. He put up five weeks' salary for the entire cast, or $75,000, of his own money into it. He laid his friendship with Jerome Robbins on the line, threatening to sue the director-choreographer for $50,000 if he failed, as threatened, to go into rehearsal on schedule.

Even though the only first-night review called the show mediocre (in *Variety*), the Mostel-Chagall-Robbins musical ran for 3,242 performances on Broadway—the longest run to date.

Hal Prince is so much the gambler that he has hung behind his producer's desk a very large Wheel of Fortune in gaudy carnival colors, with the names of his productions printed on it instead of numbers. It was a gift from Ruth Mitchell, dating from just before the show *Candide.* He says his favorite of all his works is *Company.* The floor of his office is equally fun house—crazy flame shapes in red, black, and white. He says he considered doing the ceiling in the same, but now surely he is joking. He appears, in context, the very picture of a trickster.

"This is where I do my producing," Prince explains in reference to the odd decor. "Producing doesn't interest me in the least. At home there is a white box I work in when I am directing; my wife designed it."

It must be just another joke that he doesn't like to produce, for there are mementos of everything he has produced lining the walls of the outer office. One wonders whether legitimate theater is a subsidiary of the Broadway poster business. We see signs of Anouilh's *Poor Bitos;* Zero Mostel in Sholem Aleichem and Jerome Robbins' *Fiddler on the Roof;* Liza Minnelli in George

Abbott's *Flora, the Red Menace;* Lotte Lenya in Christopher Isherwood's *Cabaret;* Hugh Wheeler, Leonard Bernstein, and Stephen Sondheim on Voltaire's *Candide;* Wheeler and Sondheim again on Ingmar Bergman's *A Little Night Music;* Sondheim's *Follies* and *Company;* Kazantzakis' *Zorba the Greek;* and the slightly artier Duerrenmatt's *The Visit,* Congreve's *Love for Love,* and O'Neill's *The Great God Brown.*

In the greasepaint-sawdust-all-tricks-go! atmosphere of this office, there is not much room. The areas are rather small and contained, in an old-fashioned style, perhaps, like interlocking corridors and enclaves. The funny little space, with a Christmas tree and presents underneath it honoring the holiday, houses, besides Prince, George Abbott, John Flaxman, Howard Haines, Celia Linder, and the companies named Cabaret, Chelsea-Candide, Follies, Smiles, and (not Fiddler but) Tevye. One considers for a moment, and then rejects the possibility, that the Australian Broadcasting Company, and Republic of Zaire Purchasing Agency, which are just down the seventeenth-floor hallway, are in any way connected with Prince.

Who are Hal Prince's investors? When asked directly, he takes the Fifth, except to say that they are the same backers he's had all along, since he first raised the money for *Pajama Game* in 1953. He refers one to his autobiography. There we learn that in 1953, Prince, George Abbott, and Rosalind Russell's husband, Frederick Brisson, producing partners, followed the usual practice of auditioning bits of the play in donated living rooms before prospective angels. In one night they "eliminated every major theatrical investor in the country" by being too honest about the theme of *Pajama Game,* which was a strike in a factory. After that, Prince writes, there were ten more auditions, as they "canvassed people who didn't normally invest in shows." But without divulging either the number or the identities of his patrons, he acknowledges raising a quarter of a million dollars. He thanks Edie Adams for the use of her living room and credits Brisson with raising $28,000 himself. Not even financial investigative teams have been able to penetrate his secret; all *Business World* could learn was that Prince has a loyal group of 170 people.

Hal Prince values "concept" and he values "classical antecedents." What he seems to worry about most, in the construction of a play, is that it not be boring, though he doesn't mind if it "courts ambiguity." His opinion of David Merrick's hit *Hello, Dolly!* is that it was "mindless, unmotivated, inconsistent." And he says further: "The theater needs language, imagery, imagination, to separate itself from the realism of the six o'clock news."

He calls himself a "unionist" but tells several stories, in his book, about times when union regulations cost him too much money. He includes a letter he wrote to the musicians' union Local 802 accusing them of systematically killing the theater.

Prince is the kind of trickster who has a nostalgia for the Mafia. He can actually write, about Jerome Weidman's *Fiorello!* that the subject was a lament "for a bygone manageable New York, for the loss of heroes, of the innocence of speakeasys and payoffs and gang wars."

He admits to changing the homosexual at the center of *Berlin Stories* into a heterosexual in *Cabaret,* for the sake of "the musical comedy audience which required a sentimental heterosexual love story with a beginning, middle, and end."

The first thing I had noticed about Prince, from his *Who's Who* listing, were the names of his children. Charlie and Daisy. Impeccably American. Sounded like they came out of a musical comedy about Smalltown USA. "Because they're not related to any family on either side, for ever and ever, Amen!" Prince explained. "And they don't have middle names for the same reason. But Daisy's after Daisy, Daisy in Scott Fitzgerald. We liked that. And Charlie: I haven't a clue. Just a good name. It's not Charles!

"My wife's Judith and I'm Harold, and those are two *horrifying* names."

The first sentence of Prince's *Contradictions* reveals that he is "privileged, upper-middle lower-rich class, Jewish, both parents of German families which settled here soon after the Civil War." And his wife, he explained to me, is Russian-Jewish, which usually means poorer, and more recently arrived in America.

Students of the fine points of Jewish sociology might argue that the Russian Jews traditionally regard the richer German Jews as boorish, literally "without sensitivity." Could this be why, in his dedication, Hal Prince refers to his wife as "Judy, a snob about the theatre"? or why he calls himself an "optimist"?

I told Prince I had seen his name in a gossip column, as listening to Dave Brubeck with the Stephen Smiths. He admitted he liked Brubeck but denied having been there or being friends with the Kennedys. He explained that restaurants can send your name to the papers strictly on the basis that they've sent you an invitation; "it's all to do with restaurants, publicizing restaurants."

"I don't know a very lot of rich people," he said. "I don't find rich people as interesting as a lot of people who aren't rich. So I don't number among my friends a lot of those fancy names you're talking about. Rich people, you see, are as creative about money as you and I are about literature, or the theater. So they tend to talk about money the way we talk about theater. So we're not very good company for each other."

I suggested to Prince he might have an "interest," in the sense of "class interest," that guided his theater choices in addition to his conscious decisions. He dismissed the thought as "asinine."

How many plays does Prince receive in the mail? He hedged. "We would be getting five a week—250 a year—if we weren't prevented from accepting one while working on another."

He said he could tell "instantly" whether or not he wanted to read a script. I asked how. He said, "Subjects. Certain subjects don't interest me."

"Can you give me an example of some subjects that don't interest you?" I asked.

And he replied, "Sure!" Paused a moment. Then laughed at himself. "I said, why sure!" He groped for an answer. Then: "The subject of *Auntie Mame* didn't interest me. Or *Hair*. Or *Equus*."

"What was the subject of *Hair?*" I asked. "Hippies?"

"The subject of *Hair* was, What was the generation in the early '60s doing to protest its total frustration and inability to express itself, in that period, politically?"

"What's the highest compliment you could give a colleague?"

"Talented. Honest. Self-disciplined. Disciplined."

In 1967, Prince visited Moscow and was heavily influenced there by the Taganka Theater aesthetic, a revision of the "method" of Stanislavski. As Prince explains it in writing, "Taganka, part cabaret theater, borrows liberally from the Russian actor-director Vsevolod Meyerhold, who began with Stanislavski at the Moscow Art Theater and broke away on his own in protest of the extreme realism of that movement, exploring instead means of using theater techniques to excite, creating an audience of participants in which subjective involvement was all."

Previously, Prince had not departed radically from conventional Broadway methods of presentation. But afterward he moved into the Broadway forefront, his projects particularly highlighted by the multidimensional nonroom sets of Boris Aronson (and on *Candide*, Eugene and Franne Lee). He calls the Moscow experience "a turning point in my thinking as a director."

CUT TO: Journalist, infatuated with Prince's Broadway, singing her just-written original feminist remake of *South Pacific* into a tape recorder in the Stage Deli ladies' room.

☆   ☆   ☆

"Hal Prince is like a kitten in a bowl of cream. I'm not so taken with the whole thing of producing. I'm not stagestruck. But I do have a warm point in my heart for great artists. There's no artistic trait I respect in the abstract; I respect anarchy."

The man speaking is Arnold Saint-Subber, sitting about as far from anarchy as money can get in a double penthouse apartment over the East Sixties. One of the most notable fixtures in this theatrically furnished apartment-office is a large oil portrait, mostly in pastel colors, of Truman Capote. Saint-Subber has produced two plays of Capote's, two by William Inge, two Cole Porter musicals, ten Neil Simon comedies, and twelve other works since 1948. He is now fifty-eight years old, a wizened and terribly small man both in height and width.

Last year a Jewish women's group gave Neil Simon a testimonial dinner, honoring him as the "nation's most successful contemporary playwright." This is understating the case. Comic playwright Simon is the god of Broadway, and producer Arnold Saint-Subber is his prophet. And since Simon has had more hits on Broadway in the last ten years than any other writer—by far—Saint-Subber's position in the hierarchy of Culture Barons is a respectable one.

"I never decided to become a producer," he says. "I was an exceptionally ugly child, due to an accident, and I used to think I

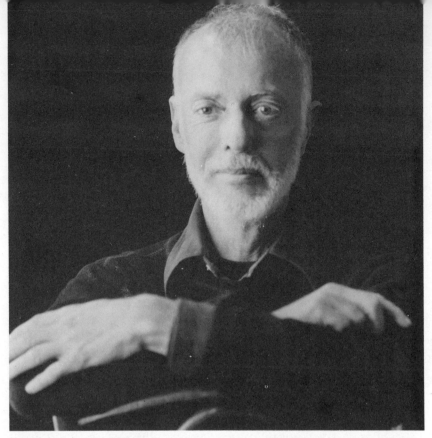

Arnold Saint-Subber, producer of Neil Simon and other Broadway play-wrights

had come to the wrong planet. I still think so. So I was sent away to school in England (my father, Saul Saint-Subber, worked for the government in Washington). When I was about fourteen I had a chance to be in a play. All I could think of was 'Get me out of this school.' So I was in the play, and that was the end of my education outside the theater. I can't do anything else, I don't know anything else—I can't even make toast. I call it fate.

"I don't put any of my own money into the plays I produce. My backers change all the time. Neil Simon virtually produces his own plays—if you want to know about his finances, you'll have to ask him. He gave me his first play to produce when he was work-ing in television. It was *Come Blow Your Horn*. I held onto it for two years while he did twenty-two rewrites. In the end I dropped it because it was a Jewish play, and I'd just done *The Tenth Man*. *Come Blow Your Horn* had nothing to say to me. Of course I adored it, because it made me laugh. But somebody else finally produced it. He gave me his second play as well; that was *Barefoot in the Park,* his most autobiographical work. I produced that, and nine since then, the bulk of Simon's work. I stopped after *Prisoner of Second Avenue* in 1973. Neil Simon is an enormous craftsman. But maybe he's floundering now, to find himself, as so many artists do.

"What is the process of collaboration like? Well, take *House of Flowers,* for example. I went to Truman and I said I want you to adapt *House of Flowers* as a musical book, and halfway through that I went to Harold Arlen and said I want you to write the score, and because it was Haitian black I got Oliver Meskill to design it, and then I got Peter Brook to direct. I go to one or at most two of the people at a time, and I bring their talents together as I see they're needed. Nobody presents either me or Hal with a finished musical. He's in there from the very beginning, as I am.

"Besides Hal, I would be hard pressed to continue the list of producers I admire.

"I don't select plays to produce. Before page one is written I've committed myself to an idea. For instance, I decided to musicalize *The Taming of the Shrew,* the onstage and offstage battles. That became *Kiss Me, Kate.* With *The Grass Harp* I had to hold Capote's hand; the same with Chayefsky on *The Tenth Man.* When Carson McCullers worked for me I went to her first and said, "Let's do a play together." I have hundreds of ideas. *1600 Pennsylvania Avenue* was my idea (that became the Bernstein-Lerner musical) because I've always been interested in government. Not politics so much as government, Washington, D.C., the White House. I'm interested in particular themes at particular times—until a play embodies the essence of my knowledge, and that way I get the theme out of my system. No, I don't know what themes I'll be interested in next. I don't solicit plays. Nobody submits plays to me. Sometimes backers come to me.

"Then I try to match the play with a director. I've worked with the greatest directors in the world. I was the first to use Peter Brook in this country, the first to use Tyrone Guthrie, before he was knighted. I've worked with Elia Kazan, Bobby Lewis.

"I'm not in favor of state subsidy of the arts. I'm a loner. I cannot work with somebody over me.

"I worked my fanny off for Lincoln Center when it was going bankrupt. Amyas Ames and Jules Irving asked me to bail out the repertory theater. I produced Lillian Hellman's *The Little Foxes*, with Anne Bancroft, George C. Scott, and E. G. Marshall—and for no money at all. Once it was a raging hit, they didn't even send me a thank-you note!

"I'm as young as the times are. I was a part of the Revolution of the '60s. To me the theater is a church of freedom. It's absolutely holy to me. I don't think women or blacks are any less liberated than anybody else. I'm for the liberation of men and women and children and old people.

"Any nice girl can find a man to marry her. Any good food will find someone to eat it. Any play that's worth doing will find someone to produce it.

"I despise statistics. First you must love yourself, and then other people will love you. First you must please yourself in making a play. I'll defend those young men's right to wear their hair long, and if they love themselves more by doing that, then other people will love them for it. But what the hell are we if we're not all of us unique? All of us cannot do without the next person or the next person's point of view. There's no defining a marriage, any more than a successful collaboration in the theater—no two are the same.

"I believe fiercely in God. When we die we just become another sort of energy. Whatever he wants me to be, I'll be. If I please him best by becoming a worm or a mote of dust, then I'll be a worm or a mote of dust."

☆   ☆   ☆

Since the invention of the LP record in 1949, record company involvement in the Broadway theater has significantly increased the proportion of musicals being produced. When Columbia did *South Pacific* in 1949, it was a breakthrough. In 1956 CBS subsidized *My Fair Lady,* and four years later did the same for *Camelot*—irrevocably stamping a metaphor on the incoming presidential administration. A year later Columbia, Capitol, and RCA Victor paid for fifty percent of eight shows. In 1963, Columbia gave $3 million to producers Feuer and Martin, in the biggest theatrical deal in history. In 1966, RCA Victor gave $1.5 million to David Merrick. Capitol also financed *Funny Girl* for Barbra Streisand and gave a relatively untried Hillard Elkins $250,000.

Alan Levy, in *The Culture Vultures,* asserts that the alliance between Tin Pan Alley and Shubert Alley has increased the proportion of musicals on stage from 1 out of 4 to 12 out of 22. He explains: "There is so much album money to be spread around that it's easier, cheaper, and less risky for a producer to mount a mediocre $400,000 musical than a good $75,000 one-set drama."

PAINTING:
Among the Princes

Painting has always been at the command of wealth in the West, though not in the old integral cultures, where even a utensil had meaning. First the churches got them to paint religious stuff, but that was all right because they were so holy, it was a kind of community. Then the kings got them to paint how great royalty was. Then the capitalists got the artists to show the ridiculosity, the great big meaningless joke of the society. . . .

Now it's the wives really who run around playing with the art. The husbands are in their offices earning their zillions of dollars. The wife shows him, "Oh look, honey, isn't this darling?" and if he says, "That stupid thing?" she'll sneak some of his zillions away from him to buy it just because he's such a philistine.

A piece of art, a new dress—they're just baubles, toys, 'cause there's nothing they can possibly do with all their money. With the money they put into the hunks of "public sculpture" on Wall Street they could have built a swimming pool for the kids to play in: splash, having fun in the water, send a kid to camp.

—Paul Siemering,
art teacher, Boston

Yes, in many ways the Rockefellers are like the Medicis.

—David Keiser,
director of Lincoln Center, Inc.

The Rockefellers are enlightened. They are preparing the way for a gradual, competent assumption of cultural responsibility by the public sector.

—Akrim Medany, dean, School of Fine Arts,
Carnegie-Mellon University, Pittsburgh

Our confrontation with Hoving was what broke us.

—Sylvia Goldsmith
Art Workers Coalition and
Guerrilla Art Action Group

THE ROCKEFELLERS are the Royal Family of America. Or at least the Dukes of Earl. With dozens of children now into the fifth generation of them, perhaps "princes" is the right word. Like the Medicis of Renaissance Florence, they bankroll the flourishing arts by their patronage of several museums, especially the Modern, by virtue of the existence of Lincoln Center, which they conceived and nursed through infancy, and by means of the New York State Council on the Arts, Nelson Rockefeller's gift to an increasingly socialistic citizenry.

Naturally the Rockefellers believe strongly in the capitalist system, particularly that liberal mode of it which distinguishes a Nelson from a Nixon and his authoritarianism at the center. They believe that it is the free enterprise system that has made America great—and given her a prosperous middle class of trade unionist bricklayers and electricians. They think that the family is endangered by women's liberation—although some women in the Rockefeller tribe are a bit more open than the men to certain feminist programs. And they imagine that a little belt-tightening all around is all that is necessary to solve prevailing economic and ecological problems. This is the Rockefellerian notion of culture in the broadest sense. In the more specific sense of this book, the Rockefellers ascribe to the conventional wisdom that the humanities sweeten and refine life; Nelson expresses the wish that his myriad art objects be appreciated on a "purely aesthetic" level.

Akrim Medany, dean of the School of Fine Arts at Carnegie-Mellon University in Pittsburgh, sees the Rockefellers as enlightened. In his opinion they are promoting distributive capitalism, not socialism, but they understand that, the way things are going, in one hundred years there will be no Culture Barons. Referring to his own university, Medany says, "Already there is no Andrew Carnegie, only a Carnegie endowment." Because Nelson Rockefeller is involved with political power, says Medany, he is providing for transitions and the gradual translation into laws of the assumption of popular responsibility.

Legend has it that a popular song runs "as rich as Rockefeller" even though the family tried to have the lyric squelched. They worry about their unpopularity. The Vice President and his brothers and their families live on three thousand high-security acres at approximately $25,000 per in Pocantico Hills, near Tarrytown, New York. Collectively, *Fortune* magazine estimates, they are worth several hundreds of millions of dollars, or slightly more than they admit to. According to one of their sworn opponents, deposed ex-president of Guatemala Juan Jose Arevalo, the House of Rockefeller controls corporations worth over $50 billion.

As Merrill Folsom wrote, in *Great American Mansions and Their Stories*, the Rockefeller estate in Westchester County is "as remote from the outside world as a fortified principality. High stone walls, massive iron gates, alert guards, police dogs, and miles of barbed-wire fence make the home a sanctuary."

Nelson's house, which dominates the Pocantico property, is filled with antique furniture (Chippendale, Hepplewhite, Sheraton, and Adams) and a gigantic collection of art which includes more than five hundred paintings and sculptures of the twentieth century, some nine hundred contemporary prints and drawings, and some one thousand pieces of primitive sculptures. He is now building another home, in Japanese style, to live in.

At a party in Pocantico Hills (once safely past the electrified barbed wire, untroubled by any of the thirty armed guards on foot and in radio cars, nor floodlit from a rooftop beam) one would be likely to run into people like Franklin D. Roosevelt, Jr., Margaret Truman, William F. Buckley, old and new multimillionaires, and heavies of publishing empires galore. The Rockefellers attend openings at the Metropolitan Opera and at the museums they patronize (and of course the dinner parties in the homes of great collectors or great climbers or the old Protestant elite prior to the Contributing Members' receptions and screenings—described by Tom Wolfe as The Only True Certification of Where One Stands in This Whole Realm of Art and Society), but they call themselves "not very social" people.

Most of the Rockefellers' work is in fact done austerely, with the Baptist ban from their youth on movies and other frivolity still casting its slightly unstylish shadow. Nelson wears Brooks Brothers suits—but he wears them baggy. And pointed shoes decades out of style.

The Rockefellers dominate a good part of the Rockefeller Center building, with John D. 3rd and Laurance maintaining offices on the fifty-sixth floor. Nelson is of course in Washington and makes an appearance with the others only at Christmastime, in the

Rainbow Room. David is downtown, at 1 Chase Manhattan Plaza, running that bank. On the fifty-sixth floor are also the Big Lawyers for the family, such as J. Richardson Dilworth, their top financial adviser (though neither his nor any of his associates' titles are spelled out).

Next in rank after the Brothers and the Big Lawyers come the Executive Secretaries and the Men Friday, talented and ambitious individuals on their way up—like Henry Kissinger, Dean Rusk, and John Foster Dulles, and like Nancy Hanks, once personal secretary to Nelson and now chairman of the National Endowment for the Arts—to bigger and better jobs. Collectively, the Executive Secretaries are seen by their subordinates as awesomely gentle, possessing extraordinary personal talents, given to passing the buck.

About three hundred people were working for the family in 1972. Messengers, euphemized as "office assistants," were required to reply to their superiors with a "Yes, sir!" The only employee organization was a company union, a Rockefeller Center Inc. employees' recreation association. In contrast with the vaguely differentiated responsibilities upstairs, low-level employees had their jobs defined in detail.

In the Rockefeller Family Archives, which begin in 1855, one discovers that only the "brother" generation of Rockefellers has had any significant involvement with the art world. The original John D. had large Greek and Roman sculpture. His son John D., Jr., had Chinese porcelains in a lacquered and exotic Victorian style, which decreased in value.

The current John D., however, whose art influence is more significant, has a taste for older American painters such as Eakins and Caleb Bingham ("Fur Traders Descending the Missouri") and for Oriental. His wife, Blanchette Hooker Rockefeller, is president of the Museum of Modern Art, taking up where her mother-in-law, Abby Aldrich Rockefeller, the cofounder, left off.

David Rockefeller keeps "early modern masters" such as Matisse and Degas in his house on Sixty-fifth Street and also favors pastels and watercolors. In his office at Rockefeller Center there are Braque, Chagall, and John Marin paintings.

A *New Yorker* writer described David Rockefeller's Chase Manhattan office as follows: "In his own office, on the seventeenth floor—a twenty-six-by-twenty-seven-foot chamber with a push-button operated opaque glass sliding door to shield him from sightseers—[David Rockefeller] has a large abstract oil by Kenzo Okada, a Wyeth, a Signac, a Cézanne watercolor, a Mark Rothko, and, perhaps his favorite, a bold Victor Vasarely. He also has some Greek vases of the fifth century B.C., a wooden Buddha, a Chinese lacquered chest, a twelfth-century Mosul incense burner, some Korean acrobats carved out of wood (his mother gave them to him when he was in college, and they have been talismans ever since), a Cézanne lithograph, a glass-faced chest full of small Buddhas, which was given to him by a Prince of Thailand (the Japanese royal family had presented this to the Thai royal family, and the Prince passed it along to what struck him as a prince of comparable American tribe), and a *sumgbolo*—a carved wooden box from the Ivory Coast." * Outside David's office, in a glass case, are the pistols used in the Hamilton-Burr duel. All the art and artifacts are David Rockefeller's personal possessions.

Nelson employs a curator for his collection, a Mrs. Carol Uht, whose father owns the estate adjoining the Rockefellers' compound in Tarrytown. A sympathetic employee explained: "You keep the loyalty and inner circle within a very specific socioeconomic group of people. Most of the trusted employees are from the wealthy classes. No amount of competence by itself will take you to the highest echelon." And why? "Because of their situation they want to feel secure, at ease, with their associates. They don't want to be concerned with the complications of different backgrounds."

But Nelson Rockefeller, at least, is interested in the exotic or intricate in his *objets d'art*, if not in his social relations. The Vice President has a large primitive art collection, some of which is now housed at the Museum of Primitive Art in New York and some of which will soon go with his late son Michael's collection into the new wing specially built for it at the Metropolitan Museum of Art. It consists mostly of work from New Guinea tribes, pre-Columbian South American, American Indian, and historical African. He also collects contemporary American works.

In 1969 the Museum of Modern Art gave an exhibition and

* E. J. Kahn, Jr., January 9, 1965.

printed a book of donations from Nelson's collection, curated by
Dorothy Miller. In the late '6os Nelson himself gave a lecture on
art, with slides, at The New School.

Nelson's head curator, Mrs. Uht, it is said, circulates a list of
"purchasable" painters.

Employees of the Rockefeller Center complex tend to argue
that the Rockefellers are not among the richest families in the
country. Du Pont is richer, they say; the Gettys give nothing at all
to philanthropy. While some think that what the Rockefellers are
involved in is "relatively human," others describe it as "the crush-
ing of the positive and the good."

On the macro level, this gets into the politics of big banking,
exemplified by David Rockefeller: its tendency to bolster corrupt
regimes—as, for example, in the Union of South Africa—and its
disregard for and mistreatment of economic entities below its
range of vision. The Rockefellers have their enemies, to be sure. A
$10 million damage suit was filed against Nelson Rockefeller by
August Heckscher for unfair leasing practices in connection with
the depression-era acquisition of space for Rockefeller Center.
(The suit was settled out of court.) Militant left-wing opposition
formed around David Rockefeller's plan to develop Morningside
Heights, calling itself the Save-Our-Homes Committee. (That
stalled him for eight years, but the banking titan won in the end.)

A really harsh statistic emerged in 1970 in a book called
David, an unflattering portrait of the Rockefeller banker. Author
William Hoffman pointed out that since 1965, when L.B.J. announced the first large-scale escalation of the Vietnam War, the
assets of David's Chase Manhattan Bank had shot up to almost $23
billion, nearly doubling in five years what it had taken more than
eighty years to acquire.

In more domestic terms, David Rockefeller was also scored
for not taking the displaced poor and small businesses into ac-
count when he constructed a pair of 110-story towers to house a
proposed World Trade Center, *i.e.*, the governmental and commercial services needed for the smooth functioning of international
business.

But David has his mind on higher things. Since 1954 he has
served as a charter member of a group that meets once a year,
barring the press, to discuss "their views on the state of the

world." Meeting with him in these secret sessions are such big names on the international political scene as Prince Bernhard of the Netherlands, Fulbright, McNamara, Ball, Rusk, Herter, Javits, Niarchos, Acheson, Wilson, Gaitskell, Monnet, Heinz, Henry Ford, Moyers, Pearson, Trudeau, and Mendes-France.

One aspiring artist I met felt quite tragic about his abortive attempts to get the attention of a Rockefeller. "I was only peripheral, only an underling," he said, "but there were moats, barriers, armguards protecting them, sealing them off. There is a lot of mythology involved: our own dreams. People around a Rockefeller see your ego dream and cut it down. I spent a lot of time trying to get close; I have not been successful. I was ready to accept the little bits, the tidbits, that they give out to the peasants."

This young man managed to get himself an appointment with David Rockefeller's executive secretary, Eleanor Wilkerson. But then she refused to come a few floors down on the elevator and visit an art exhibition of his in the same building. Nevertheless, when she agreed to sign his "reception book" he was inordinately grateful, even thrilled.

"Nelson's curator was snooty, condescending, and cruel to me," said the young office assistant at 30 Rockefeller Plaza. "I asked her how to break into the art market and she said, 'There's a good market for art teachers in Alaska.'"

Al Moscow, who ghost-wrote *Six Crises* for Richard Nixon, is reportedly now working on a book about the Rockefellers. Another book has been published recently by Peter Collier and David Horowitz, former editors of *Ramparts,* who interviewed financial adviser Dilworth and several of the fourth-generation Rockefellers; they sold paperback rights to their book for upwards of $300,000.

"What do the Rockefellers fear?" I asked my sources. "The Russians?"

"No," came the unanimous reply. "Kidnapping."

MNEMONIC DEVICE: Roughly speaking, the third generation of Rockefellers, commonly known as the Rockefeller Brothers, when listed in alphabetical order turn out also to be arranged in order of intellectual credentials.

David is No. 1, and has a Ph.D. and other degrees from Chicago, Harvard, and the London School of Economics, and a current interest in MOMA, the Rockefeller Institute (also known as the Nobel farm), and all his old schools. Furthermore, he is chairman of the biggest bank in New York, often considered to be a position far higher than any merely political post.

Next in line is John Davison Rockefeller 3rd, who did much by way of scionhood. That is, he set up Lincoln Center and seems to preside over or manage most of that Rockefeller Foundation's and Funds' money.

Then there's Laurance, who manages the air: Eastern Airlines, McDonnell Aircraft, etc. He has also been chairman of the board of trustees at Princeton, a job undoubtedly requiring some cleverness.

Next comes Nelson, four times governor of New York and once Veep of the United States. But before he did that, all he really did was coordinate culture and commerce across the Columbian continents. A pushover. Went to Dartmouth, home of the Winter Carnival.

And finally down at the end, the late Winthrop, convivial clown of Arkansas, Yale dropout and imitation cattle baron. His divorce cost him six million dollars.

Blanchette Hooker Rockefeller, sixty-seven, is married to the eldest of the five Rockefeller brothers, John D. 3rd. A graduate of Miss Chapin's School and Vassar College, she has worked at the Museum of Modern Art for forty years, serving on its Painting and Sculpture Committee for twenty of those years and as president and chief executive of its board of trustees for seven years, all of which positions she now holds.

Blanchette Rockefeller is not the most powerful of the Rockefellers. But she was willing to speak to me in her capacity as president of the Museum of Modern Art. I interviewed her on the assumption that her opinions would have some positive relation to those of her more powerful brothers-in-law and husband, and she would therefore in some sense be speaking for the Rockefeller establishment.

It was several months after negotiations that she greeted me in what appeared to be a paper-supply closet on the fifth floor of the Museum's office building, one door down from the museum. She is a strikingly tall woman, and had well-blended rouge but a slightly uneven pencil line on her lower eyelid; she was wearing a white-on-black polka dot dress with long sleeves and a middle-of-the-road hemline, diamond and platinum wedding rings beside a

The Rockefeller Dynasty

FIRST GENERATION
John Davison Rockefeller
Established Standard Oil; became richest man in the world
m. Laura Spelman

SECOND GENERATION
John D. R., Jr., b. 1874
m. Abby Aldrich (sister of Chase Bank pres.), who cofounded Museum of Modern Art
railroads, leather; 1915: miners shot at Ludlow; lawyer Ivy Lee: philanthropy

THIRD GENERATION

3 daughters
m. Harkness
Pratt
Whitney

b. 1903
Abby
m. Milton (div.)
Pardee (dec.)
Mauzé (dec.)

b. 1906
John D. R. 3rd
Princeton

Chairman:
Rock Fdtn.
Gen. Ed. Bd.

President:
Rock. Bros. Fund
AYH

b. 1908
Nelson
Dartmouth

Vice Pres:
U.S.A.

Governor:
N.Y.S.
(1958–74)

b. 1910
Laurance
Princeton

Director:
Eastern Airlines
McDonnell Aircft
Canadian Nickel
O.M. Chemical
African cloth
Vitro nuclears
Viking rocket

b. 1912
Winthrop
Yale DO

Governor:
Arkansas

b. 1915
David
Harvard
London Sch. Econ.
U. Chi. Ph.D.

Chairman & Pres.:
Rock. Institute
Morningside Hgts. Assn.
Downtown Assn.

Chairman:
Chase Manhattan Bank
#1 N.Y.C.

Trustee:
Princeton
Williamsbrg.
AMNH

m.
Blanchette
Ferry
Hooker

Sandra
John D. R 4th
Hope
Alida

div.

m.
Margaretta
(Happy)
Fitler
Murphy

Nelson A.
Mark

Cross-Continental
Culture & Commerce
Coord.:
i.e., in charge of
So. America

m.
Mary
Todhunter
Clark

FOURTH GENERATION

Ann
Steven
Rodman
Michael (dec.)
Mary

div.

Chairman of Board
of Trustees:
Princeton

Trustee:
Sloan Fdtn.
YWCA
IDA

m.
Mary
French

Laura
Marion
Lucy
Laurance

#2 U.S.A.

Overseer:
Harvard

Trustee:
MOMA
U. Chi.

m.
Bobo
Sears

div.

m.
Jeannette
Edris

d. 1973

m.
Margaret
McGrath

David, Jr.
Abby
Neva
Margaret
Richard
Eileen

plastic watchband, clear plastic-frame eyeglasses, and one large flecked opal ring. Her hair was in a high beehive bun, and her eyes were blue and sad.

I was glad to be speaking with her, having spoken quite enough already with Elizabeth Shaw, the public information officer of MOMA. Shaw is a formidable woman with a bass voice and flouncy clothes and has in her office a microfilm reader surrounded by surreal and primitive posters.

Not surprisingly, Mrs. Rockefeller was charming but not particularly informative.

We spoke briefly on the mechanics of the Museum of Modern Art and the various controversies concerning art museums currently in the newspapers. She made the point that the lay people, such as herself, should not be confused in people's minds with the directors, such as Dick Oldenburg (brother of Claes Oldenburg and now director of the Museum of Modern Art). She explained why the Museum's Professional and Staff Association (PASTA) had not been able to win a seat on the board of trustees: because their superiors, the curators, didn't have a seat. She told me how the Metropolitan Museum had solved its educators versus curators problem, but later this became a subject on which she preferred to pass.

"I think we should work very hard in helping the American people to improve their judgment of modern art," she said, while acknowledging that there are galleries now doing what the Museum of Modern Art was originally founded to do.

Like many other Culture Barons, she complained of the inflation: ". . . with all of the museums, and the ballets, opera, all of them—we're being strangled by the creeping up of costs."

I asked her if there were fewer of the very great patrons than existed in the past. She said yes, there were, and that it was because of the tax laws preventing one from passing on one's fortune to one's children.

Then we got down to business, discussing values and moods. She said she would like to go to the ballet more often but her husband doesn't like it. She used to play the piano "until I got too depressed with myself about it." Sir Rudolf Bing, she was politic enough to say, "was the true manager extraordinaire of the period in Europe where he was trained."

I asked if she was affected by the cultural revolution of the 1960s. She redefined the subject as "the unrest at the universities and the young people's attitudes" and went on to blame the whole thing on the Vietnam War and contraceptives. She berated the tendency of youth to go off to the country and retreat and urged them to remember the need for leadership. One of the most curious differences she saw between herself and her children's generation was her own inability to analyze herself and her children's always-trying-to-find-out-why-we're-all-the-way-we-are.

"And then, of course, marrying into the Rockefeller family has made a very deep impression on me. I was brought up by my parents to be very gregarious and very friendly. We never were 'in society.' Not in the true sense, the snobbish, elitist type of thing that went on when I was growing up. I was always just sort of on the outskirts. I went to a good school and knew a lot of those people, but I never felt really a part of it; I never wanted to be very much. I hated country clubs. [Laughter] I loved sports. But I didn't like the lolling around the swimming pool, and the Saturday evening dances, and so on; I was just a little antisocial. But when I married into the Rockefeller family I found that there was just such a tremendous sense of mission about everybody, a great sense of obligation to use their position for the benefit of people. They were brought up with this idea—I'm sure you've heard it said, if you've read articles about the Rockefellers. They always say that they were brought up with the idea that their money was something that came to them unexpectedly, and it was a responsibility that they must use for the good of other people.

"Of course this is not the image of the Rockefellers in some people's minds: a sort of robber baron and the rebates of the Standard Oil Company from the railroads and all the evil things that helped them to make the money. But the side of them I have seen has been the later generations. My father-in-law was a perfectly marvelous man. If you ever want to know what he really believed and lived, all you have to do is go to Rockefeller Center right near the skating rink in front of the RCA Building, and there's a plaque with his credo on it, which he wrote down and taught to all his children. And above all he really tried, and very successfully, to live by it.

"He was a very religious man, and very conscientious, and he didn't seek public notoriety at all; he wanted to do what he did quietly and behind the scenes. He never wanted to be in politics or be a great national statesman. But he wanted to do these things that he was able to do, like Williamsburg and the Rockefeller Foundation and all these things—they were his life interest. And I suppose this has had a great influence on me, because I was devoted to both of my husband's parents. And I knew them very well and for a long time.

"I don't know how to evaluate what that did, but I'm sure it added to my own sense of responsibility and not wanting to be just a society person.

"Of course the Rockefellers are all carrying great responsibility in the business sector and in the political sector, and there are great pressures on them and great criticisms of them. It's very hard to do everything right. I think, for instance, the way the Vice President was 'gone over' before he was appointed was really a frightful ordeal for the whole family to go through. Because it was done always with the attitude that of course he couldn't have done all these things without having bad motives. Because nobody ever heard of anybody who did things like that for good motives. And this is where I feel the public really doesn't understand that this family have had—maybe they haven't used the right methods— but they have basically a desire to be public-spirited. I *really* *think* they have. And I'm not a Rockefeller, and I've seen them operating over many years; and there are many things they've done that I perhaps wouldn't have been enthusiastic about, but basically their motivation in life is to serve. They are highly patriotic and they believe very, very deeply in our form of government, our form of the combination of capitalism and liberalism."

After we had talked, Mrs. Rockefeller contacted me and requested that material be deleted on the subject of women's liberation, capitalism, and her own children.

☆   ☆   ☆

Perhaps the most telling of all sensibilities is the familial, or tribal, sense. As Ferdinand Lundberg pointed out in his 1937 classic, *America's Sixty Families*, "one can trace an almost unbroken

The Museum Combine

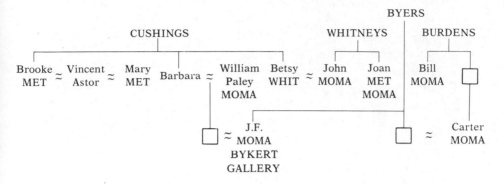

line of biological relationships from the Rockefellers through one-half of the wealthiest 60 families in the nation." The Family Connection in the museum world is awesome to a biblical extent.

First there were founders of the Museum of Modern Art, Abby Aldrich Rockefeller and Mrs. Cornelius Sullivan. And Abby begat John, who took for a wife Blanchette Hooker, and she assumed the presidency of that organization; and Abby begat David, and David, lo! he was chairman of the board and vice chairman also; and Abby begat Nelson, and Nelson, he too was top executive officer of that august and stuffy body for a while.

And Mrs. Sullivan passed control to her cousin William Paley, and lo! he was another chairman. And Paley wed Barbara Cushing, and Barbara's progenitors also begat Betsy, and Betsy's husband John Hay Whitney, lo! he too was on the MOMA board of directors. And Payne and Helen Whitney, who had begat John, also begat Joan Whitney Payson, and, greatest of marvels! she sat on the board not only of the MOMA but also of the Metropolitan Museum of Art.

And the relatives of Paley and of Cushing shall be numerous as the sands.

For Paley had a daughter who did marry J. Frederick Byers, of Bykert Gallery, and lo! that Byers did also sit on the board of MOMA. And Byers was related as the brother of one Carter Bur-

John Hay Whitney, trustee of the Museum of Modern Art; chairman, International Herald Tribune, Paris (Helen Marcus)

den's wife, and lo! this Burden was on the MOMA board, and so was his uncle William.

And Betsy Cushing, who held office herself on the board of the Whitney Museum, had another sister, Brooke, who married Vincent Astor. And Brooke and a previous wife of this same Astor, Mary (Mrs. James) Fosburgh, both sat on the Metropolitan board.

The Rockefeller wealth and lineage are not tied in with this combine. A small Rockefeller child reportedly exclaimed once to a friend, "Who do you think we are, the Vanderbilts?"

The Rockefellers do not lack for significant in-laws, however, for their money weds money just as it did in the old crowned days of Europe. They are related by marriage, and not distantly, to Aldrich (former senator from Rhode Island), Stillman (president of the First National City Bank, number two in New York City right after David Rockefeller's own Chase Manhattan), to Dodge (Remington Arms and Phelps Dodge), to McCormick (International Harvester), to Clark (the Pennsylvania Railroad), to Percy (senator from Illinois), and to Carnegie.

Other families are also significant. Alice Tully, whose name graces the auditorium in the Juilliard School ("for promotion purposes," explained the aide to a Juilliard official), is the granddaughter of the founder of Corning Glass and serves on the board of directors of Juilliard, the Philharmonic, and Lincoln Center, Incorporated. Her cousin, Arthur A. Houghton, Jr., is chairman of the Metropolitan Museum of Art, a trustee of the Public Library and of the Rockefeller Foundation, and was in the past chairman of the Philharmonic Society, vice chairman of Lincoln Center, and chairman of the Institute of International Education (which administers the Fulbright grants).

The chief curator of paintings and sculpture at the Modern is William Rubin, whose brother Larry is a dealer in New York, selling some of the same artists that the museum curator exhibits. Similarly, Carter Burden bought for MOMA some paintings out of his brother-in-law Fred Byers' Bykert gallery.

☆   ☆   ☆

Though some authors speculate about the existence of painting collections, auctions, and art sales in ancient Rome, the director of the Museum program for the National Endowment, Thomas W. Leavitt, traces the collecting of paintings only as far back as the seventeenth and eighteenth centuries in Europe. At that time, collectors personally showed their possessions to artists or other aristocrats.

In America the earliest museums were appropriately more commercial and popular in origin, dating from Charles Willson Peale's famous display of paintings, sculpture, stuffed animals, fossils, and curiosities in Philadelphia at the beginning of the nineteenth century.

Museums as they are now known coincided in their development with the rise of the great fortunes: Carnegie, Morgan, and Fuller of Boston. New York saw its National Academy and other galleries opening in the nineteenth century, and though these places began as forms of patronage by the wealthy, they were often operated by the artists themselves. When no additional collections were forthcoming, in the 1920s and '30s after the income tax laws had been passed, the most successful museum director became the person who could converse as an equal with the captains of industry.

Currently the function of a museum director, says Leavitt, is to build, to raise money by employing professional fund-raising firms, to do public relations, to provide educational services, and to solicit and make a case for public support.

But the old symbiosis of patrons and artists is gone. Writers in art magazines attribute this to the gross changes in the social economy since the Renaissance. "Society in a producer-consumer democracy makes the creation [of masterpieces] almost an impossibility," writes Bryan Robertson. "Artists became dispensable at the time of the Industrial Revolution, which removed them from near the center of the social scheme to marginal bohemia," writes Ernst Van Den Haag. There is no participatory relationship between artist and patron today, no community nor common language. It is hard to celebrate comfort and convenience, and out of the easier option—that is, derision—grows much of recent art work. Meanwhile, the museums are like ancestral graves, permanently commemorating a time or times that are irretrievably past.

Painting and sculpture are possibly the most inherently decentralized of all the arts, since they require only one person to produce an *oeuvre*. And yet Thomas P. F. Hoving, director of the Metropolitan Museum of Art, as well as the aristocratic interlocking boards of museum trustees, have the power to make certain *oeuvres* worth much more in a twinkling of an eye. Many find fault with individual decisions of Hoving's, or of MOMA's, and accuse him/them of blackguardism of the worst sort. Hoving dismisses all charges heatedly.

But perhaps the more important question in the case of Thomas Hoving hinges upon the bigness of the Met, and whether or not this is a good thing. Hoving has presided over a significant expansion of the museum, moving out onto Central Park land, buying more expensive and selling more sacrosanct works than his predecessors, and arranging more impressive exhibitions. New York City alone gives the Met $3 million a year, and large grants come also from the state and the Federal government. Hoving celebrates these attentions as the rightful due of the hemisphere's most "encyclopedic" visual arts institution. But of course the bigger the Met gets, the greater his power.

Thomas P. F. Hoving, director, the Metropolitan Museum of Art (Alix Jeffrey)

Hoving's most outspoken opponents were the short-lived Art Workers Coalition. They accused the museum of being too big and argued that it should abdicate in favor of community art centers. Hoving brilliantly parried their attacks, outmaneuvering, hiring, and prosecuting the left-wing artists as necessary. Today their organization is dissolved.

Tom Hoving is an interesting man, an intriguing enemy. Like a Viking, he is determined to the point of bloodthirst to conquer, to show prowess. He is happiest when engaged in a battle of wits, when he can roll the most abstruse art-history references off his tongue, complete with European pronunciation, and stymie his opponent with his erudition, real or faked.

Not long ago he was pictured in *The New York Times* holding a piece of Scythian gold with a greedy glee in his eyes, his mouth open. (The Viking conquers the Scythians!)

Though lambasted by the popular press, the art journals, and the art dealers, and invaded by angry hordes of art revolutionaries, Hoving seems impregnable in his position as director of the Metropolitan Museum of Art. He doesn't have a whole lot of leverage, as he says, but the roots under his feet go terribly, terribly deep.

His bastion, the Met, looms like a huge fortress or mausoleum, presiding over the East Side of New York, dimly portending the destruction of some new pharaoh. Sculpted on the façade are the faces of Italian artists whose work cannot be found inside. There are many pillars, many steps, many water jets in the long oblong pools on the concrete plaza. And just beyond the gates to the north and to the south there are an enormous ameboid metal sculpture and a mundane construction-work fence—both covered with neighborhood graffiti.

A pass from the main desk gets me by the mezzanine attendant and into a railroad flat of Museum administrative offices flanked by two plaster busts: Voltaire and Rousseau. All I can think of to explain their presence is William Blake's line: "Mock on, mock on, Voltaire, Rousseau!"

Hoving's Miss Mescall motions me into the immediate waiting area where I have time to consider, as possible reading material, some of the books on his shelf: *Inside the Third Reich,* numerous *Who's Whos, Artforum, Art at Auction 72–73, Dürer 1471–1971,* three volumes of letters of Van Gogh, *The Central Park* by M. Scott, and a French dictionary.

Then TPFH leads me—late and therefore running—into his own office, a not-large room filled up by a circular table and many chairs placed casually around it. I notice a slide projector, a papier-mâché mock-up of the expanded Museum, a photo of the windswept face of a young girl. Miss Mescall seems surprised Hoving has let me in at all; when I informed the lady at information of my appointment she had replied saucily "Well, aren't you lucky!" Perhaps I am being treated like a possible subversive because I am wearing a new T-shirt, a gift, which has John Lennon's eyes and nose across my breasts and the command, on my back: "Listen to this T-shirt."

Thomas P. F. Hoving—to a New Yorker, at least, the name conjures up princely images: polo, cycles, such genteel crusades through such graceful localities as Central Park as befits the son of the chairman of Tiffany's, and, of course, friendship and camaraderie with New York's own Yalie prince movie star, John V. Lindsay.

Hoving, I understood before I met him, is born to the kind of social status where a little bit of intelligence goes a long way. He was a vigorous child, flunking out of four prep schools, all utterly exclusive; yet he came back with a summa cum laude from Princeton. His father, a Swedish Presbyterian, was the head of Bonwit Teller's and Tiffany's. And so Hoving went straight from college into the kind of job fellows of his set walk into—assistant curatorship of the Cloisters, the uptown branch of the Metropolitan Museum.

Retelling the next stage in his life is risky, since the last person who tried it, *Times* reporter John Hess, afterward transferred himself to the restaurant beat, as Hoving merrily points out. Hoving rose to prominence over the heads of his elders thanks to one particular demonstration of prowess. He went to Europe and saw in a Zurich bank vault an old ivory cross with an anti-Semitic inscription in Latin on it, and he said, "That may be the great Bury St. Edmund's Cross! [*snap snap* on his little spy camera] and we've *got* to have it for New York. We'll pay anything!" (This is the way people think in the power elite. They make decisions fast and smooth them over later.) He paid plenty; the Louvre chipped in; and they don't even call it the Bury St. Edmund's Cross anymore. But Hoving was promoted to the head of the Cloisters all the same.

Just at that time (1965), his boating companion John V. Lindsay was running for mayor. Hoving drew up a paper on how to revitalize the city parks. And presto! he was Commissioner of Parks, Recreation, and Cultural Affairs.

Within the year he was lusting after the Met. For that his liaison was the late Ted Rousseau, senior curator, who also knew and was liked by most of the Met trustees. Friend Rousseau sponsored Hoving to them, and Hoving impressed them with a brilliant 1966-style speech about rejuvenation. And lo! vice president of the Met.

I interview him in his capacity as director of the Met, one of the sixteen members of the New York State Council on the Arts, member of the executive board of the Public Broadcast Laboratory, director of IBM. "Oh, my credentials aren't very impressive," he demurs modestly.

But he surprises me for not looking the aristocrat. His body is slightly pear-shaped, though not fat, rather like the shape of Leutze's George Washington or the pharaoh Akhenaten. His nails are desperately short, dirt-rimmed, and jagged—almost as if he is indeed hanging by his thumbs over there at the Metropolitan because of all the vociferous criticism.

His fingers are stained yellow, and they tremble as he smokes.

When he catches sight of my tape recorder he says, "Oh no!" and, "I have a Nixon fear!"

So I set my little Sony down on his mock-up, and we deliberate the subject of taping. I tell him I would be happy not to tape if it bothers him. He suggests I am lazy; he suggests I let him practice answers and then tape the finished version. I say No to both. Finally we agree to let him make the decision on the basis of the first question, which, fortunately, is a decoy. I ask him if he is related to Hoving and Winborg, an art auction house in Stockholm. He says No, the name Hoving is Dutch, and I can turn on the tape.

Hoving has been greatly criticized in print for the choices he has made or has been responsible for in the past few years in the buying and selling of Museum properties. Many people do not understand how or why the Museum can plead poverty and force the State Council to increase its allocation and then promptly turn around and spend $5.1 million on more than four hundred works of Japanese art. Some feel that the sale of works by several well-known impressionist painters (for example, Van Gogh and Rousseau) was not justified by the purchase of very expensive nonobjective metal sculptures. Others feel that, given the tight money economy and community needs, there is no justification in general for spending six or seven figures on single pieces of art.

I ask Hoving to justify his recent controversial purchases of expensive art objects.

He gets angry. He insults me. He criticizes the writing style of the question. Then he says he is limited by law, by bequest, by the Museum's state charter, to the use of certain money for certain things.

"Somebody gives you six million dollars in 1908 for the purpose of buying art, you cannot use it for buying milk. And you cannot use it to start a community museum. You can't do it! The attorney general'll walk in and take your . . ." He did not finish the sentence.

He tried to get the Cleveland Museum or the National Gallery to chip in on the Velázquez, he says, but they refused. And anyway, he continues, the Met's purchases average in the five figures, not six. "How much money do you think we take in, in an average year, of works of art, by gift, purchase, and bequest? Guess! Twenty-two million dollars. Average. Now, every single one of those works of art, probably nine hundred or a thousand, are not in seven figures. We buy things for five hundred which we consider as important as some of the six-figure ones. We're an enormous institution, with twenty departments; we're not just the paintings gallery. A lot of things we buy are *very* minor in price and *extremely* important. You have to remove the emotion of the thing from really the hard facts. A rather stunning figure, isn't it?"

Well, what about the charge made by radicals that museum directors seek to "monumentalize" themselves by the purchase of enormous objects serving a quasi-religious function?

"I don't know what the hell that means," replies Hoving.

He spells out the Museum's acquisitions policy.

"We prefer, since we have three million works of art in the Museum," he says, "really, at this point in our history, not to continue to buy numbers, but wait, and from time to time go after those things that are extraordinarily rare and therefore extraordinarily expensive."

Hoving doesn't like my question—especially the word "monumentalize"—until I rephrase it as a direct reference to the recent abundant criticism of him.

Then he launches into a long and detailed defense, apparently referring to the charge made in *Art in America* and elsewhere that he improperly disposed of Adelaide De Groot's legacy. He refers me to his White Paper on Transactions, issued by the Museum. He claims that New York State Attorney General Lefkowitz had drafted with the Museum some guidelines on accessions and disposal and found nothing illegal—which defense was unreported in the press, he says. He counters with a criticism of Eugene Thaw, past president of the Art Dealers Association, "a purist," after whose tenure the group "adjusted back to reality." He characterizes the criticism as "shrieking around."

"I was the Folk Hero and the Press Hero of New York City for a year and a half, and then I became the Skunk at the Garden Party. For a while. Both were based upon an image. I couldn't have done what they said I did. I couldn't have been as great as I was when I was Parks Commissioner and they overlooked deliberately things that were not good."

Then I notice the cartoons on his walls of old-fashioned bicycles (which Hoving and Lindsay capitalized upon during their mutual heyday) and of the front of the Met with a big sign: "Welcome, Mr. H.!"

Not long ago John Walker, the director of the National Gallery, wrote a book, *Self-Portrait with Donors*, and an article, "Confessions of a Museum Director," describing his job. It consisted, Walker said, primarily in the locating of sponsors or purchasers for works of art, upon recommendation of the curators.

"Don't believe anything in John Walker's book!" Hoving exclaims.

In the light of his virulent off-the-record remarks, I can understand that Hoving had a Nixon fear. While the recorder is running he says only: "I wouldn't consider that my job at all. My job here is chief executive officer of an extremely large organization, over which I have total supervision in all aspects. Particularly emphatic, right now, is obviously the completion of the building. Which we are undertaking to do. And seeing that finances are in good shape. And seeing that, uh . . . the great international mark of the Museum is made. We are a national institution. We would like to be known as the National Museum. And we're now getting very deeply into the international."

Hoving hardly seems to be talking about art anymore but rather about his aspirations to higher political office. Similarly, the Museum's board of trustees, which governs the institution with him, consists of men noted for their "experience and wisdom in being involved in the running of large organizations," as Hoving puts it, rather than for their concern with the muses.

I ask about the procedure for electing a new member to the board. First he mentions that trustees serve six-year terms and cannot be nominated after the age of sixty-five or re-elected after seventy. "The nominations are discussed by the nominating committee. Anybody can put in a name. Staff puts in names. Several

times. Board members come to a full board. The name will be discussed, and then it must be laid over until the next full meeting of
the board, which is three months later. I can't recall ever that
somebody was voted down, because if that were to happen it
would happen prior to the name coming out of the nominating
committee and going to the board. Because the word is let out,
and if anybody has an objection, then it never comes to the point
where you would vote on. Which seems only reasonable. It's a
very tightly run operation."

On this nominating committee, which effectively screens all
possible candidates for the board of trustees, are two former Pen-
tagon employees and three members of the Council on Foreign
Relations, which Richard Rovere defines as tantamount to the national presidium on foreign affairs, superior in influence even to
the President. All five men either work for the Rockefeller bank or
live in the very same building on East Sixty-fifth Street (or a few
houses down around the corner).

With all that cold war, Rockefeller-family muscle on the important nominating committee of the Met, it is not surprising that
an article on the museums and the CIA was ripped out of the Don-
nell art library issue of *Artforum*.

In the flurry of radical political activities of the last decade,
the trustees of the Metropolitan and other museums, along with
Thomas Hoving, were confronted with an ideological assault by
the Art Workers Coalition. The Art Workers accused the museums
of being classist, racist, and sexist; they documented in art journals
the connection between museum policies and the cold war (for instance, the official cultivation of some dangerous Mexican mur-
alists at a time when radicalism in that country was threatening
the oil interest). And they challenged the right of Museum officials to use public money in private ways.

Right after the invasion of Cambodia and the Kent and Jackson State killings, numerous artists sat on the steps of the Met and
called for an "art strike." In early 1971, Met trustees banqueting on
the Louis XVI furniture were invaded by protesters bearing
cockroaches and claiming that such use of a period room was
wasteful and elitist, especially when the Met requires public donations and accepts city money. Sometime later the Art Workers
had a private encounter with Thomas Hoving about which one of

their leaders reports: "Our confrontation with Hoving was what broke us."

Later, there were a few more individual demonstrations by implacable art workers, but the Met and the Modern successfully prosecuted the perpetrators (in the case of Tony Shafrazi and Jean Toche) or hired them (in the case of Tom Lloyd).

"How do you feel about your dealings with the Art Workers?" I ask Hoving.

"Satisfactory," he replies. "We had several meetings with them which were not particularly productive because they were obviously not there to have a productive meeting. And they wanted to take over the Great Hall at one point, and actually didn't: they wanted to have us say No. Knowing that, we allowed them to do it. And I insisted upon the same type of paraphernalia that groups of that nature demand upon Establishment institutions, which threw them off. But we'd boxed them into a point where they had to do it. But legal advisers with arm bands and all this paraphernalia. And they came in, and they had their series of lectures in the Great Hall, and no member of the public really looked or cared, and they closed up shop after two or three hours 'cause it was obviously a fizzle. What they wanted to do was for us to close down the Museum and bar the gates so they could be photographed "locked out," which we decided would be really rather politically unsophisticated. And quite frankly, since that time we haven't really heard anything of them."

And how about the black protester who was hired to head up a community survey project? I ask if Hoving is also satisfied with that. He says he is not, particularly, but refers me to the "other people doing arts in Jamaica [New York]." And he uses the phrase "not productive" three times in a rambling, unfinished answer. I notice that Hoving has a problem of repeating words. In a statement about the Museum's good terms with the public, he indicated four times that the bad publicity has had "no effect."

"How do you make a judgment of the quality and importance of a work of art?" I ask.

"That's easily measurable," Hoving replies. "It's totally definable. You have three great pieces of eighteenth-century French furniture by Riesener. You can tell which one is the better one by its size, by what it was, for whom it was made, by the elegance of it, by the act of the commission, and so on.

"Quality is judged in comparison within the individual's own work or something very close to it in time or school. For example, I know what quality is within the works of Rembrandt. I know what quality is between, within Rembrandt and Rubens. But Rembrandt and Poussin? Rembrandt and Velázquez? No comparisons can be made because they're so separated in all respects. They were all baroque seventeenth century, but it's totally hazardous to say baroque over rococo or baroque over Momoyama." (Hoving coughs out his "baroque" with a Continental accent.)

As for debatable purchase, for instance a very rare Hans Baldung as an example of early sixteenth-century German painting and whether it is good enough: "These choices and these things are discussed at considerable length in the professional ranks."

I ask what the Met's reasoning had been in the hanging of James Rosenquist's huge piece of pop art "F-111."

"Actually, we hung 'F-111' because it was to us a rather fascinating example of history painting. And you know that the important thing about the show was that we had Jacques Louis David in the same room, Emanuel Leutze, and two other historical machine painters. The 'Death of Socrates' by David was a political picture. It was made just at the time when there was this change from monarchy to a republic, so-called, when they were stressing the republican virtues, which meant that a broad constituency decided the fate of the country. And 'F-111' is a statement about the state of the United States.

"We would no more say 'Ughch! that's bad!' morally, or something, huh? about the salon painters Meissonier or Chassériau than we would say that the hierarchical style in Byzantium was any worse or better than the classical style. Both went on at exactly the same time, for slightly different purposes. Therefore I cannot possibly give you anything about Conceptual art or any of this; it's not good, or bad, compared to anything else; it is. And that's simply what we're here for; we're here to protect, and to get things, that are.

"We were accused of being morally turpitudinous for showing 'F-111.' But we frankly read that review and couldn't figure out what the guy was driving at. 'Cause we don't think *hanging* a work of art can *possibly* be morally turpitudinous!

"The issue was, that people had taken a moral stand on a

style: pop art. Which we think is ridiculous, to take a *moral stand* on a style. That's like Count Neunkirchen, who said that 'this Manet' and 'this Monet' were immoral. 'Cause they didn't paint highly glossed historical pictures. Mmmhm?"

"Do you think it's possible to see relationships between the ruling elites of any given historical period and the artwork that flourished under their direct—"

"Oh, sure!" Hoving interrupts.

"Do the Rockefellers in any sense influence the artwork produced, like the Medicis in Italy, or the church patrons?"

"Not at all," Hoving answers.

"Rockefeller is a total blotter. He likes to think that a broad spectrum of what is being created, that he can pick out what is very good, in his opinion. But I wouldn't think that any painter or sculptor ever said, 'Now, what am I going to do that will appeal to him?' and therefore the whole art movement would change. That just doesn't work.

"Rockefeller buys historical things in the African area, and very little of that, actually. His main thing is pre-Columbian. American Indian. And New Guinea."

As for the general theory of museums, Hoving explained, "We feel these things are World Ownership, in a sense; and Pure Possession is probably not particularly important. Pure Conservation is. I mean they [the Great Masterpieces] ought to be pinned down, so you can take care of them."

(Akrim Medany, dean of the School of Fine Arts, CMU, feels that too much interest in conservation may be hazardous to art because it is related to the obviously fallacious desire for personal immortality. The only reason Rembrandt's work seems so uniformly dark to us, he points out, is that varnish has been applied to preserve it.)

One last question: "Mr. Hoving, are you related to the Rockefellers in any way, or to the Paleys and Burdens?"

"No," he practically snarls. "I'm not related to any of *them!*"

"Where'd you get those questions?" he asks me as I am packing it in. I laugh mysteriously. So then he warns me "not to make this into anything political, because it's not political and it will snap right back in your face." Strange. Just the opposite might apply to him. He thought his actions as museum director were

above politics, and because they were not, they snapped back at
him.

☆   ☆   ☆

From a certain perspective it is sensibility that determines the
power structures in all the arts, particularly the visual arts. Affini-
ties between cultural *gestalts* and modes of diction may play more
of a part in the manipulations of money than any purely sociological factors.

Analyzing the Culture Barons this way, we perceive at least
ten or eleven distinct sensibilities, half of which can be called
"hip," or "decadent," while the other half are square, pedagogic,
tending to teach people they are inferior.

What the hip or decadent sensibilities have in common is a
use of tertiary colors (*e.g.*, pink, gold, lavender), and interest in the
"thingness" of the thing, an excising—since Warhol—of the "ar-
tiste" personality, or the opposite tendency, as with Pollock, to
pee in the patron's fireplace.

Exponents of the hip sensibilities are pre-eminently the homosexual artists and theater people, both of which groups adhere
on the basis of the exclusion of nonliterates from inaccessible gay
modes of speech. Homosexual artists are said to be less chauvinis-
tic than homosexuals of the theater world but simultaneously more
isolated and more alienated from straight society.

Another hip sensibility has been described as the "affectless,
psychopathic womanizer," and as such might include some of our
Culture Barons.

L.A. comics have a hip sensibility of their own, which includes the smart *Artforum* critic Peter Plagens and the "dumb"
photographer Eddie Ruscha. Plagens sees in New York City the
polarization of human relations; the austere, efficient, wasteless
common sense versus the militant clinging caprice. And he thinks
Pasadena is like Manhattan.

Texans make up a special category of hip because "rich people like to have exotic Texans in their house."

New York aestheticians have a tough time with decadence.
They prefer a straight or square Elizabethan sensibility, seeing art
as a basic counter in the social game, a way of increasing elitism in

response to pressure from the rising monied masses. Or they hold a tragic Germanic position: "High art is morally serious." Or they have a Patriarchal Bourgeois New England Transcendental Capitalist sensibility (and studied Euripides at Harvard but not algebra): "Art is good for us, and I possess it all." All these outlooks seem perverse to the subversive decadent avant-garde artist.

Art dealer Leo Castelli's image and sensibility are a unique elegance (looking like Maximilian Schell, wearing lace cuffs, sitting in the Prater talking to Ad Reinhardt)—and he also keeps in contact with the artists of Soho, that is, the grass roots, by looking at a lot of slides and therefore having a solid base for his taste.

Tom Hoving demands a special camp for his Viking sensibility. In the art world they speculate about the deep dark sources and motives of his behavior but resign themselves to never learning the true story. Does he feel like a sissy for going into the Museum instead of the stock market? Has he macho pretentions? Financial macho? Did he think Van Gogh was shlock, popularized and grandmotherly, because of the erosion-debasement of the Dutchman's once courageous value, and did he think Clyfford Still chichi, and did he think he would be praised for making such a hip move as trading in the one for the other? Square sensibilities get in trouble when they venture too far into hip turf.

But "hip" and "bohemian" are not the same thing.

It is not unusual for a Culture Baron to be fearful of artists and therefore conduct a kind of psychological warfare against them. He speaks of the artists he works with in a disparaging tone of voice. He promotes the Myth of the Artist as Bohemian. What this actually means could use some careful study, but it may be remembered that Hitler took the gypsies as one of his special enemies at least partly because of their mysterious lore and unsocialized habits. Were artists ever really Bohemians? Or does the label serve merely to make them socially taboo, even sexually taboo, like "niggers"—and thence available for economic exploitation? The artist who thinks of himself as a Bohemian will be that much less likely to protest his crummy working conditions.

THE MONEY POOL

The National Endowment is not a Federal bureaucracy. The people who run it are well-informed, sympathetic, open-minded people, willing to make changes.

My work consisted of reading through all the applications in a big ring binder and then going to Washington for one big three-day meeting once a year, at seventy-five dollars a day. The applicants submitted tapes or scores, or preferably both; if you're a musician you can tell in a few minutes whether they're any good or not.

—Dan Morgenstern,
former jazz panel consultant,
National Endowment for the Arts

W HERE do the Culture Barons get the money to keep their projects rolling? Curiously, they complain, almost to a man, of having "no money." "No money" is given as the official problem of the arts in New York by a special NBC-TV program on the subject. Sociologist Alvin Toffler and Princeton economists William and Hilda Baumol agree that the "cost-benefit" ratio of the live performing arts simply cannot compete with that of the mass-producible arts, and so the high arts are doomed to economic disaster. Arguments deriving from this basic premise filter down to each of the individual arts. One hears of the "death" of the theater. Though Harold Prince suggests the Musicians Union is to blame, another producer, Bernard Sahlins, faults the Broadway landlords and the main theater advertising agency. A computerized survey sponsored by the Ford Foundation last year concluded that the operating deficit of symphony orchestras, operas, ballet and modern dance troupes, and theaters all around the country now stands at $62 million and is projected to inflate fabulously in the coming years.

All this talk about having no money seems curious because the money is obviously there. One hundred and fifty million dollars changes hands each year for the purchase of original paintings and sculptures. The right two people—Peggy Douglas and George Moore (one of the leading lights at First National City Bank), for example—can raise seven million dollars between them in a short time, as they did for the new Opera House at Lincoln Center. Millionaires like Mitzi E. Newhouse and the late Vivian Beaumont, when approached just the right way, are willing to strip off a million bucks or three million for the Repertory Theater at the Center. And Miss Alice Tully's contribution to the Performing Arts Center was so great they don't even publicize the amount but named a hall for her *and* made her one of the only three women on the board.

Mrs. De Witt Wallace, widow of the hundred-millionaire publisher of the *Reader's Digest,* recently gave the Juilliard School $5 million for salaries of professors, as well as $650,000 to the Metropolitan Opera. She has also given the Metropolitan Opera several $1 million packages. For fifteen years Martha Baird Rockefeller paid for one or two of the Met's annual four new productions, and when she died in 1971 she left $5 million to the opera.

And as Mr. and Mrs. John T. Adams were giving $215,000 to Amherst for a music fund, the National Endowment for the Humanities was laying out $4 million for "The Adams Chronicles" on public television.

Such coin is in evidence all over the country, not only in New York, the financial capital. The Ford Foundation discovered that local private contributions are supporting the arts throughout the United States to the tune of four and a half times as much money as is being donated by government or foundations. In one season, 1971, that amounted to $36 million in cultural charity, or half as much as the arts themselves earned.

The paradox lies in the circular definition. Some arts are indeed commercially viable in the United States at this time—film, popular music, literature, and television—and they are therefore constantly making and disposing of money through the given economic structures of their respective media. They are full-scale industries, self-supporting, in good repute with the populace, the banks, and organized crime. Indeed, business is so good that there is not much need, in the commercially viable arts, for powerfully eccentric or individualistic impresarios; increasingly, their head men are accountants, lawyers, packagers, even rack jobbers.

Perversely, these commercial arts are not considered full arts. "Publishing has very little to do with literature," comments Michael Korda, editor-in-chief of one of the most important publishing houses. The prevailing view is that, if it makes money, it's not art: consequently the arts, that is, the real arts, are losing money. Q.E.D.

The economically noncongruent arts, also called real or high culture, now operate on huge deficits. They are dependent on charismatic individual impresarios and their entourages to importune their own sector of the populace, the private rich, and beg for charity. In the recent past, this method has worked sufficiently well.

☆   ☆   ☆

PUBLIC SECTOR

It is a cardinal point of faith, among Culture Barons as well as among labor attorneys representing the artists' unions, that inflation has wiped out the private patron of culture. However, the events in the political sphere in the 1960s are having an effect on the culture statesmen at least equal to the events in the economic sphere in the 1970s. What the Culture Barons mean when they speak of having no money for the arts is that they want to establish themselves in some sense with the public sector, to alter fundamentally their pattern of support, to put a claim on all that money that now goes for unpopular things like weaponry ($81 billion on defense in 1975, or 30 cents of every Federal dollar spent) and traffic circles (at $25 million apiece). If this doesn't work, the Culture Barons are still ready to commit grantsmanship with the foundations and corporations, but long-term economic planning indicates that the state is the soundest source of money.

Broadway composer and lyricist Stephen Sondheim says we are the only major country whose government does not subsidize art. "Maybe it's free enterprise, but it's bad. Only mass arts like movies and TV can support themselves. But theater has needed support even since the Roman coliseum."

Likewise Amyas Ames, chairman of Lincoln Center and of the New York Philharmonic, director of the Rockefeller Foundation and overseer of Harvard, holds that the arts must have government support if they are to survive and flourish. Ames is fond of pointing out that in the United States the government spends 29 cents *per capita* on the arts, while in Canada the government spends $1.40 and in West Germany $2.42. *Fortune* magazine contrasts the percentage of opera subsidized by several major governments: U.S.A. 2 percent, Britain 40 percent, Germany 45–72 percent, Sweden 90 percent, the U.S.S.R. 100 percent.

The real kicker to these statistics is that the American public is willing to let their government support the arts. A 1973 poll by the National Research Center for the Arts, a new division of the Lou Harris organization, revealed that 64 percent of the American public would be willing to pay an additional five dollars a year in taxes to maintain and operate cultural facilities. And of those people, more than half would be willing to pay an additional fifty dollars.

In the summer of 1975, Representative Fred Richmond, a Democrat from Brooklyn and former member of the N.Y.S. Council on the Arts, filed legislation in the House of Representatives which would implement this polled willingness. The bill would allow taxpayers to designate an amount of their choosing, either from tax refunds or as a donation, for use by the National Foundation on the Arts and the Humanities.

Richmond expected that a billion dollars could be raised in this way for the National Endowments.

UNITED STATES

The government is already funding the arts. The National Endowment for the Arts, a 1965 L.B.J. creation, gave $61 million last year to just over two thousand individuals and organizations. This comes to an average grant of $30,000, with very few grants exceeding $150,000, like the one of $1 million to the Metropolitan Opera or the $900,000 to the New York City Ballet. In 1974 about one third of all applicants were granted some money by the National Endowment, a high percentage of success.

Decisions on grants are made by staffs who screen, panelists expert in the various fields who weed out, and ultimately by the National Foundation on the Arts and the Humanities, (the overall agency comprising the National Endowment for the Arts (Nancy Hanks, chairman) and the National Endowment for the Humanities (Ronald Berman, chairman) appointed by the President, who meet quarterly to approve grants to the survivors of the other processes. Chairman of Arts Nancy Hanks has the power to veto applications or to make grants of up to $10,000 by herself.

The Endowment panels include: (for dance) Merce Cunningham; (for music) Gian Carlo Menotti and Risë Stevens; (for theater) Joseph Papp and Harold Prince; (for literature) Donald Barthelme and Simon Michael Bessie.

On the National Foundation on the Arts, the overall policy-making body are Nancy Hanks, Maurice Abravanel, Angus L. Bowmer, Richard F. Brown, Henry J. Cauthen, Van Cliburn, Kenneth Dayton, Charles Eames, Clint Eastwood, Judith Jamison, James Earl Jones, Charles K. McWhorter, Jerome Robbins, James D. Robertson, Rosalind Russell, Thomas Schippers, Gunther Schuller, George C. Seybolt, Beverly Sills, Billy Taylor, E. Leland Webber, Harry M. Weese, Eudora Welty, Dolores Wharton, Anne Potter Wilson, Robert E. Wise, James Wyeth, and Michael Straight (deputy chairman).

Funds are allocated into Architecture and Environmental Arts, Crafts, Dance, Folk Arts, Literature, Museum, Music, Public Media (including the American Film Institute), Theater, and Visual Arts. Under the Expansion Arts Program, professional artists who have chosen to work in their local communities and are "deeply involved in the cultural expression and traditions of their neighborhoods, communities, and regions" are funded through their organizations. Matching grants up to $50,000 are given to community-based cultural centers that have had a continuing program in at least two art forms for at least three years.

Though the Endowment gives plenty to the Metropolitan Opera, to Balanchine's New York City Ballet, and to art museums around the country, its main impact is to support such homey-folksy things as pottery workshops, jazz clubs, street theaters, totem-pole preservations, graffiti in Philadelphia, clowns in New Orleans, guitars in Baltimore, or three months on a raft for the Otrabanda Theater with filmmaker Dom Pennebaker.

National Endowment money is funneled through fifty-five state or territorial arts councils to support projects like the building of an eagle made of auto bumpers in Alabama, preserving cowboy rock drawings in Wyoming, and reviving Appalachian quilting. Endowment money went to a totally nude "Bacchae" by the Performance Group, under the direction of Richard Schechner. Eskimos and Indians in Alaska have been funded through the schools to teach children ivory carving and leather working. In Leominster, Massachusetts, kids are learning printing. And in Brunswick, Maine, a sculptor is creating a mammoth outdoor work with the help of vocational school students.

The Endowment (along with the New York State Council) also funds a group called Volunteer Lawyers for the Arts, founded in 1969, which gives free legal assistance to indigent artists and arts groups with arts-related legal problems.

The philosophy behind the National Endowment's encouragement of cultural decentralization was summed up by David Dempsey in *The New York Times:* "The big Eastern cities are parochial today," he wrote, "whereas the expanding university towns and upstart metropolises of the South and West provide the talent, energy and creative ferment that are changing the tastes of the art Establishment."

At least one midwestern Culture Baron is not comfortable with the aesthetic promoted by the National Endowments. William F. Turner, a television executive in Iowa, castigated the Foundation on the Arts and the Humanities in particular for publishing books edited by George Plimpton, one of which included a poem that consisted entirely of the word L-I-G-H-G-H-T. "George Plimpton's editing work alone cost the United States $200,000!" he complained. "And for a word that's not even spelled right!"

At an appropriations hearing of the Senate Subcommittee on

the Arts and Humanities, former Endowment official Brian O'Do-
herty, in shoulder-length hair and fringed jacket, defended the
"progress toward realism" that Endowment artists were making.
"After all, they use real objects," he argued.

Another opposing view of the National Endowment's aesthetic was voiced by New York theater man Joseph Papp. In 1973
he objected to the ceiling of $150,000 set on grants by the Endow-
ment. Such a limit tended to penalize large theaters, he felt. And it
fostered the decentralization the Nixon people were attempting to
effect in other areas of communication: in public broadcasting and
in network programming, "watering down the influence of the intellectually suspect communications centers so repugnant to the
cautious and rigid-minded President."

Close enough: The Endowments admitted, in an article in
The New York Times, that they "would like to see Americans less
dependent on TV and more accessible to living performers."

Chairman of the National Endowment for the Arts is Nancy
Hanks, aged forty-seven and approximately the fifth highest
woman appointee in the current administration. A graduate of
Duke University in political science, she spent thirteen years previous to her appointment working in philanthropy, some of which
were as personal secretary to Nelson Rockefeller. Though she is
cagey enough to imitate a southern accent while lobbying in
Congress for money, reporters have called her "unsophisticated,"
noting that she makes crewelwork covers for her typewriter. She
lives in Georgetown during the winter and in East Hampton,
Long Island, in the summer.

In a ninety-six-page book of condensed guidelines for the programs of the National Endowment for the Arts, Miss Hanks's staff
spells out the various grant requirements and eligibilities. In theater a resident professional company to be eligible must have a
yearly operating budget of $200,000 and pay Equity salaries. A
choreographer must be an "experienced professional," and even if
he does not have his own permanent dance company, it is the
dance company that must apply for the choreographer's grant. In
museum grants, the size of the institution is not a criterion but
rather that a specific project suggested be of national or regional
impact and of aesthetic and cultural significance. Craft and Folk
Art grants are administered under other programs, such as Music

Nancy Hanks, chairman, National Endowment for the Arts

or Visual Arts, Education, or Expansion Arts. An orchestra with an annual operating budget of $100,000 for three seasons may qualify if it has national or regional impact or if it serves unique geographical needs; the more expensively run may request funds of up to $150,000.

In literature, to be eligible for grant consideration, a writer must have accomplished any one of a long list of different literary achievements. He must have published two or more short stories in two or more literary magazines, or published a volume of short fiction, or published a novel, or published ten or more poems in two or more literary magazines, or published a volume of poetry, or published two or more essays or critical articles related to literature or writers in two or more literary magazines, or published a volume of essays or criticism, or had produced by a professional theater company a play in any form and of any length, or published a play of any length in a literary magazine or theater publication or book form, or have a letter of recommendation (in the case of a playwright) from a professional theater person. The fellowships in literature are for $6,000.

Of all the arts and humanities, creative writing is the most oversubscribed—or underfunded. In 1975 when the stipend was only $5,000, 1566 applications were received, with the largest group being 729 poets; there were also 393 fiction writers, 333 playwrights, and 111 essayists, critics, or biographers. Only 154 writers throughout the United States were awarded the grants, or fewer than one out of ten. This is a far worse statistic than the Endowment average. Elsewhere in the Endowment competitions, one out of three grant applications was successful.

In the Expansion Arts program, community-based artists are funded according to the following criteria of selection: (1) merit of the project, (2) organizational stability, (3) capacity to achieve objectives, (4) constituency served by the organization, (5) demonstrated need for support requested, and (6) capacity of the organization to raise funds in addition to those provided by the Endowment.

Cultural centers, which are also eligible for $50,000 matching grants, are chosen on the basis that they 1. Be professionally directed and community-based. 2. Have demonstrated a commitment to the pursuit of the highest level of artistic achievement. and 3. Have demonstrated high standards of performance and administrative ability.

Most of the qualities sought out by the National Arts Endowment are the same as those theoretically valued by the state arts councils: community relevance, professional and experienced leadership, solid financial grounding. In theory these criteria are also the same ones used by the Ford Foundation, the other giant of the money pool. But in practice Ford's grants in the arts conceal their populism under a thick coating of aristocrat. The longtime director of Ford's Humanities and Arts division was slightly boastful that his standards were higher than those of the government agencies. "A government agency has to fund certain things that we just don't have to," he said, probably referring to some of the colorful local activities. "But we," he said, "have the opportunity to set standards." By which he means Balanchine's ballet, the Pennsylvania Ballet, Houston's Alley Theater.

Head man of the National Endowment for the Humanities is

Ronald Berman, aged forty-six, holder of a Harvard Ph.D. in Shakespeare and Renaissance studies. He is a champion half-miler, he says. He wrote a scathing history of the American intellectual left in the 1960s.

☆   ☆   ☆

The National Endowment for the Arts and such state agencies as the New York Council on the Arts are split right down the middle between those who feel the money should go to an ever larger and more widely distributed group of people, and those who feel the programs are already too experimental and decentralized. The culture revolution of the 1960s provides the positive values (not always consciously so) for one side of this argument, while the other side defends standards, academia, and professionalism. Correspondingly, about half the Endowment money now goes to the untried or grass-roots artist, about half to the established. The debate continues. But even as it does so, a safer, more conservative course of action is implied by the attempt to "build audiences," that is, to promote popular appreciation for the arts when the program fails to promote popular participation. This is a cop-out.

Governor Rockefeller himself placed an emphasis on popular participation in the arts as one of the goals of the New York State arts program in his original address to the legislature in 1960.*

Of course there must be hundreds, even thousands, of candidates for government funds who failed to get them, though deserving. But one such case is the California Ojai Festival, which was refused National Endowment money and where there appeared last summer what *Daily Variety* called "probably the most musically accomplished rock group in the world" (Tom Scott, John Guerin, Max Bennett, Larry Nash, and Robben Ford) and an orchestra conducted by Michael Tilson Thomas.

---

* The relevant paragraphs from Rockefeller's State of the State message were:

I have pointed out that the goal of economic development is individual self-development. This goal finds its fullest realization when the individual has the opportunity for cultural expression, participation, and appreciation.

I recommend the creation of an advisory Council on the Arts to be composed of private citizens who have distinguished themselves in the several

☆   ☆   ☆

NEW YORK STATE

The other significant governmental body contributing money
to the arts is New York State. In 1974 the Albany legislature approved the spending of $34 million on arts organizations—slightly
more than half the amount allocated to the arts by the Federal government that year and *far* more than the other forty-nine states put
together. Nelson Rockefeller, when governor, had initiated the
Council on the Arts with $50,000 in 1961 in the spirit, it would
seem, of the culturally oriented Kennedy Administration. The allocation zoomed from $2 million in 1969 to $20 million in 1970 apparently on a whim of the Governor's, taking the Council administrators by surprise. Under Rockefeller's successor, Malcolm
Wilson, though still by Rockefeller's will, the budget hit its record
high of $34 million in 1974 and again in 1975 and virtually para-
lyzed the men appointed to give it away.

But it must be understood how different are the various
groups of people, one from another, who are involved in the slow
functioning of the New York State Council on the Arts. The primary group is the legislature in Albany, men with proud photographs of themselves on the new Mall, Democrats still congregat-
ing in the smoke-filled bar of the De Witt Clinton Hotel. The word
of Nelson Rockefeller may come down, and be impossible to resist, but they maintain a fierce guardianship over the rights of their
many little rural communities. In 1974, Wilson's hard-working
State Senate and House decided to guarantee that all those millions of dollars would not be given out just in New York City. So
they slapped a provision onto the 75-cent *per capita* dole that
every county had to receive its correct *per capita* share. Simple,
democratic, obvious.

But not to the taste of the Council itself, the second group of
individuals to be reckoned with. The sixteen governor-appointees

---

fields of cultural activity. The U.S. is in the process of a tremendous surge
of public interest in art, music, the drama, and other forms of cultural
expression. New York State must make a contribution to this cultural advance commensurate with its unequaled cultural resources.

are a kind of sieve; they want to keep the classy in and let the populist out.

At the tail end of the Wilson Administration the Arts Council consisted of Seymour Knox of Buffalo, banker and art gallery owner; Kitty Carlisle Hart, television personality and former opera singer; Max Arons, president of local 802, the Musicians' Union; Romare Bearden, painter; Miriam Colon Edgar, director of a Puerto Rican traveling theater; John Hightower, president of the Associated Councils of the Arts; James Houghton of Corning Glass; Thomas Hoving; Edward Kresky, one-time aide to Nelson Rockefeller; Mrs. David (Vicky) Levene of Binghamton, SUNY teacher; Arthur Levitt, Jr., broker; Alwin Nikolais, choreographer; Frederick Richmond, U.S. representative and president of Carnegie Hall; Mrs. Richard (Dorothy) Rodgers; Andrew Wolfe of Genessee Valley, publisher; and Henry Allen Moe, MOMA trustee and adviser to Nelson Rockefeller on artistic matters.

These sixteen prominent citizens were appointed to serve on the Council by the Governor and approved by the State Senate. However, the job is not merely honorary, though unsalaried. At the subcommittee level these people are in a position to affect drastically who gets money and who doesn't.

And they are not all exactly Renaissance men. Outgoing executive director Eric Larrabee commented of his neighbor in Buffalo and then Council president Seymour Knox, "He couldn't care less about symphony. He's only interested in his gallery."

Dorothy Rodgers, on the music subcommittee, is a matriarchal queenpin and an ardent supporter of the Metropolitan Opera. Terribly elegant, she is also very tough; another Council member, Vicky Levene, and the entire Performing Arts department staff jump when she talks; people pale when they sit near her. She demands, "Would you get me a sandwich!" to the nearest Arts administrator. And she says, "Oh, let's give the Met another $250,000," when that means eight small chamber music groups will have to get nothing. A staff member of the New York State Council on the Arts says she killed a senior citizens' show at Town Hall single-handedly.

Thomas Hoving, they say, "cuts a swath when he talks."

The new members of the Council are always a little "parochial" at first, but they learn the cultivation of an objective value judgment pretty soon, says an insider.

Perhaps the best of them is Richmond, president of Carnegie Hall, who went on from New York City councilman to the U.S. House of Representatives, where, in 1975, he introduced a bill putting an optional arts donation on every income tax form.

Then there are the panelists, who pass judgment on the professional quality of applications for state subsidy—approximately one hundred people, whose names are a well-guarded secret. Their deliberations over applications form yet another sieve, one of "professionalism."

And finally there was Eric Larrabee and his staff of eighty in New York City, working out of a stolid turn-of-century office in the Fisk Building on Fifty-seventh Street, trying to orchestrate the whole process.

Eric Larrabee, past executive director of the N.Y.S. Council on the Arts, was a Social Register socialite in an office full of blacks and Latins and Jews and musicians who looked like Hell's Angels. Apart from him (and perhaps one blond arts assistant), the state subsidy office could have been a Gauguin painting. But Larrabee was a self-admitted member of "the Arts Mafia," a group of people who have known each other a long time and have a lot to do with what goes on in culture in New York State as well as in the U.S.A.—and that was perhaps his downfall.

When the rule came down that there must be *per capita* representations in every county, the Director balked. "There's nothing in Queens except people!" one of his higher staff commented, though younger staff persons thought there was nothing inherently wrong with the new distribution requirement. Larrabee complained that there were no funds for a computer; a staff person muttered that he hadn't even tried using a calculator.

All that money and a reluctance to spend it: it reminded me of the rupees frozen in India, paid for American wheat, but unexportable. Grantees found themselves waiting overly long times for the money they'd been promised. Albany threatened to make drastic cutbacks. The head of the Ford Foundation's division of Humanities and Arts (the big boy down the block) commented, "The state council has a history of being slow. Part of the bureaucracy and red tape is the legislature in Albany's fault, part is their own fault. I think it'll gradually go away."

One other group of people the State Council on the Arts is concerned with are the vocal artists and critics of New York City,

most of whom feel they are not getting their just deserts. Even
before the 1974 snafu, Upstate was clearly getting the better end
of the bargain. Five out of six Upstate arts organizations applying
for aid received some; but only one out of three New York City organizations, and only one out of thirty-three individual artists.
These ratios were clear enough from newspaper reports—but, surprisingly, were not general knowledge around the Council office,
where it was understood only that there was "pressure for decentralization." *The Village Voice* reported provocatively that there
was an "upwelling of sentiment against Eric Larrabee, but gentil-
ity seals everyone's lips." Art critic Annette Kuhn said that they
"didn't see the forest for the trees," and were "ad-libbing decisions
instead of making long-range policies, despite the bigness of the
organization." A letter to the *Times* complained that choreographers, if they were to get grants, were required to maintain a
dance company, which was economically difficult. One employee
of the Council admitted to "some egregious faults" but refused to
elaborate, being afraid "to lose his job" or "screw it up with the
legislature."

One well-known playwright who had been funded by the National Endowment but not by the state called the state agency
"unserious, they're a mess of incompetents, and they're playing
with our lives," and referred me to their reasons for rejecting a
serious opera composed by a friend of hers: "They said it was too
impressive, too strong, that it wouldn't find an audience of more
than one hundred people." But it was a serious piece of music!
she protested, "not a situation comedy!" "That shows you what
state subsidy can do," she commented finally. "They're all there
because they failed in business."

I went to speak with Eric Larrabee, when he was still executive director, holding possibly the most powerful arts position in
America today (according to Knox, then president of the Council)
though it paid only $40,000 and though he had repeatedly con-
demned the idea of a Superministry of Culture. I went to see him
where he worked behind the skylight of the twenty-sixth and top
floor, to which the elevator does not go, at 250 West Fifty-seventh
Street.

The first thing I noticed in his medium-small cubicle was a

Eric Larrabee, former executive director, New York State Council on the Arts (Nancy Foote)

huge oil painting behind his desk in floaty-pink and gold abstract expressionist gauzy homage to impressionism. The thing was, it matched him! He also had goldish hair, white eyebrows, a healthy pink and white skin. A smallish man, pursed and twinkly, probably a tennis player under his crew cut, he looked handsomely rabbity and spry, honed to a finely ambiguous point from the necessities of incessant compromising of taste and values in the Jello-y medium of politics and public relations in which he moves.

A leather cigarette case, inscribed in gold to EL, Harvard, lay in a noticeable spot on his desk among the papers. But he indicated that twelve years at *Harper's* magazine had made more of an impression on him intellectually and politically than had the university (where, however, he met his wife and the friends who later offered him jobs).

Most unnerving was a moving steel sculpture close to my edge of the desk. Looking something like a book, it opened and closed with a slow, pulsating rhythm, making me momentarily believe it was mirroring my own pulse.

Larrabee acknowledged that there was a concentration of power in the arts, even volunteering that "there is an Art Mafia." He mentioned as members Nancy Hanks of the National Endowment, and Ralph Bergard, John MacFadyen, and John Hightower, all connected with a group called Associated Councils of the Arts, and the latter two former holders of Larrabee's seat on the New York Council. "Sure, we've all known each other for years," he said, "but it's not important. The connections are accidental and have no effect on events."

He said the Arts in Government group were unlike the Arts Council members or the boards of big institutions—ostensibly because they are more whimsical, more casual, and have more sense of style. He sees MacFadyen at the Coffee House Club for lunch, an anticlub club that producer Hal Prince also frequents. He gets together with Hightower at the Century Club, which he smilingly refers to as "the citadel of the Establishment." It is also the most literary of the exclusive men's clubs in New York (some of its other members being George Plimpton, C. P. Snow, John V. Lindsay, and Nelson Rockefeller).

Taking Larrabee at face value, I concluded that in the case of the New York State Arts Council and the National Arts Endowment as well as their related auxiliary lobbying bodies, there is an emergence into partial visibility of the old boy network of wealth, blood, and schools. Heretofore, the major museum and opera governing boards and the administrations of the big foundations have always been examples of the same power structure, but this was not in the public notice.

Executives of the agencies and arts administrators are defined by their adherence to the well-spoken politeness syndrome— "we're all gentlemen here, we can talk it out"—and in the end, whoever has the most power makes the decision and the others agree.

These are the kind of men who—like C. Douglas Dillon, Roswell Gilpatrick, and Tom Hoving, all now on the board of the Metropolitan Museum—are eased into military and political offices by virtue of being asked by the higher-ups to do "studies" of selected topics. Respectively Dillon, Gilpatrick, and Hoving "studied" the Navy, the defense establishment, and New York City's parks system, before being appointed to power positions in those areas.

Mayor Beame's Commission to Advise the Mayor on Cultural Policies, said Larrabee, was an invention of Stephen Benedict and John Booth at the Twentieth Century Fund. Though no one had been appointed to it as of our interview, Larrabee was using "we" quite naturally. "We will foot the bill," he said. "All the Mayor has to do is ask for a report." And the idea behind it, Larrabee revealed, was to move culture out of the Parks, Recreation, and Cultural Affairs office and put it into the Mayor's office.

Executive Director Larrabee was fondly speculating on who would be named to the Commission (later called Commission on Cultural Affairs), indicating that he could probably name one hundred people around the city from among whom the appointments would come. When the names were announced, some months later, it turned out that many of them were familiar from my explorations into Culture Barony: Amyas Ames, chairman of Lincoln Center; C. Douglas Dillon, president of the Metropolitan Museum of Art; William S. Paley, chairman of CBS; Mrs. Vincent Astor, foundation president; Barbaralee Diamonstein, member of the Landmarks Preservation Commission; and critic Brendan Gill. Also the publisher of the *Amsterdam News*, John Procope; the chairman of the Brooklyn Academy of Music; two Spanish names; the aristocrat Robert Goelet; a suburbanite representative of the Staten Island Council on the Arts; the director of the Museum of the City of New York; a nun; the president of the actors and artists association; a lawyer; a law professor; a trustee of the Modern; and the chairman of the Foundation for American Dance. Chairman of the Mayor's Committee was Martin Segal, an investment banker and president of the Lincoln Center Film Society.

As we talked, Larrabee recalled his early career for me.

At Harvard he studied seventeenth-century French and English history and literature, or in other words he read Molière (whose name turned up frequently on Council grantees' programs) and Shakespeare and studied the reigns of absolutists Louis XIV and Oliver Cromwell. After Harvard he went to Paris, tried the free-lance writer life, found he wasn't suited for it. Then, working for a long while at *Harper's* and a very short while at *Horizon* and *American Heritage*, Larrabee had gotten involved in the nomination of Adlai Stevenson. The experience was emotionally absorbing, he says; he wept at the convention. Much more recently, he helped a friend write a book on Adlai and was startled to find him "very unpleasant," the story "searing." Now he was politically adrift and disillusioned, he told me, having gotten inured to Nixon.

In 1960 he published a book, *The Self-Conscious Society*. He wrote wittily, "Culture is the attempt, art is the success." And, "Originality is the assembling of a new audience." Various essays in the book dealt with politics, jazz, and the homosexual bias in the arts, particularly theater, literature, TV, and film. He deplored it as perverse, especially in view of the fact that heterosexual motifs are censored. So I asked if there was an antihomosexuality bias in the workings of the Council. He denied it. "My personal predilections have no effect on what we support," he declared.

If anyone were to ask me, I would say that America's contribution to world culture has consisted mainly of Hollywood movies, jazz, blue jeans (utilitarian and very sexy), and perhaps such diversions as abstract expressionism. But to Eric Larrabee the real breakthrough was Henry Ford's mass productionism.

We discussed a fair amount of Larrabee's economic and social philosophy. In terms of real social impact, he named Henry Ford as the most important person of the twentieth century, inventor of the assembly line and mass production. He mentioned Ford in the course of defining what he meant by "industrial democracy," which is something he values. He takes, by Melvin Lasky's definition, the Rooseveltian view of America as pragmatic and active, which replaced the Jamesian view (idealistic and brash) and the Jeffersonian (America as innocent and pastoral). When Henry Ford began producing the automobile, a new way of organizing the society came into being, Larrabee said, which contained democratic imperatives as its very essence and which would not endure if those democratic imperatives were not respected. (I was sorry to hear Jefferson left in the dust.) But Larrabee held that the industrial system would not work without this new type of democracy, Rooseveltian individualism, being protected. This political and intellectual view he had assimilated while working as an editor of *Harper's*, where he was exposed to the influences of Bruce Catton, Russell Lynes, and others.

Larrabee saw the many complicated aspects of the state subsidy mechanism as a good feature, a kind of checks and balances system, insuring no undue concentration of power in any totalitarian manner. He outlined the application-screening procedure, starting from "our tedious and annoying application" (thirteen pages, to be completed in triplicate) and working on through the legal complications other staff members in his office have called "Byzantine." Copies of the application go to the programming and fiscal staffs, who do their different kinds of analysis on it, which, it is hoped, will "merge." The fiscal staff asks whether the arts organization has reasonable budgets, if the earned to unearned money ratio is reasonable, and if there is "evidence of economic vitality, non-dependence on us." In other words, a little symphony somewhere upstate has to be taking in at least one third of its total expenses at the box office.

Then the programming staff checks to see what the group does, what its management is like, and how promising the group is. "The so-called personal considerations in choosing grantees," a staff member said, "are mainly oriented around not sensing that the management is *bad*. We see if they have a community connection, community support, if they're trying to get an audience, that they're not *selfish*." My informant glanced a moment at the white-painted walls of his office. "If they don't have these things, then they have to be of *extraordinary* experimental quality." He laughed. "Ideally they have both."

Sometimes there are fights between divisions of the Council on the disposition of money. The Visual Arts department's grant of $750,000 to the Bronx Zoo was highly unpopular with the Performing Arts department. "They gave all that money to the monkey house!" was the complaint. (Actually, it was for "architecture and environment" and didn't go to monkeys at all.)

Within Performing Arts, staffers have strongly differing opinions on how much money should be going to such significant representations of culture as the Metropolitan Opera, the City Center, and the Brooklyn Academy of Music, with personal favorites and animosities only one factor in the larger game of political lobbying.

Next, fiscal and programming staffs present one "all-purpose-form" on each applicant to one of ten panels on the arts, each composed of ten or twelve "community liaisons," representing the disciplines, coming from all around the state. The panels principally speak to the question of artistic quality, said Larrabee, determining if an applicant is professional enough. No sources at the Council would name any of the panelists.

Then Larrabee divulged a step omitted from all previous published accounts of the process. "The real work goes on at the next level," he said, "when the staff deliver the panels' recommendations into four subcommittees of the Council, which are statewide and therefore have a broader perspective." Five or six people from the Council sit on each subcommittee, "but two or three do the most work."

From the perspective of a lower-ranking staff person: "We only consider applications for seven weeks a year. I recommend twenty or thirty for music grants, and so does everyone in my department, for a total of about one hundred. These are brought to a secret panel of music professionals in the board room of Lincoln Center just prior to submission before subcommittees of the whole Council—which is the critical stage—and where projects find "champions" so as to enable them to proceed smoothly to the much too busy meeting of the full Council. I have to defend my music choices against, say, Dorothy Rodgers, in subcommittee with our entire staff; I'm not invited to the Council meeting itself." The full Council meets in May, July, September, October, and November. Only about half the membership is in attendance.

A lot hinges on whether a grant application catches the fancy of a Council member in subcommittee, since at that stage no applications are entirely rejected but merely recommended for more or less money, and the full Council of sixteen people, meeting only five times a year, is "much too busy" to consider every one of the applications that has come through the screening process so far.

Though professionals look at the applications at an earlier stage, it is the tastes and interests of the Council members, and particularly the more active ones, which ultimately determine the outlay of state subsidy money.

One might wonder about the qualifications of these appointees. In the Visual Arts, there was a painter, a gallery owner, a museum director, and a museum trustee–Rockefeller adviser. In the Performing Arts: the wife of a composer of musicals, a former opera singer, a concert hall president, and a labor leader. In

TV-Film Media, there seemed only to be one publisher. And there were only two minority group members to weigh the merits of Special Projects; all the rest of the Council being, by Larrabee's admission, "from the upper class." The other guardians of culture in the State of New York 1974 were businessmen, brokers, and bankers.

Meanwhile, Eric Larrabee was caught between the Council, the legislature, the hungry and the well-fed artists, and his own staff. Reports were that he did not get along with dowager Dorothy Rodgers. His staff criticized him for not making decisions fast enough, for sending memos instead of taking action.

He was pleasant and open with me. He was as cool and un-flustered to admit as I was shocked to hear that the "Special Projects" department was a euphemism for ghetto, and duplicated the services of the Visual Arts, Performing Arts, and Media departments on an admittedly different, and lower, level. He acknowledged that there were programs in Special Projects that wouldn't survive analysis in the other programs' staff sections. "This department nurtures groups till they want to move on and be treated like any other. . . . Ideally, we should be integrationist. But for now we have something valuable." Only a diplomat could put together a statement like: "There is a way to bring together minority community needs and aesthetic professionalism." After that I caught only fragments and phrases: "identity . . . particular kind of power . . . special impact and significance."

Larrabee was a polished liberal, of the upper-class cosmopolitan sort, favoring British government, German music, and French cafés. In the offices outside his, there was an abundance of black women secretaries (compensatory discrimination?). At home in Buffalo he lived in a Frank Lloyd Wright house, with an architect wife and Navajo vases. Larrabee unapologetically equated his own preferences in art with the "American high culture": Frank Lloyd Wright, jazz, Van Cliburn, *Moby Dick*, Robert Frost.

Since he had written paeans to jazz, I asked him if perhaps symphonies are losing money because people want to hear rock and jazz. "We don't know what people—in quotes—really want," he replied. "They have to want what they know about. Who the audience is, is a great unknown."

Larrabee himself had been exposed to the rock audience, at

least, during his tenure in the late '6os as provost of the volatile
State University of New York at Buffalo. His first memory of the
'6os period was of tear gas and broken windows; because of it he
is "a little more discouraged about the Cultural Renaissance" he
had seen coming in 1960. Indeed, he said he taught a class in
guerrilla warfare at Buffalo, to "SDS and their girl friends and
dogs. . . . The rhetoric in class was appalling, it blew up badly,"
he recalled, then went on to recount the story of the school strike
in 1968, "when the University shook itself out like an old coat."
Suffice it to say that a nonstudent was convicted for draft evasion,
that several hundred students occupied a building, and that by coincidence there occurred the same weekend what Larrabee calls a
"drug conference, with O'Leary and Ginsberg" (others call it an
Arts Festival). The president of the university convoked the entire
body of students and faculty one hour before the strike was scheduled to begin. Larrabee worried about "one maniac with a match"
but stood up anyway on the school's largest stage. Two dozen
demands for the Art Department were met on the spot; suspicions
about the French Department were granted as justified; and the
provost talked down a girl in bright purple cape and granny
glasses haranguing him. "I'm here to do a piece of work with or
without your help," he remembered saying. And he remembered
a fellow in the front with a tape recorder cheering him on: "Keep
going, baby, you're beautiful."

The whole experience was for him "complete and richly satisfying." What matter that the succeeding president at SUNYAB
called four hundred cops? It was the "radical leadership that was
on the edge of violence" that made it go sour. "People who ask,
'Where did it all go wrong?' took the counterculture poetry and
rhetoric, like *The Greening of America*, for literal truth. There was
no communication. There was no effect."

Larrabee was asked onto the Arts Council by Henry Allen
Moe, a Rockefeller adviser and trustee of the Museum of Modern
Art. At first Larrabee had political qualms, being an Adlai Stevenson man. But he was convinced when Chairman Knox told him,
"They'll be the most interesting years of your life." For three or
four months a year, now, he said, he thought about nothing else
but drumming up money from the legislature. The Council submitted to Albany a budget the thickness of a telephone book. Then

Larrabee's job was to keep track of things. "The natural condition of Albany is rumor. What's going on is what people say is going on. My job was to find out individual legislator's qualms about the Council and talk them out of them.

"So I talked to them over a few drinks at suppertime and I told them why we'd turned down some one of their constituents. They were grateful for a reason!" With the faintest trace of upper-class snob, he summed up the men in the State Senate and House: "Some of them are first rate. Some try. And some have a lot of courage."

Those in his staff who accused Eric Larrabee of lack of leadership perhaps failed to understand the finesse necessary to his position, having to deal with and harmonize such diverse groups as the dowager queens and Culture Barons of the Council itself, the chafed-elbow, loosened-tie legislators in the De Witt Clinton Hotel bar, and the striving and restive ghetto talent. It appealed to Larrabee's liberal spirit to be overseeing the noblesse obligatory dole of several millions of dollars: delicately, he was keeping control in the hands of the clique he actually calls "the good guys." Unconsciously, he stands for the country-house, city-house lifestyle; explicitly, he calls himself "gently reared." He ran the kind of operation that could give, when challenged, the ultimate reason: "That isn't the kind of thing we do" (as an Arts assistant said when explaining why Guy Lombardo could not be sent to Hormel, N.Y.).

The State Council on the Arts had been accused of cliquishness. Larrabee rationalized it away. He deplored instead "the crowd scene" downstairs on the twenty-third floor, where the Creative Artists Public Service program gives money to individuals rather than, as the Council does, to groups. The previous year there had been only 125 successful applicants out of nearly 3,000 attempts, and CAPS director Isabell Fernandez admitted she had to turn down two or three times as many qualified people as she had accepted. This year the applicant rolls had swelled to 5,500 so far. And CAPS, a combined project of the state, the National Endowment, the city department of cultural affairs, and several major corporations (Xerox, Exxon, Avon, Cluett Peabody, etc.) followed the same selection procedures as outlined for the N.Y.S. Council proper. In other words, they have a high overhead, with many artists employed on the screening panels. "At least it's getting money to them somehow!" Larrabee smiled. Angry rejectees claim that CAPS awards their subsistence grants of $3,500 and $4,000 to the same few artists year after year, the friends of artists who are on the selection panels, and that the artists on the selection panels are hardly—themselves—selected with the same democratic-bureaucratic rigamarole.

"Do you favor an artist who is established, and fully achieved in his career, over a new artist?" I asked. "For godsakes don't ever make that decision!" Larrabee exclaimed dramatically. He reaffirmed that the nitty-gritty selection principles are a jealously guarded secret. All he would reveal of grant-making policies is that the museum community is highly organized; that the Council's approach to them is "tell us what you need."

By his lights Larrabee stood for civilization and the cosmopolitan, for the continuance of a successful "industrial democracy," a "society that makes individualism possible." Yet there were fallacies in his explicit goals which eroded the moral foundation of his position. For instance, his and his staff's heavy reliance on "professionalism" was unexamined. Another problem was in the "individualism" he purports to value. Governor Rockefeller also spoke of the individual in the speech he made to the legislature recommending a council on the arts. But individuals are dealt with by the State Arts Council not at all; they are shunted to the "crowd scene" at CAPS. Only as consumers, as audience to be "built up," as "appreciators," are they taken into consideration. It is arts organizations that are funded, not individual artists, professional or amateur.

The bias toward "the professional" and away from the individual toward the organization undercut Larrabee's claims to individualistic cosmopolitanism. What to him looked like universal culture looked to me like the Harvard fallacy of assuming an identification with the kings of England and the statesmen of Western Europe.

Nevertheless, partly in despite of the work of his own State Arts agency, Larrabee touchingly predicted "the emergence of the artist from second-class citizenship."

Eric Larrabee's professional plane went down in a blaze of political accusations. Governor Nelson Rockefeller had—according to his sister-in-law Blanchette—tried hard to appoint a "bipartisan" Council. But when Malcolm Wilson's Albany statehouse was cleared out to make room for Democratic Governor Hugh Carey, half of the old Council members, including director Larrabee, were cleared out as well.

Replacing "Shorty" Knox as chairman of the Council was a woman, Joan Davidson, who, unlike her predecessor, has been working from the Council offices in Manhattan. And she takes a more active role than he did. She ran unsuccessfully as a Democratic senate candidate in Manhattan in 1974, but she promised the legislature that confirmed her that she would never tolerate political pressure on the council.

Then she finalized the dismissal of Larrabee, commenting that the Governor needed to recast the Council in line with his own ideas. Larrabee's successor was Kent Barwick, age thirty-five, former executive of the South Street Seaport Museum and director of the Municipal Art Society, which promotes a more aesthetic-looking New York.

The Davidson-Barwick council will differ from its fifteen-year forerunner. At first Davidson threatened the elimination of the secretive advisory panels, which in previous years intervened in the grant selection process midway between the staff recommendations and the council subcommittees' approval. But later she contented herself with just making the usual personnel substitutions of a new regime.

In the first flush of her administration, Davidson committed several political gaffs, for which she was rebuked by *The Village Voice*. She had the nerve to criticize council member Max Arons when his musicians' union went on strike, closing down much of Broadway. And she had the bad taste to take money away from the highly organized museum community. Less than a year after the new regime took office, *The Voice* repeated rumors that Nelson Rockefeller and his friend *Reader's Digest* owner Mrs. DeWitt Wallace—a major patron of the Metropolitan Opera—were scouting around for Joan Davidson's replacement.

☆   ☆   ☆

N.Y.S. Council on the Arts, Before Carey
Staff Flowchart

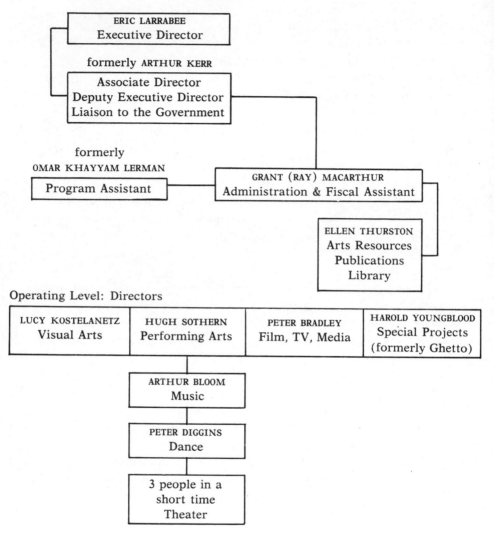

ERIC LARRABEE
Executive Director

formerly ARTHUR KERR

Associate Director
Deputy Executive Director
Liaison to the Government

formerly
OMAR KHAYYAM LERMAN

Program Assistant

GRANT (RAY) MACARTHUR
Administration & Fiscal Assistant

ELLEN THURSTON
Arts Resources
Publications
Library

Operating Level: Directors

LUCY KOSTELANETZ Visual Arts	HUGH SOTHERN Performing Arts	PETER BRADLEY Film, TV, Media	HAROLD YOUNGBLOOD Special Projects (formerly Ghetto)

ARTHUR BLOOM
Music

PETER DIGGINS
Dance

3 people in a
short time
Theater

N.Y.S. Council on the Arts, After Carey
Staff Flowchart

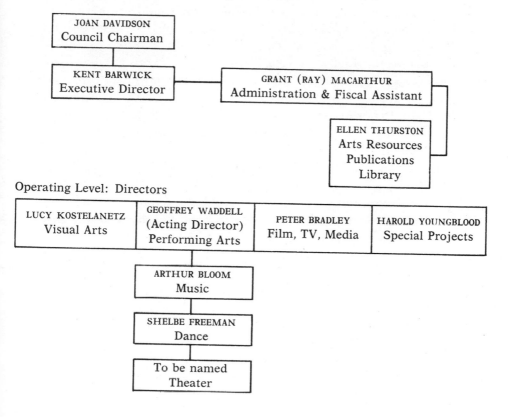

Operating Level: Directors

NEW YORK CITY

Financially, the city is in worse shape than either the state or
the Federal Government, which collect more money from their
citizens in taxes and consequently have better credit-ratings with
the banks. Nevertheless, the city has made some notably large
contributions to the arts. About $5 million has gone to Joseph
Papp to support first his free Shakespeare in the Park and later his
Public Theater operation in the Astor Library. The Metropolitan
Museum of Art, a tenant of the city through the Parks, Recreation,
and Cultural Affairs jurisdiction over the Met's site in Central
Park, receives over $3 million in annual aid. The mayor is the hon-

orary chairman of the New York State Theater's principal tenant, the City Center, and through this connection the City of New York contributes $300,000 per year to the upkeep and ordinary functioning of Julius Rudel's City Opera and George Balanchine's City Ballet.

Before the Federal or state arts agencies were created, New York City donated $15 million to the building of the culture complex at Lincoln Center, the money primarily going to Damrosch Park, the Performing Arts Library-Museum, and the underground garages, all of which the city continues to administer.

Though nearly half of the city budget comes from state and Federal funds, Lincoln Center administrators such as Schuyler Chapin, former general manager of the Metropolitan Opera, asked for more city money in the upkeep of the Center. Specifically, Chapin requested that the city pay the $200,000 that Lincoln Center, Inc., was then spending on a private security force.

Others among the Dukes of New York have recently maneuvered "culture" out of the PRCA office and into the mayor's office, by means of the establishment of a commission to advise the mayor on cultural policy. One of the leading spokesmen of this group is Hugh Sothern, one-time head of the Theatre Development Fund and then acting program director of the Performing Arts for the New York State Council on the Arts.

Because there is as yet no hard and fast power structure dealing with New York City subsidy of culture, there is a certain accessibility, a certain scrambling for money, in the dignified motions of the local nobility.

☆   ☆   ☆

PRIVATE SECTOR

CORPORATIONS

Corporations are tied up in the arts to almost precisely the same degree as foundations: in both cases a tiny percentage of their capital, less than the tax-deductible limit. The Ford Foundation survey found that corporations and foundations had each con-

tributed $8 million, in the 1971 season, to a group of 166 perform-
ing arts troupes around the country.

Some corporate sponsorships are conspicuous and well
known, such as Mobil Oil's million-dollar grant to NET, the public television network, for each season of Masterpiece Theatre,
and Exxon's million-dollar grants for Theater in America. Xerox
also sponsors television drama. In fact, these donations are indica-
tive of a trend. Corporations supported public television with $15
million worth of grants in the 1973–74 season alone—a much
higher level than their support of operas, theater, ballet, and symphony. At the same time, however, the Ford Foundation picked
up nearly four fifths of the tab for public TV.

On the opera front the most notable gifts are Eastern Airlines'
and Texaco's millions to the Metropolitan Opera, for productions
of the Ring Cycle and for weekend radio broadcasts respectively.

Art-collecting corporations are the Chase Manhattan Bank (Is
it David Rockefeller's taste they adhere to?—Observers say he
likes modern masters.), S. C. Johnson and Son, and Philip Morris,
which sponsors museum exhibits. Cummins Engine Company of
Columbus, Indiana, spent $2.5 million on architects, giving the
city a uniquely experimental skyline.

And increasingly, media-entertainment corporations are cross-
ing over into branches of the arts with which they ordinarily have
no concern. A decade ago CBS backed *My Fair Lady* on Broadway; just last season Twentieth Century Fox put up some of the
money for the successful show *The Wiz*.

☆   ☆   ☆

FOUNDATIONS

The foundations play a part in the dream life of every artist
and arts organization. For they represent, to artists, scientists, and
professors, that most parental of symbols, the socially sanctified
dole. How many artists (and scientists and professors) have spent
how many hours pouring their hearts into letters or filling out
applications or making up high-sounding phrases to describe
what they do or intend to do, dreaming of that cornucopia of gen-

erosity from the Establishment? And how many millions of disappointments!

☆   ☆   ☆

Foundations, those peculiar entities, were created by charter in the U.S. Senate between 1910 and 1914 and were conceived of as a new type of beast, over which some national, and yet private, checks should be exercised. The senators actually considered whether foundation trustees should be approved by a majority vote of the President of the United States, the Chief Justice, the president *pro tem* of the Senate, the speaker of the House, and the top officers of Harvard, Yale, Columbia, Johns Hopkins, and the University of Chicago! Since then we have come to accept that the "educational and cultural" activities of a foundation may be nothing more universally enlightening than the preservation, for public view, of a Du Pont mansion.

But it may well be that the foundation, with its oddly humanitarian justification and its solid tax-exemption, is the emblem of the American economic system. As Blanchette Rockefeller points out, no such tax breaks are given in Europe.

In 1940, under Roosevelt, economists identified thirteen families in control of the top two hundred U.S. nonfinancial corporations. These were Ford, Du Pont, Rockefeller, Mellon, Carnegie, McCormick, Hartford, Harkness, Duke, Pew, Clark, Reynolds, and Kress. To protect it from taxes, most of the money of these families was locked into foundations, with Pew and certain branches of Mellon and Du Pont identified as tied to the right wing.

Under President Nixon the big foundations came under heavy pressure from the Federal Government to stop the funding of the arts, the usual reason given being that the economic crisis in the United States was serious enough that money should be diverted to needier areas. A bill went through Congress in 1970 prohibiting any explicit political activities by foundations and requiring tighter control over the financial records of their grantees. The right wanted to know "what foundations were up to." Sol Hurok, quoted in *New Republic*, asserted that foundation money was, indirectly, taxpayers' money. Foundation spokesmen explained the crackdown on their tax privileges as a move by the oil lobby, to take attention away from oil depletion allowances.

☆   ☆   ☆

Ford

One of the obvious targets of the Nixonian antifoundation drive was the Ford Foundation, with one sixth the assets of the entire group of 25,000 foundations in the U.S. and by far the largest. Ford had been funding community projects in New Mexico, which looked to the Right like financing revolution and to the Left like buying it off and diverting it. But Ford was also fueling the arts at $20 million annually, more than $300 million over the last two decades. This was four times as much as the second largest foundation, the Rockefeller, though only a tenth of Ford's total output. A financial journal, contemplating the Ford Foundation's $3.25 billion assets, proudly hailed it as "the largest philanthropic endeavor in history."

The Ford Foundation's current sympathies with radical separatist movements—supporting, besides La Raza in New Mexico, CORE in Cleveland, and community control of schools in New York City—are a long way from the eccentric individualism of the founder and original source of its wealth. Henry Ford, the automobile magnate, had a gang of hired thugs some called a private secret police. He was a well-known anti-Semite, and supported the scurrilous Dearborn *Independent* in the 1920s. He thought cows and horses were wasteful animals and should be eliminated; considering crime a result of poor diet, he was ardently antisugar and prosoybean. By 1945, in his old age, journalists considered him mad. (His grandson Henry Ford 2nd, a Yale dropout, sometimes carried a gun to the office, said *Time* magazine in 1970.)

Right after the old man's death, however, two scientists named Compton and Gaither from MIT's radiation laboratory revamped the Foundation along more idealistic lines. Paul Hoffman, a Marshall Plan statesman, was the first president. Under the leadership of the University of Chicago's Robert Hutchins, the Ford Foundation imposed educational reforms upon the Establishment with grants of $100 million in the early '50s. "Omnibus" was sponsored on television, the forerunner of intellectually wide-ranging public TV. Later the Foundation put so much money into NET itself that the Ford people, around their office, jocularly referred to it as the Ford Foundation network. Ford established the Center for International Legal Studies at Harvard and supported the Fund for the Republic, which was, in 1953, a target of the Mc-Carthyites. The late President Henry Heald hired W. McNeil Lowry, director of the Ford Foundation's Education Program, to head the new Humanities and Arts Program approved by the trustees in 1957.

After 1966 the new Foundation president, McGeorge Bundy, cut spending back so the body of the capital would no longer be used. A refugee from the Kennedy Administration, Bundy put another Kennedy-ite, Robert McNamara, on the board of trustees. And after the assassination of R.F.K., Ford found reasons to grant comfortable stipends to several of the men who had been on the late Attorney General's staff. It was this measure, along with the community projects around the country, that seems to have broken the back of congressional and oil-interest tolerance. The result was the Tax Reform Law of 1970, forbidding foundations to involve themselves in politics.

On the present board of trustees of the Ford Foundation are Henry Ford II and Benson Ford; McGeorge Bundy representing the staff; Robert McNamara; Kermit Gordon, director of the Federal budget under both Kennedy and Johnson and currently president of the Brookings Institution; Alexander Heard, chancellor of Vanderbilt University (a sensible southerner); John H. Loudon, board chairman of Royal Dutch Petroleum, replacing another official of the same company; Edwin H. Land, the Polaroid scientist; Walter A. Haas, Jr., chairman of Levi-Strauss; J. Irwin Miller, chairman of Cummins Engine Co.; Indonesia's Dr. Soedjatmoko; and six others: investment bankers, lawyers, professors, women.

The average age of a board member is sixty. Joseph C. Goulden, an observer who had occasion to study "Rule by Trustee," described the system as arbitrary, secret, lifelong, hereditary, aloof, disdainful, personal, whimsical, remote, contemptuous, suspicious, conservative, wasteful, passive, and old.

In the case of the Ford Foundation, one grant application is approved out of every one hundred received. And for that one, staff members estimate there are twenty-five reasonable candidates.

☆   ☆   ☆

A former Ford Foundation executive explained to me how the trustees decide where to put the Foundation's money. "It depends on the enthusiasm of the individual program officer," he said, "of whom there are usually five or six. And their enthusiasm depends on whom they know."

"Is that all?" I asked.

"No, not really. Not officially. Officially they evaluate what's best, or supposedly best. They make preliminary judgments and decide what to go to bat for in the divisional meetings. And their judgments are made according to what's in *vogue*, how excellent someone's *credentials* are, *and if they know them*. Yes, it always gets back to that, because executives at a place like Ford think they're "good," so the people they know must be "good"—they think.

"The pattern of the grants is to the major cultural institutions. To build up strengths rather than to nurture the smaller or experimental projects."

☆   ☆   ☆

Others have also pointed out the personal nature of the grant determination process. One professional fund-raiser, Charles A. Brecht, vice president of John Price Jones, Inc., did an analysis of ten Foundation grants to colleges, of over $50,000 each; he discovered that in eight of the ten cases, there was some trustee-to-trustee contact between the two institutions. Goulden reports that in 1968 fully one fourth of all Ford Foundation funds earmarked for education and research went to Harvard, Yale, and Princeton, with more than half of that amount going to Harvard alone.

Nevertheless, Ford cannot be accused simplemindedly of elitism, since more than $250 million has gone for black rights since 1950, almost exactly as much as has gone to the arts in that time. It is not easy to pinpoint the interests of this giant $3 billion operation, planning the libraries of the future, financing the Wilson fellows in graduate school, making trouble for the status quo in Cleveland and New Mexico and the boroughs of New York, nurturing the Kennedy people. It is not even clear what is meant by a journalist's accusation that the foundations are more interested in hardware than people, that they are "schizo-utopian."

To check out the mood of the organization first hand, I had to insinuate myself into the physical plant itself. Ford is an architectural masterpiece that stands one hundred yards to the west of the United Nations international zone, one hundred yards to the northeast of the *Daily News*, largest-circulation morning paper in the country, on the busiest artery of the city, facing a high school for commercial arts where adolescent black girls lounge on the front steps looking at Forty-second Street.

I walk tremulously up to the big building that is halfway between the UN and the *News*. "Ford!" "Praise Ford!" and "In the Year of Our Ford!" are echoing in my ears. The magnitude of the place, what it means! It is like the sublimation of the automobile, of the original Henry Ford's assembly line, of all the capitalist-religion that now lives and pollutes!

It's not a government. It's not a business. It's not even a university. Though it seems to be doing the work of all of these, it's a whole damned eco-system! This great space into which I now step, alongside tourists talking Russian and pointing at the library, is a grand, high, old Roman atrium. A distant shell of offices soars above. Just ahead is a full-scale tropical rain forest, seething with vitality. Somewhere, I know, there are computers printing out. But here there is primal drama. Russians and a rain forest. And a library (behind glass).

The rain forest implies a proper eco-system rather than the parasitism of most large buildings.

Praise Ford! The Foundation pumps dimly and gigantically, like a heart I have stepped into. One might like to romp in and smell these greens some long childhood's afternoon.

But one thought stops me. I contemplate the mystic puzzle of the plants. All this green growth entangled in the great center of Ford is like an inner sanctum, into which—perhaps—the noxious may be transformed into the nurturant, for that is the genius of plants. In other words, do the Ford Foundation executives urinate into the jacaranda?

W. McNeil Lowry, former vice president, Ford Foundation, Humanities and Arts division

Oh well. Perhaps the rain forest is meant to imply only symbolically a proper eco-system.

There is an atmosphere, in the Ford Foundation, of being in the ultimate ivory tower. Two very inconspicuously beautiful women are riding up in the elevator with me, the black one saying to the Russian-named one how perfect the job is at H/A (Humanities and the Arts), reading papers and things, how happy she is here.

At the tenth floor a midwestern-looking secretary in slacks is taking coats from the middle-aged men there waiting for a conference with Ford head McGeorge Bundy. Though I am younger and female, one of the men introduces himself to me (he's come in today from Philadelphia), assuming I am waiting for the Bundy conference also. I am flattered.

McNeil Lowry, whom I am going to see, inspires many different kinds of comments. To one writer, he is "a nice man." To another, he is "perhaps the single most important money man in the arts in the U.S." There's no getting around the fact that the head of the Ford Foundation's division on Arts and Humanities has given more money to performers and entertainers than any other individual in the United States.

Born in the American heartland, on the borders of Missouri, Kansas, and Oklahoma, he was a precocious redheaded fourteen-year-old who impressed the ladies in the Methodist Church by making a scholarly speech debunking the fashionable biblical scholarship of 1927. He spoke then about what sect of Jews Jesus represented and who the kings were that are mentioned in the Old Testament—with references to Plotinus, Zoroaster, and the Orphic religion. In his office at Ford there are drawings of pillars on his wall from the loggia of the Vatican, and a cartoon of a Pompeian hall leading to an Eleusinian cave as Picasso might have sketched it. But at sixty-one the man doesn't go to church anymore. His doctorate at the University of Illinois was taken in Aldous Huxley (the man who first said "Praise Ford") and D. H. Lawrence: "the Revolt against Reason in the Twentieth Century." And when asked about his part in the social upheavals of the '60s, he answers with a quotation from Mao: "Let a hundred flowers bloom."

His erudition is such that he says "art history" to one audience and *kunstgeschichte* to another. What is, by salon diction, avant-garde, becomes in a college auditorium the "self-professed rebels."

Of the Humanities and Arts chief, Foundation head McGeorge Bundy commented, "He makes choices like an aristocrat, but scratch him and you'll find a populist."

In fact, "populism" as a political credo is very dear to the former midwesterner. As handed down to us by the great Americans of the last century, he says, it stood for the return to the people, in a democratic framework, of the resources and results of production. It was not Marxism, it was not socialism-as-in-the-U.S.S.R., but it was also not what Samuel Gompers and the AF of

L, speaking for the laboring classes in the cities, thought it was either: that is, potentially a landholders' movement, just because it was agricultural.

"The dissolution of that movement was a tragedy," says Lowry, investing as much immediate passion in the election of 1896 as most people put only into recent matters. "There are populists now among the young," he amended, "who also believe in preserving artistic standards. And they know, and write in their publications, that Ford is not inimical to them."

The only manifesto of the 1960s which gave Lowry serious trouble was the stipulation that all artistic activity was equal to all other artistic activity, that participation created the alleged art. (*Newsweek*—Dec. 24, 1973: Many concept artists think of "every event in life as art;" for example, Terry Fox, who has recorded his breathing during an operation.)

When the H/A head gives me a seat in his office, a chair by the sofa, opposite and equivalent to his, I am immediately dazzled by the originality of the artwork there, all individual pieces with a surface humility that have escaped through asymptotes in the art history courses. There is a view of the New World seacoast in watercolors, which appears to be done in the style of a Mughal or Rajput miniature! As if India discovered America? It defies analysis. Sitting among his Vatican "cartoons," as he calls them, and a drawing by the late Ben Nicholson that inspires me to make of it a diagram of the Foundation: a linear design of a three-sided square inside a circle inside a petallike pattern of curves inside an ultimately jagged exterior, I seem to have come upon Lowry pondering his own fate within the great org—now that he has been interrupted in his meditations on the great input mulch, and the output of art unto longterm history or the needs of the moment or the timeless philosophical dimension.

Lowry's new Foundation for the Humanities and the Arts had already been touted in the newspapers as "the country's first private national foundation devoted solely to promoting the performing and creative arts." I wondered why Lowry would want to leave such a nice job at Ford, and why, if so, he was still there in a lame duck capacity, perhaps.

But first I think it only right we discuss the business of Ford, where he has presided over the cultural software for more than twenty years.

"How did the 1970 Tax Reform affect Ford?" I asked.

The 1970 Tax Reform Law did not have a big effect on Ford, he said. It had only increased paperwork; more information was on file. If a grantee took in less than a third of its total operating budget at the box office, Ford was required to have independent records, to do an outside audit, and to bear responsibility for the grantee's expenditures. As an example he mentioned Ellen Stewart's La Mama theater group, which must be able to demonstrate to the Internal Revenue Service that Ford demands regular reports.

The real reason for the law was the government's desire to cut back on the autonomy of foundations, he said, their "freedom from constituencies." But in that end they had failed.

Lowry directed one of the very first Arts and Humanities grants in 1957 to the New York City Opera, after visiting nearly 200 communities in his first five years in office. He did it to test whether there was an audience for contemporary American opera. It turned out there wasn't, he said.

In reference to the Metropolitan Opera, the major rival of City Opera, he took a humorous position. The Met's $25 million annual budget he called "disastrous," "mostly wasted," and "a disproportionate emphasis." The Opera is used for social status and upward mobility; the social *éclat* connected with the migration of a few very big voices may not be an altogether bad thing. But the Met, "whatever we say, you and I, it's going to continue. Forever."

In the twenty plus years of his tenure at Ford, music received funding equal to all the other humanities and arts combined. Why was this so? I asked. Lowry explained that this was because of a special symphony orchestra program, initiated when Ford was still spending capital. There had been a Foundation-wide competition for suggestions on how to spend the money from a special reserve fund. The Humanities and Arts division submitted two ideas, involving $80 million, one for symphony orchestras, the other to go to sixty odd museums' professional staffs. The trustees chose the former. And if the symphony orchestra program were subtracted from the music total, music would have only the plurality, not the majority of funds.

Of the music money, none had been earmarked for rock. Rock, it was considered, was supporting itself quite well alone. A few projects in jazz were undertaken—the Tulane Jazz Archives and the New York Jazz Museum. "Jazz doesn't seem to have any trouble getting performed," he said, as if the musicians could live on the love they receive at little clubs.

According to the press, an enormous amount of Ford Foundation money went to George Balanchine's New York City Ballet and American School of Ballet, leaving all other dance companies in the cold. Lowry took exception to that. Granting that there was $2.5 million given to Balanchine's school over a period of ten years, and to Balanchine's company $2 million over a period of ten years, there was also a $2.9 million grant to Barbara Weissberger's Pennsylvania Ballet, $2 million to the Joffrey Ballet, and grants to ballet in Boston, Washington, Salt Lake City, and San Francisco. In other words, Lowry maintained, Balanchine, contrary to newspaper reports, did not receive anything like five-sixths or seven-eighths of the dance allotment. A young lady journalist actually apologized for the error, he contended.

"The only major ballet company we did not support in 1963 was the American Ballet Theater. But that was for the following reason. First of all, in their application they presented us with a three-line budget asking for five million dollars, and not explaining, as every applicant is expected to do, the income and outlay that would make that request necessary. And second of all, as you probably know, Lucia Chase has put more money into the A.B.T. than the N.Y.C.B. has already spent! More money than Rebekah Harkness was putting into her ballet, and she was putting in nine hundred thousand dollars a year until last year.

"Of course," he admitted, "if you asked me if we thought that Balanchine represented leadership and standards in his field, I would say Yes."

"Why were there cool relations between Ford and Joe Papp for so long?"

"Papp was a consultant to our theater program. He was interested in a sort of free band concert municipal thing. We were interested in the continuity of companies, and interested in their interest in income. We do believe artists must be in touch with what the society is willing to pay for. We thought his natural support was from the city itself or individual patrons with an interest in New York City. We didn't want to subsidize and then withdraw. We are always pushing for groups to earn."

He described how Ford's Theater Communications Group had worked for subscription sales to the resident theaters outside New York and how this had resulted in guaranteed box-office sales up to 20,000 apiece for Washington's Arena, Houston's Alley, and San Francisco's ACT theaters.

Since 1967, Joe Papp has been charging money for his plays at the Public Theater and since 1973 at Lincoln Center. And like the A.B.T., he is now receiving money from Ford under a Cash Reserve Grant Formula. This is a four-year nonrenewable fund declining from fifteen to ten percent of the operating budget, plus half the deficit, upon which they can borrow. At the end of the four years the money belongs to the grantee, but Ford hopes it will continue to be used as working capital rather than be spent.

Lowry waxed somewhat warmer on the subject of the Alley Theater in Houston. A sketch of it hung on his wall, behind his desk, just over a manual typewriter with a plastic cup balanced on the platen. It appeared to be a Corbusier-like swirly-geometric façade, with grandiloquent black and white paths radiating from the front door. The theater wasn't built until well after Houston had an excellent company working in an abandoned fan factory with 240 seats. "I had to go out with a lantern to find Nina Vance," Lowry bragged, "only a few years ago. Very few people knew about her. And she's one of the great theater directors in the U.S."

The proper procedure for initiating a regional theater, he said, was to get a good theater person first, "give him or her their head," and then build the structure only after a working theater is already in operation. He deplored the mania to build arts centers first, a phenomenon he and others have labeled "temple complex" and "edifice complex." "All they had in Atlanta was the symphony, under Robert Shaw, a good, modest, second-rate group, when they built the Municipal Arts Center. Now the Atlanta Arts Alliance has a terrible time filling it. . . . Yes, it was the Woodruff Foundation, Coca-Cola, that put up most of the money. But the whole population of private donors and businessmen in Atlanta are to blame, not just Woodruff."

Lowry then revealed the primary mechanism for determining

where in the arts Ford is to give its money: the consultation group. At the beginning of his tenure, in 1957 and 1958, he had personally visited almost two hundred communities around the country, talking to art directors and theater directors, painters, sculptors, composers. This enterprise had given Lowry a personal knowledge of—he estimated—five thousand artists and artworkers all over the United States.

"We are figuratively into bed with all the leading artists and art directors in the country," he said. "And we are peripatetic. We could always get on our horse and go anywhere." What he does with this vast acquaintanceship is, firstly, store the names, addresses, professions, and titles on a huge revolving drum file downstairs—abbreviated "revo" and containing, Lowry declares, "the most complete list of artists and experienced people in art fields ever compiled in America." Then they are, group by group, invited to the Ford Foundation building as conferees and consultants.

"In 1958 I spent several days locked in with theater directors," Lowry recalled. "And I went from that directly to painters and sculptors. I said to myself, 'If my job were any more exciting I don't know if I could stand it!' " It's better than being head of any state agency for the arts, he added, because state agencies are obligated to fund certain types of groups that a foundation is free to refuse. "We are more independent. We set the standards."

Conferees are paid an honorarium of $125 for two or three days with Ford. They are sworn to secrecy in advance, by means of a letter headed "Confidential," and their hot and heavy proceedings are neither taped nor reported to the press in any way.

"Our aim is to discuss the issues in the artists' own terms," said Lowry, "as you would discuss science in a scientist's terms. We want to know from that what the problems and standards and trends are and what the artistic criteria mean to a professional in the field. The most eloquent expression of hairshirt actual problems and trends comes from someone who's in the midst of twelve or thirteen of his peers in the same field."

When John D. Rockefeller 3rd was looking for theater directors for Lincoln Center, Lowry reported, reminding me of the difficulty there, he had asked Ford for a list of consultants. Lowry sent him four hundred, from all over the United States. Rockefeller requested more help, saying, "Couldn't you put a red pencil mark next to four or five?" But Lowry refused, explaining that they do not consult with the same person for different fields and are not interested in who's a VIP. "What we care about is who's experienced, how well someone can re-create for us the problems and trends and standards in their field."

The Humanities and Arts division of Ford, under McNeil Lowry, has been interested in and concerned and involved with the status of art fields, as such, though not as defined by the academic world.

"Our acquaintance with artists is so extensive we thought we could know where qualified leadership is. Some other foundations operate mainly through applications and interviews in their offices, but we don't." Lowry talks on the telephone frequently to Nancy Hanks of the National Endowment and Eric Larrabee of the State Council on the Arts. "We tell each other everything we know about an organization. Why shouldn't we do that? We cooperate to the hilt." But he has seen Larrabee in meetings only four or five times, alone only once. If there were an Arts Mafia, "with people sitting around and only knowing each other, that would be a very unhealthy situation, static," Lowry said.

He gibed at the Mellon Foundation. "They have only six people on the board and four on the staff, who are mostly all officers. They stay home and read and phone and make people come there. Only very recently have they let David Saltonstall [the director] go out and look at things for himself."

I heard a distinct sadness in Lowry's voice when he juxtaposed an expression of profound contentment with the job he had constructed for himself with the observation, "McGeorge Bundy is looking for my successor."

But a moment later he was more cheerfully explaining the plan for a new Foundation for the Humanities and the Arts, the first national foundation to be solely dedicated to the support of the arts. It is hard for private patrons of the arts to influence the national value system systematically outside the framework of a foundation, he said. Still, such patrons wanted to show support for entities like the Pennsylvania Ballet, as a way of saying that standards in a craft or technique are important, that the experience people of any age have in attending a ballet or theatrical performance has something to do with our sense of human values. Ford, for example, he pointed out, is able to support the whole field of resident theater. But individual patrons are not able to do that, and that's why his new foundation was necessary.

I asked him why it was necessary to leave Ford and set up a foundation that would in effect duplicate Ford's work in the humanities and the arts. Lowry's answer was startling and moving.

Lowry had, in short, been a victim of the prejudices about age that rack our society as badly as the prejudices about sex. For all the utopian pretensions of the Ford Foundation's little world, which he himself shared, he is a kind and scholarly man, booted out of paradise. One worries about the stature and gifts of his successor.

Lowry said a policy decision had been made at the Foundation the previous year, that vice presidents had to retire at age sixty. Before that, retirement age had been sixty-five. Lowry himself had reached sixty when it happened.

"But there was a special exemption written into the policy for me. Written right into the document—my name, exempted. To stay until I was sixty-five. So I said No to that, I didn't want any kind of personal exemption. I thought the policy should come up before the board on its own merits.

"Bundy said, 'That'll cut the board right in half!'

"But he won. That was in June of last year. I hoped it was not a personal issue. Such things might be suitable for Exxon or GM or IBM!

"In October they offered me a vice presidency without the power to make grants. A kind of 'house guru.' 'Consultant.' I turned down that opportunity. Can you imagine coming in, sitting in my chair [I gave an involuntary start], and having me be still around? I'd rather tell the next person in the job exactly nothing.

"In December I announced my new foundation.

"There is always a minority of people here who understand that being a foundation professional is different from working in government or business or even the university. The rest thought that any bright generalist could make a foundation work. But to know how to structure for impact and how to target priorities requires a sense of mission and dedication to the institution as a whole. Even at the highest levels, often, there has not always been this sense of mission.

"Too many on high levels have thought of Ford as a private government. Their sense is only of sitting in councils and having

Self-Image of the Ford Foundation

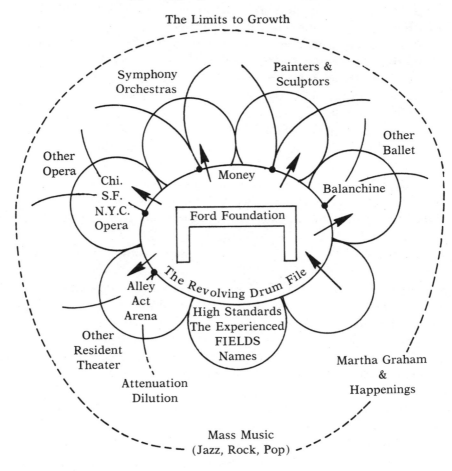

an influence. In the fifties Ford was giving only five to eight million dollars to India, much less than A.I.D., and yet all sorts of people here thought that our involvement was crucial in preventing India from coming under communism. The officers and trustees were just wrong; they lost their sense of proportion.

"De Tocqueville said that voluntary agencies are a counterweight to political centralization in America, making for pluralism. Yes, 'pluralism' is a Talcott Parsons word, only I construe it more bluntly politically than he:—'to keep decisions from being made all in one place, *i.e.*, Washington.' If all our tax money goes there, will all our cultural decisions come from there? The genius of the American system is that this is not the case. And yet the pluralism is being reduced."

☆   ☆   ☆

Rockefeller

The Rockefeller Foundation is the second largest foundation, in amount of assets, and it gave slightly more than $70 million to the arts in the last fifteen years. Like Ford's, that money went primarily to Establishment music and dance, to contemporary opera and resident theater. Rockefeller is also known for funding eight playwrights a year; one year, seven out of those eight applied to Joseph Papp's Public Theater to work off their creativity with him.

In 1974 the amount of the Rockefeller grant to the arts hit a new low, $2.5 million where it had previously been $4 million. Howard Klein, head of the division on the arts and reputed to be a Buddhist, a vegetarian, and very gentle, told the press "the arts boom of the sixties is over." Rockefeller money would henceforth be diverted to the population explosion, health, and food, he said.

In fact, the Rockefeller Foundation has been better known for its work in science than in art. In the Rockefeller Foundation natural science department in the 1940s the electron microscope was invented, as well as the oscilloscope and the ultracentrifuge; spectroscopy and chromatography were developed, as was radioactive tracer technique. Rockefeller financed the University of California cyclotron, sponsored fellows to the Manhattan Project, and in general can be said to have played a major role in the development of nuclear weapons.

Waldemar Nielsen, affiliated with the Twentieth Century Fund, also writes that the Rockefeller interests saved hundreds of Hitler-threatened scientists and intellectuals.

Earlier the Rockefellers had sponsored antimalarial programs in sixty-two countries and anti-yellow fever and antityphus vaccines.

☆   ☆   ☆

Other Foundations

The Mellon Foundation, another one of the giants, gave about $45 million to the arts in the last fifteen years. Meanwhile, Paul Mellon's Old Dominion Foundation gave $20 million to Yale College alone. Ailsa Mellon's Avalon Foundation supported the Metropolitan Opera, the Philharmonic, and the Bronx Zoo; these two Mellon units were merged in 1969 into the Andrew W. Mellon Foundation.

Another front for the same family is the Bollingen Foundation, which supports esoteric literature. It publishes the definitive edition of the *I Ching,* which sold many millions of copies to the new youth of the '60s. A black sheep of the Mellon family was reported, in a sensational exposé in *The Village Voice,* to have been the chief financier of Timothy Leary and his lysergic acid diethylamide thugs.

Two more Mellons, Richard King Mellon and Sarah Mellon Scaife, have built up Pittsburgh, turning their father's and uncles' Gulf Oil and Alcoa and U.S. Steel money into a scientifically oriented university and numerous cultural auditoriums and galleries.

In general the Mellon scions are characterized as right wing, after their progenitor Andrew Mellon, a spokesman for the trusts and war profiteers in the 1920s and a decisive influence in the architecture of Washington, D.C.'s Pennsylvania and Constitution Avenues. Yet there is an occasional dissident. Ailsa's daughter Audrey and her husband, Stephen Currier, set up the Taconic Foundation for racial justice, which played a leading role in race politics in the 1950s and '60s. They were killed in an airplane crash in 1967.

The Mellon Foundation, however, can sound as liberal as the next fellow, putting a good bureaucratic face on it, optimistically saying No. Asked how he decides where to give the Foundation's money, David Saltonstall, one of the program directors for the Mellon Foundation, told reporter Ray Schultz: "Generally, we like to help groups that have some sort of track record. Children's theater, for example, is replete with mediocrity. When we saw Meridee Stein's Meri-Minis we were impressed with their level of professionalism. Usually an organization will write us a letter, and we will invite them for an interview. Then, formal application is made. If we can, we will visit them. We appropriate the money on a quarterly basis, so applications will sometimes stay alive for several months—you never know when you will get the money.

"About one out of every fifteen applications is accepted."

He didn't think the Meri-Minis were going to get any more money, "for general support," once their specific project had been completed. "Of course we don't preclude the possibility of giving them another grant at some later date. . . ."

Recently, the Rockefeller Foundation gave $260,000 to the Eliot Feld Ballet in New York, and the Richard King Mellon Foundation gave $10 million to Pittsburgh's Carnegie Institute.

Other foundations which have given money recently to the arts include the Dorothy Starling Foundation, which gave one million dollars to the Cincinnati Conservatory of Music; the Kresge Foundation, which gave $250,000 each for music buildings at Rollins and Lebanon Valley colleges; the Booth Ferris Foundation, which gave $100,000 for USC music scholarships; the CBS Foundation, which gave $100,000 for USC film fellowships; the JM Foundation, which gave $50,000 to Circle in the Square (a New York theater); and the Kulas Foundation, which gave the same amount to the Cleveland Musical Arts Association.

Carnegie is estimated to be one of the top foundations, both in terms of total assets and of money given out. But it has done nothing spectacular since its founder, the initiator of American philanthropy, aided in the construction of two thousand libraries. The Foundation's sponsorship of the arts and sciences is now mostly confined to Pittsburgh, where the Carnegie Institute of Technology has been combined with the Mellon interests to become Carnegie-Mellon University, and to Washington, D.C. Recently the Foundation has involved itself with education and a commission on public television.

Du Pont is another mammoth foundation. Some say the family is richer than the Rockefellers. But it would be hard to tell exactly, since there are 1,200 minor and 250 major members of this Ducal system now, many of whom are not named Du Pont. One estimate of their worth is $10 billion; another is that they control $30 billion worth of corporations. In this respect they would be exceeded only by the Houses of Rockefeller and Morgan, estimated by Juan José Arevalo, the former president of Guatemala, as controlling $50 billion and $74 billion respectively.

Du Pont accumulated its money first of all in gunpowder and explosives—single-handedly producing almost half of all the cannonballs used by the Allies in the First World War. This was not necessarily out of patriotism; afterward they made cartel agreements with the businessmen of Germany and Japan.

The Du Ponts control thirty banks in Florida and operate behind all these names: Longwood, Nemours, Bredin, Carpenter, Christiana, Copeland, Andelot, Lesesne, Rencourt, Theano, Winterthur, and General Motors. As a family enterprise, Du Pont has had the most wealth and industrial power for generations; yet as a foundation its main interests seem to be ancestor worship and the maintenance of its own chateaux.

In Du Pont's literature, a magazine called *Context*, one learns that the Foundation does support the work of scientists Jacques Cousteau (oceans) and Jane Van Lawick Goodall (chimpanzees). However, all the rest of its time and interest seems to concern the development of chemicals that it describes as pesticides and herbicides of strategic importance to the world food supply. Earlier in the century, nylon and cellophane were developed in the Du Pont laboratories.

The Pew Foundation, which was on F.D.R.'s economists' list of thirteen families controlling the top U.S. corporations, and also counts among the 33 foundations which currently possess more than half the assets of all 25,000 foundations, is a decided noncontributor to the arts. Affiliated with Sun Oil, the Foundation supports Billy Graham, the Christian Anti-Communist Crusade in California, the Rudolf Steiner School in New York City, Morality in Media, Inc. (N.Y.C.), and evangelical activities in Philadelphia and Long Island. One observer characterizes the Foundation as

Norton Simon, member of the board of Museum Associates, Los Angeles County Museum of Art

"antisocial" and another labels it, simply, "the most conservative wing of the Republicans." It publishes no annual reports.

Lilly, the foundation connected with the pharmaceuticals firm of the same name in Indianapolis, is unofficially estimated as being one of the five largest donors of money in the United States. It is another foundation which is not interested in the arts. Rather, it supports middle-of-the-road Protestant religious groups, being the largest source of such money. It gives to Radio Free Europe and set up a Hall of Free Enterprise at a recent world's fair. One of its front groups is Mustard Seed, Inc.

Among the other largest foundations in the country are Kellogg and Danforth, which support graduate fellowships; and Bush, associated with Minnesota Mining and Manufacturing.

In Texas the Houston Foundation established a Performing Arts Center in the mid-'50s and gave the Alley Theater some downtown real estate. The Richardson Foundation, whose founder was a business partner of Texas Governor Tom Connally's and whose 1959 funeral was attended by Billy Graham, deals with the Del Mar, California, racetrack and diverts the profits into a nonprofit front called Boys, Inc. The Brown Foundation built roads, a New Deal dam, and military installations in World War II and advised Texas governors for thirty years; L.B.J. attended the funeral of the founder in 1962.

Huntington Hartford's Foundation, based on profits from the A & P Tea Company, has always specialized in medical engineering and research—developing such instruments as the blood flow meter, artificial heart valves and pacemaker, laser knife, cryogenics, kidney dialysis machine, and computerized diagnosis and research. Hartford also set up a smallish "cultural center" in New York City in which he revealed a slightly *derrière-garde* taste in paintings, until it was sold in 1975.

The Duke Foundation paid $6 million to change the name of Trinity College in Durham, North Carolina, to "Duke University." The Duke money was earned in American Tobacco.

The Sloan Foundation finances cancer research through Sloan-Kettering and, since the death of its anti-New Deal founder, has emphasized black professional training, management training for urban leadership and government, and a commission on cable television. Kettering supports research on cancer and photosynthesis.

Mott operates a radical front *Spectemur Agendo,* by which the son of the single largest GM stockholder can support his pet interests: Eugene McCarthy, contraception, sexology, women's political caucuses, and ESP. He also has a spectacular rooftop garden-farm with chickens on Park Avenue.

The Astor Foundation, personally administered by Mrs. Brooke Astor, widow of the founder, is focusing on ghetto needs, youth, poor, and New York City.

Woodruff, the syndicate that bought control of Coca-Cola in 1919, got into trouble with its overly optimistic funding of the Atlanta Arts Center, which the Foundation found that, once built, it couldn't fill. It also fought for desegregation in Georgia.

Founder of the Waterman/Haas Foundation was a woman with a Ph.D. in astronomy; founder of the Kresge Foundation was a Pennsylvania Dutch prohibitionist. The Kaiser Foundation works with the AFL-CIO and sponsored a Bay Area problem-solving conference. The Fleischmann Foundation considers itself a maverick organization and works for clean air and water in the Lake Tahoe, Nevada, area. It welcomes "able mavericks" to write to the Foundation personally, regardless of institutions.

Commonwealth Foundation derives from Harkness, Rockefeller's partner in Standard Oil, and professes some radical interests in such things as ghetto health, violence and drugs, environment, and the mental health of society in general.

Land Foundation is the newest of the large foundations, dating only from 1961. Since then it has hired over twenty percent blacks for its staff and financed freshman seminars at Harvard. Edwin H. Land (of Polaroid camera) is reported to be antifeudal and the most buoyant force in philanthropy in fifty years.

Close textual analysis of their rejection letters provides a seemingly small but possibly significant insight into foundations. More than one I have seen makes use of a mysteriously illogical passive voice, the agent of rejection being not the author of the letter but a thing. One finds such expressions as: "priorities preclude me . . ." and "after consultation I shall not be enabled . . ." Can these turns of phrase be symptomatic of failure on the part of the foundation executives to take active responsibility for what they do?

THE GIANT MONEY POOL RECONSIDERED

The high arts are now dependent for survival on a giant money pool quite outside the realm of the individual culture consumer. In the private sector a handful of foundations and corporations (Ford, Rockefeller, Mellon; Mobil, Exxon, and Texaco) subsidize the arts to a significant degree; the other foundations, like the other corporations—with few exceptions—do not.

But not even Ford are unqualified "good guys": e.g., the story is that they have let their highly civilized head man, a veteran of twenty years, be "retired" on spurious ageist grounds.

More and more cultural entities, however, are bidding for public sector support, bolstered in their claim by economists who have determined the arts to be inherently unprofitable. In the Federal arts subsidy agency the issue currently raging is "decentralization," *i.e.*, the giving of money to the hinterlands rather than the big cities. In New York State's arts office, the wealthiest in the country (though a cut of two thirds is expected in its dole for next year), the story now centers around the upheaval effected in the young and perhaps fragile Rockefellerian program since a Democratic governor was elected in 1974. Large structural changes in Council procedures were announced but not subsequently carried out; about half the top-ranking staff has been changed. It is not yet known what differences there will be in the grants themselves.

Only two of the art forms discussed in this book are free of the lure of "the money pool," because they are able to support themselves through normal open-market practices. These are of course film and rock music, and I shall discuss them next.

FILM:
Whose Visions in the
Final End

There are basically a dozen movie companies that determine 80 percent of what is made and released to theaters. And it's always been that way.

—A. D. (Art) Murphy,
Daily Variety, Hollywood

Film distribution is a closed shop. Perhaps the tightest closed shop in the world.

—John Cassavetes,
Filmmaker

It suddenly seemed as though a whole genre of moviemakers were becoming that hideous little army, mechanical, full of wealth, cruelty, and lurid, meaningless color for decorative ugliness. It is not exactly camp or homosexual. It is not a comment on or a reflection of the way things are. It doesn't even look like an expression of a special taste in fun. It is an appraisal of a market, with all the hateful little sensibilities involved, a joke so in that nobody but the moviemakers is getting it.

—Renata Adler, critic,
A Year in the Dark

EVERYTHING about California is different from New York. Supermarkets sell whiskey, car washes are everywhere, people wear sunglasses and are polite to pedestrians and smell of "lemon-musk." With climate so different, it might be a different country from Cultureburg, N.Y. And indeed it used to be: the Chicanos, in remembrance, paint Aztec motifs into their graffiti.

In California they speak of America's industries as "steel, autos, and movies." And sometimes, if they're feeling generous about New York, they'll throw in "advertising" as well.

The fundamental truth about the movie business, so basic it risks sounding simpleminded, is that power is concentrated in a small number of hands. F. Scott Fitzgerald wrote it: "Not half a dozen men have ever been able to keep the whole equation of pictures in their heads. And perhaps the closest a woman can come to the set-up is to try and understand one of these men." That was in 1940. A little later Budd Schulberg had a character say, "Hollywood consists of half a dozen studios and half a dozen restaurants," and try to prove, by that, that six hundred writers in the Guild had power against one Sammy Glick.

The original founders of the electronic communications and entertainment industry were highly clever if not brilliant technicians who developed the infant radio, television, and film media from inside outward. David Sarnoff, called "the Father of Television" (and by Rudolf Bing "the General"), passed control of NBC to his son Robert, just as the Warner brothers, Albert, Jack, and Harry, passed it on to Harry's son Jack.

Such examples of primogeniture are not the exception but rather the rule. Sons and brothers of founders inherited the command positions throughout these fields, at Twentieth Century–Fox, Columbia, United Artists, Disney, Warners, MGM, and NBC.

But by the late 1940s, with the introduction of television, the motion picture industry entered a period of fallow turmoil. The economic basis of film shifted. Sons left their father's studios for the more lucrative status of independent producer. Movie companies went public. And a whole new batch of executives started coming in, two generations younger at least than the original movie pioneers, as young as the pioneers had been when they'd started in the 1930s.

The younger generations of power brokers after the original technology was accomplished in TV and films have tended to be agents, accountants, lawyers, and salesmen. At the present there are very few famous old names left in the production side of Hollywood; nearly all the studio executives are men under forty, men who have fought their way over whatever casting couches stood in their path and held on tight through a roil of industry firings.

Not long ago Goddard Lieberson, until 1975 president of the CBS Records Group, expressed concern that the record industry seemed to be "drinking that fatal glass of beer" and switching its emphasis from artistic control to mere entrepreneurism—a step that movie studios had already taken.

Now the family-owned studio system has been replaced by oligarchic public ownership, and on the surface of things power appears to be even more concentrated than before. Columbia and Warner Brothers share a distributor and the Warner Brothers studio in Burbank is now called The Burbank Studios (TBS). Paramount, owned by Gulf and Western, shares the lot of Universal, which is owned by MCA. Fox rents out sound stages, and MGM has drastically cut back on its business, its studio shared by and its films distributed by United Artists (owned by Transamerica). Still people speak of six major studios.

In Hollywood today, the television and motion picture industries are monopolized by three giant networks and six or seven large studios, run by executives with short careers who have inherited the Taj Mahals of a previous generation of moguls. The men in command of movies today—like Bob Evans, Mike Medavoy, Lew Wasserman, Kirk Kerkorian—are Culture Barons by virtue of the power and money they control but not by strength of their personalities. They are curiously self-centered and amoral in their orientation, pragmatic and often anti-intellectual. And one vice president for production reports that the situation is even worse in television, where programming decisions are sometimes made on the basis of two or three catchwords that summarize the show in question.

Daily Variety's Art Murphy, sitting in a noisy midtown Hollywood newsroom, estimates that there are six major studios and six more important minor ones or distributors, with an executive cadre of about a dozen people at each one who possess just about all the power that there is in Hollywood to make movies happen. Such baronial concentration belies the nominal existence of more than 350 film and tape production companies in New York and more than 200 around Hollywood, and hundreds of local TV stations across the country. The six studios are, Murphy says, "the corporate extensions of the original pioneers."

Those pioneers were immigrants and first-generation Americans whose tastes matched those of an immigrant America. They invested in the movie business lock, stock, and barrel. If their pictures failed, points out Murphy, they lost their house, they were out on the street. Movies were their whole life. The current generation of movie corporation executives are employee-managers of public companies traded on the stock market; they are very different from owner-managers. "They don't have the desperate drive to succeed," he says, "because it's not coming out of their hide. If they do a bad job, they're replaced."

Just so. In four months in 1974–75, three top motion picture studio executives (or exex, as *Variety* puts it) had been replaced or resigned from their positions. Yablans of Paramount and Stulberg of Fox were fired from their presidencies. Murphy explains: "There were some internal things and they lost the internal battle. But that happens in lots of companies." The third, Ted Ashley of Warner Brothers, stepped down at the peak of his career, into semiretirement, and this, continues Murphy, has stimulated a lot of speculation. But according to him, this recent turnover of executives was merely "coincidental." The real winnowing out occurred in the wake of the cultural revolution of the 1960s, when executives who had begun their careers very young and many years ago were finally revealed to have outlived their professional expertise. Darryl Zanuck, David Selznick, Irving Thalberg—men like these had begun to work for Hollywood in their twenties and had never really been replaced. In the late 1960s and 1970s a whole raft of new corporation heads came in who were themselves mostly in their thirties: Frank Welles came on to Warner, and E. Cardon Walker to Disney; Henry Martin was named president of Universal, and Sid Sheinberg president of parent MCA; Alan J. Hirschfield was made president of Columbia, and David Begelman of Columbia Pictures; Eric Pleskow president of United Artists and, and Frank Rosenfeld president of MGM.

This was the deeper and more lasting legacy of the revolution that had kicked up, on its surface, "a whole terrible plague of swinging youth pictures," as Art Murphy says.

Most of the top executives now were agents (and a few were

lawyers) before assuming studio responsibility. Lew Wasserman, head of Universal and a major stockholder in MCA, the parent company, was an agent. ("The best agent ever," according to one of his colleagues, who prefers not to be named. He adds that the man is a liberal, though his co-owner, Jules Stein, is a Republican, and Taft Schreiber, a former Universal executive now serving as a consultant, is a Reagan man. "They cover their bets, they contribute to the Democrats and the Republicans both. Like any big corporation, they support the generals in Bolivia," says this associate.) Wasserman's agency, MCA, was the largest organization of its kind until 1961, when it was forced to divest by the FCC and to concentrate on producing.

As for the politics of the movie studios in general, insiders say that the last political activity in Hollywood occurred during the McCarthy period, when management threw people to the wolves. Earlier, the studios had played footsie with gangster-controlled unions. And Metro-Goldwyn-Mayer tried unsuccessfully to crush the incipient Screen Actors Guild.

Sid Sheinberg, president of MCA, number two under Wasserman, was a lawyer, negotiating entertainment contracts. United Artists' Mike Medavoy, who's in charge of West Coast production, and Dan Rissner, who's in charge of East Coast and European production, both used to be agents. (One of Medavoy's clients was Jane Fonda.)

Alan Ladd, Jr., was also an agent; now he is senior VP for production at Twentieth Century–Fox, under corporation president and chairman Dennis Stanfill.

The top two agencies now are William Morris and International Creative Management, the latter being a product of a 1975 merger between International Famous Agency and Creative Management Associates. Both are feeder stations to the studios. The head of CMA, Freddy Fields, was in partnership with one David Begelman. Now Fields has recently arranged an independent production deal with Paramount, and Begelman has gone on to become head of Columbia. Another agent at CMA is Sue Mengers, a brilliant and brash woman, who is slated, so the gossip goes, for a studio position soon herself. There are even some interlocking family connections between the two giant agencies: one of the top exex at IFA is a nephew of Nat Lefkowitz, the New York head of

William Morris. At William Morris the agents are in general less flamboyant, says the *Daily Variety* reporter.

Barry Diller, now the head of Paramount, was formerly in television, a program production executive for American Broadcasting Company, but he started years ago in the William Morris Agency.

John Calley was a production executive for Filmways. Frank Welles was a lawyer. These two men are now respectively production VP and president of Warner Brothers, since Ashley's surprise retirement.

Dan Melnick, who is in charge of production for MGM, used to work for ABC ten years ago, but he'd been doing independent feature and television production before he came to MGM.

Sam Arkoff, a lawyer, and his partner the late James Nicholson, started American International Pictures (AIP) twenty years ago. Nicholson had been a theater owner and operator. Over the years Arkoff broadened his expertise somewhat in the creative— but he doesn't pretend to be a movie mogul. He means simply to be a movie businessman.

An important Hollywood agent explained that the agents' work changed dramatically with the changing of the studios' ownership and power structure. Once they had been employment agents, going out to hunt up jobs for their clients. Meanwhile the studios, which owned whole stables of talent, pored over the lists of the stars they had signed and selected perhaps a certain male star to go with a certain director and a certain female star and then had the whole applied to a book their story department had just purchased. Nowadays the agent selects a script by him-or-herself, makes a package that can be any one of ten things—a star and a script, a director, two stars and a script, etc.—and sees that his clients are properly accoutered when presented to the studios. Agents now are well trained to be movie production executives, says Murphy, with so many of the studios' old jobs falling to them anyway. In June of 1975, rumors were rife in the trade papers that CMA head Freddy Fields was being considered for a top spot at Warner Brothers. A week later the rumor changed: he was going to Paramount. One big agent commented that Freddy Fields at Paramount would not only get more money, he would also not have to take phone calls in the middle of the night any more from Steve

McQueen—a $10 million property. "He won't have to salute when McQueen barks."

"Twenty-five years ago the studio would hand Gable a script and say, 'Show up Monday.' Now the heads of ICM and William Morris have that much power. One big agent—Freddy Fields right now—monitors what scripts will be read by McQueen, Streisand, O'Neal, Hackman. . . ."

The big agents' offices have that wonderful air of importance one sees around Presidential advisers and other diplomats. "So and So is on seven-two," a magnificent secretary will call out melodiously, lingering on the money-dripping syllables of the name. The big cheese will discuss his profoundest ideas all in the Personal Metaphor—that is, he will use proper names as common nouns and verbs, even adverbs: "Get me a Jacqueline Susann." Hollywood is a small town with a big impact.

☆   ☆   ☆

California may be a free and easy state, but the would-be movie moguls and tycoons of Hollywood these days are uptight about an industry that is suffering, in its way, from the national economic situation. Profit is still being made, to be sure. But output is diminishing drastically, and with it employment.

As of late 1975 only half as many new motion pictures had been made as were turned out in 1974. And that was half of the previous year's production. Many of the approximately three hundred young producers with permanent offices at the six major motion picture companies wanted to know why there was a falling off of product. One blamed it on the primacy of a few big movie stars, citing Eastwood, Bronson and McQueen. (Actually, according to Quigley Publications, George C. Scott, Gene Hackman, John Wayne, Barbra Streisand, Marlon Brando, and Paul Newman were all ahead of McQueen in box-office draw, and though Eastwood was first, Bronson did not figure at all in the 1974 top ten. Other young producers were benignly abstract, indicating that nothing was very new in Hollywood—*"plus ça change, plus c'est la même chose,"* one said—rather like a Pole resigned to his Communist regime. "It's my system and I'm stuck with it."

Only producer Sandy Howard (*Sky Riders* and *The Devil's*

Rain) went on record as blaming the "goddam bureaucracy" for slowing down product.

Paramount Pictures, which in its heyday made dozens of pictures in the same time that it recently turned out only two, seems to have been suffering from some bureaucracy problems. Only a year ago national magazines hailed its young president, Frank Yablans, and young executive vice president, Robert Evans, for their brilliant successes with *Love Story, The Godfather*, and the then upcoming *Great Gatsby*. Indistinguishably powerful as Brezhnev and Kosygin, the two had identical salaries and contracts; like the Corleone brothers, said *New York* magazine, they were vying for the approval of Charles Bluhdorn, president of Paramount's parent company and source of funds, Gulf and Western's godfather. Bluhdorn of course was mad, said New York City gossips, because when he first came to power he straightaway made a slew of fabulously expensive pictures. Evans and Yablans were widely described as two dissimilar personalities, but evenly matched, possibly locked in a fruitful rivalry. Evans is frightfully attractive, while Yablans was said to be fiery and passionate and hated by executives in other companies as well as by actors Paul Newman and Robert Redford.

In any case, right after interviews in *New York* and *Esquire* magazines in which Yablans declared that he wanted to be president of the United States, among other indiscretions, and after the critical failure of *Gatsby*, both he and Evans were suddenly out of their jobs. The new chairman of Paramount was Barry Diller, a man in his early thirties. (Both Evans and Yablans were boy wonders in their *late* thirties.) Reporters described Diller as "a fascist martinet." Succeeding Evans as vice president in charge of production was Richard Sylbert, the art director of *Chinatown*, all the Mike Nichols films, *Shampoo*, and *Rosemary's Baby*.

☆   ☆   ☆

But Evans left voluntarily. He had made a lot of movies for Paramount during the nine years he was production chief. Most of them—except perhaps for *Rosemary's Baby*—are forgotten. But he will be remembered for one, *The Godfather:* before *Jaws* the biggest grossing flick of all time. Any picture that earns in the eight figures at the box office must have cultural clout, so Bob Evans must be a Culture Baron. He doesn't look like that type of man; he is too pretty, rather like a French model, smallish and delicate. But he apparently has the formula for blockbuster movies down to a science, which very rarely fails now. He is atune to what our society wants, so in tune that he is, in a way, himself invisible, hard to pin down, charmingly rough where he doesn't know the right answer to something, persuasive. He is numbing—just like the dish on the table in front of him as he talks, that contains every different brand of cigarette on the market.

Two years ago Bob Evans had, according to *Time* magazine, "the hottest reputation in Hollywood." The son of a Manhattan dentist, he had early in life harvested some millions from the garment district profits of his brother's Evan-Picone sportswear. *Esquire* said he held "a tighter rein on production than any other studio head today," passing on the script, the producer, the director, and the cast, and rarely "giving away the final cut" (that is, allowing the director or some other party to make the last decisions on how the picture actually would run), as was done at Warner Brothers.

"Running a studio is close to an impossible job," said a friend last year, "but Bob did it with grace."

☆   ☆   ☆

Granted an audience by Robert Evans at his palatial Beverly Hills residence, I felt as though I had stepped into a movie and kept expecting that any minute someone would yell "Cut!!" The setting lacked nothing for grandeur—black Cadillac, pool and tennis courts with Greek and Etruscan statues around them, leather-bound French books (Montaigne, Molière, Taine . . . plus Poe, Dante, histories), wilting red and white roses, an intricate mother-of-pearl mosaic mirror-frame, Indian brocaded-silver ashtrays. . . . The photogenic and frisky small child of Evans and his ex-wife Ali McGraw plied the guest with questions like "Can I play with your tape recorder?" while the French maid, in uniform, skittered around behind with an elaborate silver coffee service. Evans himself was dashingly casual for a Saturday noon in powder blue cotton pajamas and a white terry robe cut with lapels like an overcoat.

Mustering up all my businesslike demeanor, I asked him about the circumstances surrounding his change of status at Paramount, from production VP to independent producer.

"I was head of production at Paramount for nine years," he said, "which is a longer tenure than any other head of production since the 1940s. And I had six more years to fulfill my contract. I just had enough. My nerves were at an end. More than that, I wanted the opportunity of making film rather than overseeing other people's problems. The last two years I've been after this freedom, and the company didn't want to give it to me; they wanted me to stay and fulfill my contract. It took me two years of negotiations to finally work out my new deal. One of the things I had in my contract was that I could make a picture a year. That was the only way I would stay. But that caused a conflict of interest within the company—when I made *Chinatown* and it became a very successful picture a lot of people thought I was doing two jobs at one time and that I'd have to—you know, it wasn't right, it was causing a lot of friction. So that gave me the opportunity of going to my principals and asking if I could just remain as making my own pictures. Which I've wanted to do for a long time. So it's not really a promotion or a demotion, it's just a change of life. Within the company. I'm under exclusive contract to Paramount; I'll be making three or four pictures a year for them. I love it.

"It's not a job. I'm in business for myself now, rather than a job. That's just what I love about it.

"Yes, I have the opportunity of making more money, because I have a percentage of, a large percentage of, the pictures, which I didn't have before."

On Evans' last semi-independent deal for Paramount, the *Chinatown* project, which was reputed to be the hottest such deal ever secured by an executive VP, he'd reaped ten percent of the multimillion dollar profits, in addition to his regular $250,000 salary. On his independent deals he will now be keeping in the neighborhood of fifty percent of the films' profits.

Evans' nine-year reign over production at Paramount left some permanent changes there. When he arrived in 1966, Paramount was last among the seven large studios, in terms of income and prestige. When he left it in 1975, by both these indications, informed sources say, Gulf and Western's Paramount was first. Right behind it were MCA's Universal and Warner Communications' Warner Brothers. United Artists came next, with Columbia Pictures and Twentieth Century–Fox both having financial difficulties, from which Columbia was allegedly recovering. The distribution of MGM product, which, according to *Daily Variety*'s Art Murphy, is where the power is, was being entirely handled by United Artists.

Following these majors were solid minor companies, American International Pictures, Allied Artists, Avco-Embassy, and Disney. (Though their film end is "minor," Disney Productions is actually quite capable of making the same $50 million net overall profit as does Warner Communications.)

"The only pictures Paramount was making when I got here," continues Evans, sitting comfortably in his French Regency style home, classic female nudes on the walls, a greenish statue of a boy with a sword overlooking an elliptical swimming pool, "were Dean Martin and Jerry Lewis pictures, Elvis Presley pictures, and Marty Allen–Steve Rossi pictures. We changed it quite a bit."

One of Evans' friends has described him as "experienced but also gentle." I asked him what had gone wrong with *The Great Gatsby*. "I don't think anything went wrong with *The Great Gatsby*," he answered, hardly a trace of annoyance in his mellow baritone. "I have no excuses for *The Great Gatsby*. I just think that if anything went wrong with it, it got too much publicity. And the cover of *Time* magazine a week before it came out called it 'the merchandising of a motion picture,' which put every critic's nose out of joint. Maybe people were expecting too much. But if you look at the old *Gatsby* and look at the one we made, I think you'd appreciate the one we made all the more. *The Great Gatsby* is a very successful picture from a financial point of view. Extremely successful. We'll do over thirty million dollars on it.

"I do believe however, in theory, that when you make a classic you're damned if you do and you're damned if you don't. If you stick too close to it, they criticize you for not opening it up. If you veer away from it, they say you're veering away from it and not staying to the story. Which is what happened to us. When *My Fair Lady* was made into a movie it was criticized because they stuck too close to the play; they didn't open it up enough. Which is a classic play. It did big business, but it was critically torn apart because of that.

"I personally think *Gatsby* was a very good picture. I don't think Bob Redford was the right Gatsby. I think he didn't have the grit, he didn't have the mystery—and yet from a commercial point of view—I think the ideal Gatsby would have been Humphrey Bogart. I think Jack Nicholson would have been a terrific Gatsby. That's who I wanted for Gatsby, but we couldn't make his deal, and Redford very much wanted to play the part and did the part for nothing, for very close to nothing."

We moved on to another movie he'd been instrumental in producing. *"The Godfather* was the biggest book before it was the biggest picture. Number one best seller of the decade. And it was the first time that a film telling the story of a Mafia family ever got into the texture of the people and really made the family mean something. And I—Francis deserves the credit for that 'cause he, he was a second-generation Italian, and he really got the feeling of the Italian people and the families and the love and the children and the double standard that they live by, which has never been shown, outside of superficially, before. It was hard—people walked out—you had to hate these people and yet you loved them; you felt for their families, and you knew what they were doing was horrible. It was a strange mixture. *Godfather I* to me was one of the great pictures I had ever seen in my life. And I had a lot of trouble making it too. It was a marvelous film.

"I bought *Godfather* from a thirty-page treatment. In fact, I bought it because Mario Puzo needed money desperately—he owed gambling debts. I paid him twelve thousand five hundred dollars. And he had to pay his debts. So I had twelve thousand five hundred against seventy-five thousand for the book. I didn't have to pick up the option on the book until eighteen months after it was published.

"By the time eighteen months had passed I was offered a couple of million dollars for the property.

"It was called *Mafia* from the beginning. That was what the treatment was called. And I just kept on feeding Mario five thousand dollars at a time to continue writing it, you know, just to pay his bread bills. When the book came out it was too big a book to make it an exploitation picture. When you have a big best seller like that, you have to go all the way with it."

"Why," I asked, "are so few films being made by the major studios?"

Evans took that one as if it were a hot potato. He stammered. Began several sentences. And then finally finished one.

"Because, maybe, there are not so few, it's the films, people, quantity doesn't make any difference today; nobody's making production slates to sell to theaters. Units don't mean anything, it's the picture that means something. And people are putting more and more effort into the picture, rather than a slate of films. Because you make fifteen pictures and none of them even get back their negative costs, but you make one and it gets back everything. People are concentrating more on honing each picture as a creation unto itself rather than saying we have to make twenty pictures, let's make them no matter what they are. It's a much healthier situation now. It may mean less employment. But it will make better pictures."

Another slant on the decline in motion picture output was provided by Evarts Ziegler of Ziegler-Ross, the agency that represents such stellar Hollywood writers as Mario Puzo, Irving Wallace, and Joan Didion. Ziegler held that the reason for declining output is simply increased costs, an inability of the studios to fund the twenty-eight or thirty movies that they were previously able to make, an increase in costs across the board that is evidenced by the $3.50 and $5.00 tickets at the box office. He thought there was also a disinclination on the part of the public to accept a whole program of mediocre films, which they can easily get on television. Ziegler and other Hollywood sources were all speaking of "the event film," such as *Earthquake*, which the public presumably now prefers.

I asked Evans how the making of a blockbuster begins.

"There are a thousand nuances," he replied. "The medium of the movie, I would say certainly, is *the* major art form of our century. The motion picture. Whether it be for television or whether it be for theaters. And to create, develop, make, and sell that to the public is a major effort, from the beginning. And unlike other product, there's no close-out value for it. Like if you make a Chrysler car and it doesn't sell for five thousand, you can sell it out for two thousand; there's a buy-out for it; there's a close-out value. On a movie there's no close-out. You make a film and people don't want to see it, you can charge twenty-five cents and people are not going to go in to see it. So you have one time around to make that picture work. It goes into the theaters, it goes around the country, and then it's taken away. You have one shot. So you have to really work on that picture and develop it and make the public aware of it, interested and wanting to see it; you have to cause an undercurrent for the moviegoing public.

"You see, the habit of going to the movies is over; however, the desire to see A Movie is bigger than ever. People don't go to the movies like they used to in the '40s, three times a week. Families go usually—people—the young people are more interested in movies than ever before. In A Movie especially. And in maybe a dozen movies a year. And you have to be one of those dozen movies a year.

"I keep in touch with what people want by surrounding myself with young people. People about your age."

I tried to ask him about some of those thousand nuances. "When you make a blockbuster," I said, "does it start in the interaction between a producer and a writer? Where does it start?"

Evans: "It starts with what's on the page. To me the biggest star of any film is what's on the page—in other words, the writer. I don't care how many actors or stars are in the picture, or who's directing it or who's producing it or what company's releasing it—if it isn't on the page, it's not going to work. That's your biggest star—your writer.

"In other words, I would rather have the next five commitments of Robert Towne" (last year an Oscar winner for the screenplay of *Chinatown*) than I would the next five commitments of Steve McQueen or Robert Redford. To me Robert Towne is a bigger star than any actor. 'Cause once it's on the page you can get anybody.

"The story is your biggest star. In other words, what the writer puts down. Not only the story but the people, the relationships, the beginning-and-the-middle-and-the-end, a relationship of the audience to what's on the screen—is much more important than starring this one and that one and this one and this one." (He cited *Nashville* and *Jaws*, two then upcoming releases from Paramount and Universal respectively, and predicted them for big successes, despite an absence of stars.) "There were no stars in *Love Story*," he went on. "They made stars of them, but they weren't stars when the picture was made."

He made no other references to his ex-wife.

☆   ☆   ☆

So much of art has love at its root. Bob Evans started *The Great Gatsby* for his wife, Ali McGraw. John Christie started the Glyndebourne Opera (where Bing worked before coming to the Met) as a showcase for his wife, Audrey Mildmay. Blake Edwards produces and directs his wife, Julie Andrews. Carlo Ponti produced his wife, Sophia Loren. Lucille Ball produced herself and husband Desi Arnaz. Joan Baez promoted her love, Bob Dylan. And Jack Haley, Jr., married to Liza Minnelli, stuck her into the company of all the older MGM greats in *That's Entertainment.*

☆   ☆   ☆

"There were no stars in *The Godfather.* Marlon Brando was a *finished* star. An Italian producer came to us and said, 'If you release *The Godfather* in Italy with Marlon Brando, no one will go to see it in Italy.' And it was the biggest picture ever to play in the history of Italy! Biggest American picture ever to be in Italy!

"The point being that in the book, the story, the people were there. And that is your star. The biggest pictures I have been involved with have been without stars, because the star was the property. And some of my biggest failures have been pictures with stars. And I'm not saying that stars are not important in films; I think they are. But more important than the star is the story.

"Yes, I think the writer is more important than the director. The best proof of that is First Artists. When they went into business they had Paul Newman, Steve McQueen, Dustin Hoffman, Barbra Streisand, Sidney Poitier, and they made all failures."

Perhaps some of Evans' dismissal of star actors is due to the fact that he had a rather brilliant fledgling movie acting career going in his early twenties. "One of the highlights of my career," he mused, "was playing Irving Thalberg as my first role on the screen, and having happen to me in my life what happened afterward, in retrospect looking back, is rather interesting.

"And my first scene as an actor in film was with Jimmy Cagney, who was one of my favorite *favorite* actors. And to think that here I was—my first scene as an actor—to play with Jimmy Cagney. And he sat there and he said, 'Listen, kid,' he said, 'I'm going to give you some advice. Look, I'm only five feet four. However, when I walk in to do a scene I could be with an actor who's six foot three and when that scene's over I'm the guy whose six foot three and he's five foot four.' It only taught me one thing: size doesn't make any difference on the screen. Which is best evidenced by some of our top leading guys like Dustin Hoffman or Al Pacino or Bobby De Niro or, for that matter—size makes no difference. It's an interesting thing to have happen, that my first scene was with my all-time favorite as an actor.

"Another weird thing happened, that would read like a press release but it actually happened, is I was discovered for films at the Beverly Hills Hotel pool by Norma Shearer. And then three months later rediscovered sitting at El Morocco in New York. And people both times approached me; I didn't approach them. Now, if I were an actor, and up for either one of the roles, most probably I wouldn't've gotten them. But it was the sense of discovery, by the people who saw me, that got me the part. In both pictures.

"Both totally unrelated. One was *The Sun Also Rises.* Zanuck saw me in Morocco and asked me if I wanted to play a bullfighter. And the other one was playing Irving Thalberg [in a Lon Chaney life story] when Norma Shearer saw me at the Beverly Hills Hotel." (Evans now lives less than a mile from the scene of his first discovering.) "My mannerisms resembled her husband. And the way Zanuck picked me for *The Sun Also Rises* was he saw me dance on the floor and he said, 'That's the guy who's going to play opposite Ava Gardner.'" (Something of Zanuck's Evans' Hemingway's bullfighter was still potent. Touched on the neck by her interviewee, the interviewer goes weak in the knees, practically careens into him.)

"Which makes you feel," he continued, "that Zanuck had certainly a lot of style.

"Another highlight in my career, I have to say, is when I was in Morelia, Mexico, shooting *The Sun Also Rises.* I hadn't started shooting yet, I was rehearsing, and everybody thought I was wrong for the role. And Zanuck was in London and I was in Morelia. And, I remember, Mel Ferrer thought I was wrong for the part, and Ava thought I was wrong for it, and Tyrone didn't think I was right for it, and the director was very worried because all the actors were complaining: 'This is a pivotal role, and he's going to ruin our film.' And they called—Henry King was the director, and he was very concerned. He wired Zanuck a note saying: FLY OVER IMMEDIATELY I THINK WE HAVE TO REPLACE BULLFIGHTER PLAYED BY EVANS.

"Zanuck flew into Morelia, and I had to get dressed in my suit of lights and do my *chitas* and *verónicas* in front of him in this huge bull arena. And he took the megaphone and stood up and he said, 'The kid stays in the picture, and anybody who doesn't like it can leave!' And that showed: a leader. I was so scared I was going to be thrown off the picture, tell my mother and father and everything that I was off the film—oh, it was a terrible feeling. And when he picked that megaphone up that showed why this man was head of Twentieth and why he was a leader the way he was."

"Have you been that kind of studio executive yourself?"

"Well, I would say so. Yah, very much so. There was a case where in *Love Story* when we finally decided Ryan O'Neal should play the part. The director [Barry Hiller] said, 'I won't use Ryan O'Neal, because the script is too much like *Peyton Place* to begin with, and if we use Ryan O'Neal, everyone's going to compare it to *Peyton Place*.' And I said, 'Ryan O'Neal made the best screen test for it, and I want to use him.' And he said, 'I won't make it with him.' I said, 'You can quit the picture.' And he quit the picture that day but came back on Monday. And he made it. You have to stand up for what you believe is right. You may not win a popularity contest, but you'll survive.

"My plans now: I'm going to do *Marathon Man,* with John Schlesinger, as my first film, then I'm going to do *Black Sunday* as my second film, with John Frankenheimer. That's a best-seller book that's out now. So is *Marathon Man,* last year. Then I'm developing a book that Romain Gary wrote, which I like very much, called *White Dog.* I hope to be doing, following—I shouldn't use the word 'sequel,' because it's not a sequel, but following the story of J. J. Gittes, the central character in *Chinatown,* following his story. And I'm possibly doing a remake of *Notorious,* which is a nice Cary Grant–Ingrid Bergman story that Hitchcock did in 1946. And then there's a new book which I just bought, I'm doing with this book like I did with *Godfather.* I took it from a thirty-page treatment, and I'm working with the author and having the book written, which I will own. The book won't come out till August 1976, and I'll have a screenplay written for it by that time. I'm working with the writer. That's the difference between a creative producer and one who just buys million-dollar properties.

"I respect people in this business who have a—it's a tough business, and I respect people in this business who can continually do well, it's so difficult. You're not dealing with utilities now, you're dealing with personalities. And you know, there's the old saying that this business is very wary of the press because, unlike utilities, one bad word written about you is worth one hundred good ones. People who can survive in this business I have a lot of respect for, going from Hal Wallis to Ray Stark to Howard Koch to Zanuck and Brown. I can go on and on and on. There are a lot of directors whose work I certainly admire. And a lot of studio executives. Studio executives, unfortunately, have a very big turnover. That's always been that way in this business.

"No, it wasn't like that in the old days, because they owned their businesses, they weren't public companies, they were all families who owned—Louis B. Mayer owned his business, Zanuck was a big stockholder in his, the Warners owned their business, Harry Cohn, he *owned* Columbia" (and ran it like a concentration camp, according to Joan Didion). "They were family-run and there was great nepotism in that business years ago.

"When I came in as head of production at Paramount in 1966, at United Artists David Picker was there—he was the son of one of the major owners; Kenny Hyman was there who was the son of Eliot Hyman, who owned Warner Brothers–Seven Arts at the time; Dick Zanuck was at Twentieth, whose father was the major guy; at Columbia there was Stanley Schneider, whose father was head of Columbia, a big owner of Columbia" (and also brother Bert, till he left to form an independent company, BBS Productions). "At most every studio there was total nepotism. Not that there's anything wrong, not that there was anything wrong with the people who were running them. They were very bright peo-

Francis Ford Coppola, filmmaker and director of *The Godfather*

ple. But it was a very family-orientated business. Very closed. Now it's totally changed.

"It's changed to a lot less personalization. It's more publicly controlled. Which in a way makes it healthier, makes it much healthier."

"Doing what I did for nine years is a long period; you lose your—it's almost too much, your nerves just get frazzled by it. And I just couldn't take it anymore. And I became a bit maybe resentful of everybody else who's made so much money around me, and I never had the opportunity of really—I've made so much money for so many people and yet never had the opportunity myself. This at least gives me the opportunity of being in business for myself.

"I've never been happier than I have these last few months. I just feel like I've had an office building taken off my shoulders, you know, and I can breathe again. I am not less busy, but at least what I'm doing I'm doing for myself. I'm not putting out fires all day long, seven days a week, fifty-two weeks a year. I think that's the best way I can explain it."

As I left I noticed for the first time a long row of magazines spread out in the living room like playing cards. If the game was bridge he had a winning hand: singletons in *People* and *Newsweek*, long and strong in *Vogue* and *Bazaar*.

☆   ☆   ☆

Bumping into Francis Ford Coppola, the genius director behind *Godfathers* 1 and 2, the Renaissance talent all Hollywood is
hailing, I ask him if he is the new Thalberg.

"What did he do?" Coppola asks with a touch of belligerence.
"He didn't make movies."

His wife and child edging away from us warily, I ask the
compleat filmmaker for a quick interview. (He is waiting for his
car to be delivered up to him.)

"No, I'm going underground," he says.

"Underground," I reply. "What does that mean?"

"I mean I'm not giving any more interviews."

☆   ☆   ☆

Mike Medavoy seems to be important. He is West Coast head
of United Artists pictures, the producers of *Rollerball*. He gets
around Hollywood, raises a lot of dust. But his real significance is
slightly less than that. He is only one of four policy chiefs of the
busy movie company, even if the other three are in New York and
as soon as anything really difficult comes up, it's the conference
phone. His assistant in California, Marcia Nassiter, plays a role in
the decisions out there.

United Artists was especially busy in June 1975, having just
secured all distribution rights to old MGM films, and Medavoy
had been in his office on the MGM lot for only a week when I met
him. Previously they'd been located in the Goldwyn studios, but
now they were well settled into Culver City behind a sign that
punned: "We are glad U Are here." I found him in a large room
designed for him with a distinctly African motif, animal-colored
rugs and sofas and artifacts from that continent on neat display.
Among the marble, glass, and chrome of classically rectangular tables and shelves were gaudier accents: a bowl of apples and
oranges, a gumball machine, a pipe rack, a cup of Flair pens
in every possible color, and several nonobjective paintings on the
floor which looked like close-ups of ice hockey.

Medavoy was very up. On the phone he joked that Kirk Kerkorian—fifty-one percent owner of MGM stock—could possibly be

Mike Medavoy, vice
president of United
Artists, West
Coast Production

bugging his conversation. Medavoy had picked up the receiver
with an exuberant "What are you doing???"

It turned out he was born in Shanghai, his parents having fled
Bolshevik persecution; at the age of eight he moved with his family, then evading Chinese Communist arrest, to Chile and grew up
there speaking Spanish, Chinese, and Russian. College age, he
came north to study at UCLA, majoring in history, especially Renaissance Europe, which was to color his thinking in his future career. He began in the mailroom of Universal Studios, then primarily strong in the television production area, and proceeded
from there to become a casting director for them and then an agent
with a small agency called GAC. The crucial change in his life
came when GAC merged with the much larger agency CMA.

At CMA in the late '6os, Medavoy was able to put into practice a hunch that the movie industry needed an infusion of new
writing and directing talent. "I was able to project or visualize
what I thought would be a need in the business in the years to
come," he said. "And in order to carry out the change in the
business—I couldn't get to the established people, so I had to go
out and start new people. The fact is, those people that I started
out eight, seven, six years ago suddenly became the new stars of
the business." He cites Steve Spielberg, Terry Malick, Phil Kauf-

man, Carole Eastman, John Milius, George Lucas, Gloria Katz, and Willard Huyck. "The names go on and on." He added, "somehow or other I seem to have hit the nerve of the business, of the young people as they were coming up." By this time he had gone from a vice presidency at CMA to heading up the whole motion picture department at IFA, upon the invitation of Marvin Josephson.

"I think we're in a Renaissance period in this country," declared Medavoy, whose earliest impressions of the United States were gleaned from watching romantic adventure movie exports to South America. (He remembers *Robin Hood*, Errol Flynn, Humphrey Bogart, and Clark Gable in particular.) "But I think we're in a Renaissance period, not a classical period. I mean, just like the Renaissance in Europe was a copy of the Greek and Roman period, I think we are now really a copy of the thirties and forties—which were a classical period. That's my own interpretation," he demurred. "I'm not sure that it's gospel or even correct."

Interestingly enough, Medavoy's position on acting stars seems to be slightly at odds with the official position of his company, United Artists. As an agent, he says, he was neither very interested in them, nor could he get along with them terrribly well, since they needed, as he says, "nursemaids." So he concentrated on writers and directors. But his company is famous in the business for placing the box-office value of stars above all else. On its upcoming schedule was a feature called *Missouri Breaks* starring Jack Nicholson and Marlon Brando, and another called *New York, New York* featuring Liza Minnelli and Robert De Niro, directed by Martin Scorsese.

"Medavoy is interesting," Renée, a producer's assistant at another lot, had said earlier, "because his hands are tied. He has to either take over or leave."

Just at that moment a call came through for Medavoy from Vienna-born Eric Pleskow, the recently elected president of United Artists who was film officer for the U.S. War Department during the late 1940s. Medavoy's superior; the big cheese in New York. Though he'd told his secretary to postpone all calls, Medavoy reached for this one with alacrity.

"Pleskow's motto is 'We only want to make movies with stars,'" I had been told by Renée.

Off the phone, Medavoy described how he makes decisions on what movie to produce. "Instinct about what people will want to see," he said. "The timing vis-à-vis what we have in the house now, the cost vis-à-vis what we think it's gonna return, the marketability, the artistic value of it, there are so many . . .

"I don't have the ultimate power in this place," he went on. "There's a committee—four people. We all try to influence each other in one form or another if we believe in something. They are Arthur Krim (for twenty-five years the chairman and virtual owner of Transamerica, UA's parent company), Eric Pleskow, Dan Rissner, and myself."

United Artists produces about fifteen films a year, in addition to distributing independent producers' pictures and all MGM product through its worldwide distribution arm. As such it is one of the more active film companies. Though Medavoy pointed out that Krim's long tenure at Transamerica means that United Artists has had the longest continuous management of any movie company, he did not feel that a factor like management stability was significant in making a movie company strong. Rather it depends on luck, timing, business cycles, and the nature of the product in the previous year, he said. "I don't think any one movie company is going to stay on top for long.

"UA has traditionally been a very low-profile company," said Medavoy.

"Can you tell me," I asked, "what qualities you value in a filmmaker?"

"Yes," he said. "Style, sense of timing, rhythm, visual concepts, storytelling ability; basically that's it—and a belief in what he's doing."

Noticing two bound volumes of *Rolling Stone* all alone on one of his lower shelves, I asked Medavoy what magazines he subscribes to. The answer was *New Times, Time, English History Illustrated, Smithsonian,* and two film magazines—*Film Quarterly* and *American Film Institute Magazine.*

I commented that he looked a little like Richard Dreyfuss and wondered whether the movie *Duddy Krawitz* was about him. "I hope not," he said, "because I don't consider myself motivated that much toward pure achievement, toward power. I don't see myself as wanting to be Irving Thalberg or anybody else other than myself. I take pride in my work, and I take pride in doing things well and hopefully successfully. But I'm not looking for my name in the paper, or to elevate myself to some kind of position, or to be a millionaire. I just enjoy what I'm doing. I do it the best I know how. I enjoy the game.

"The motion picture industry is very healthy," he said. "I think it's going through its best period since the forties. Certainly in terms of income, certainly in terms of the way—the only reason that fewer pictures are being made is that costs are going up. There was a shift in the balance of power in the business. The period when the studios really had the power is over with. I think there will be a balance between the studios and the agencies with the stars vis-à-vis the studios.

"An era ended in about nineteen forty-six, forty-seven, with the advent of television. There was an appearance of the European film, and they came in and took the Renaissance beyond the steps of our own filmmaking process. The fifties and part of the sixties were really a dead period in American film, in my opinion. Then there was a kind of Renaissance. In the late sixties and the seventies."

The turnover of management, he said, dated from the end of the old studio system. And Medavoy answered Yes, he did think the diversification of ownership of the studios had a direct effect on the kind of movies that were made—but he would not elaborate.

"Listen, I don't know if the present management scheme is going to exist for a long time or not," he said. "We can't tell."

He then spoke of the old guard—"old in terms of years, not in ideas"—and the new guard. They are, he said, now existing side by side, but not as antagonists. "The old guard has profited from a melding with the new guard."

He estimated that every aspect of opinion making, from stars and writers to producers and studio executives, in the movie industry, was encompassed by about 125 people.

Medavoy indicated he votes liberal Democratic, though the 125 power brokers in the movies are split pretty evenly between the parties, in his opinion. He called them "pretty intelligent, well meaning in most cases, fairly intellectual, highly motivated, politically minded, generous."

Film critic Pauline Kael had recently issued a broadside in

The New Yorker, saying alarming things about the future of movies, the incompetence of the businessmen in control of film production, and the need for revolutionary changes in attitude among writers and filmmakers. Medavoy acknowledged Kael to be "a very bright lady" but dismissed her accusations as "presumptuous," contending that only total involvement in the filmmaking process qualified someone to be an expert on it.

I asked about the movie makers' social responsibility. Medavoy answered, "We all have a responsibility to ourselves, to our family, to our parents, or whoever, you know. We all feel that sense of responsibility. None of us are looking to endanger any group. We also have a responsibility to those people who pay us. The public, whatever. We're not looking to change values. I think films reflect mores; they don't attempt to change anything.

"Does the company that decides to make *Last Tango in Paris*? Do you consider that decision to be immoral? It's the old thing, Is it art? Does it reflect its time? Or is it a business decision? And you may think it's one, and somebody else, I promise you, will think it's something else, and it all depends on the different stakes, on the different areas in this country. You know there were people in Iowa who felt it was irresponsible to make a movie like that. And there are people in New York City or L.A. or Detroit or wherever who don't feel it was irresponsible.

"We're motivated by commerce rather than art, in most cases," he said, "but we don't feel we're doing something that will be earth-shaking."

Suddenly Medavoy switched his tack, and admitted a certain goal he longs to achieve one day—to be as close to Presidential eras as his boss Arthur B. Krim has been—and Krim was chairman of the National Democratic Finance Committee from 1966 on and, before that, adviser to Presidents Kennedy and Johnson. "If I could one day achieve *that* position in life, of being able to function in areas of life other than the motion picture business, and being able to help other people, it would be terrific. I would feel as if part of my life was worth living." Besides his direct political work, Krim, said Medavoy, gives lavishly to liberal, humanitarian causes, including medicine and medical research, "far beyond the reach of most businessmen," and is conservative only in "the money sense, an economic sense, and rightly so."

"How do you actually get the money that you need?" I asked.

"Banks," was Medavoy's terse reply.

"What's the process of going to the banks?" I continued.

"I don't do all of that, so I can't really give you enough information."

Medavoy professed an interest in African art, which was all around him. But he missed the round table in his old office, he said.

And he was not quite ready with the content of what he would advise a President.

☆   ☆   ☆

The six major motion picture companies—Warner's, Paramount, Universal, United Artists, Fox, and Columbia—together spend about $300 million a year on theatrical feature films. A handful of the minor companies—American International, Disney, MGM, Avco-Embassy, and Allied Artists—spend an additional $100 million. Most of this money, *Daily Variety*'s Art Murphy told me, comes from open lines of credit at the banks. Money coming in from previous films, the "cash flow," also helps finance new pictures.

The amount of credit being used at the banks varies from company to company. Every major movie company has a slightly different profile, in terms of its total operations. For instance, Fox and MGM both own successful film laboratories, which develop and make prints for their own pictures and outside producers. United Artists, Columbia, Universal, and Paramount all have successful music-publishing operations. MCA and Warner's and Columbia have record companies. The glamor is in the movie operation, but if they show a loss on their films, movie companies can often offset this loss with profits in another division.

On occasion the banks have caused management changes in the movie companies, Murphy acknowledged, citing the firings that were done at Columbia in 1973. "But contrary to rumors," he went on, "banks do not look very closely at the day-to-day management of a movie studio, they don't read scripts, they don't say, 'Why did you make this particular widget?' They're in the business of renting money. They rent a lot of it, and they want to make a profit, so when they see something wrong, their attitude is simply, 'Your whole program is failing. What are you going to do about it?' "

There is really only one bank in the world which is active on a grand scale in motion picture financing, Murphy declared, and that's the First National Bank of Boston. Bank of America in California used to be but is not anymore. "The First National Bank of Boston is the prime source of movie funds for Hollywood, and by extension, for the world."

The Boston bank got into pictures because of a certain White Russian named Serge Semenenko, who came to this country in the 1920s and went to work for the First National Bank of Boston in the middle of the American depression. He saw that there was money to be made in the motion picture industry, and over the years he and his staff at that bank, which is otherwise involved in routine conservative functions, took a big gamble on Hollywood. He was the only banker besides A. P. Giannini, the founder of Bank of America, who really understood the motion picture business.

Serge Semenenko was a unique financier. Almost every major movie company from time to time borrowed from his bank. And because he understood the movie business so well, the movie executives went to him as they would go to a doctor or lawyer or clergyman; they'd tell him their secrets, knowing that he wouldn't tell their competitors. He was highly respected.

Semenenko and Giannini, like the Culture Barons of opera and ballet in New York City, and like the original movie moguls, proved to be bulwarks of the American arts though they were newcomers to this continent.

Semenenko retired from the bank in 1968 and is currently on the board of directors of Columbia Pictures in New York. He helped engineer their "survival program" which is going on now. He was succeeded in Boston by William Thompson.

First National Bank of Boston has credit lines out to Twentieth Century–Fox, Columbia, Warner Brothers, and Cinerama at this time. MCA (Universal) does business with the Bank of America and First National Bank of Chicago—the only movie business involvement of these two banks. Paramount, because it is part of Gulf and Western, gets its financing from them. United Artists works through its parent corporation, Transamerica.

With two big Culture Barons moving in on them from other art forms, Twentieth Century–Fox has lately taken some parliamentary steps to insulate themselves from the hassle of outside takeover bids. Two years ago both David Merrick, of New York theater fame, and Norton Simon, the West Coast visual arts mogul and industrialist, bought sizable chunks of Twentieth stock. But they were foiled in the attempt to gain a voice in management by the executive board of chairman and president Dennis C. Stanfill. Simon responded by lashing out at the current board, but last year he changed his tune at the annual meeting and praised Twentieth's management.

The movie company decided to stagger the elections of its officers and to provide chief executive officer Stanfill with one of the most unusual contracts in the film industry. Stanfill is guaranteed his job (at $200,000 basic salary and a bonus of more than half again that much) unless he receives a whopping four years' notice of termination. This provision renews itself every year, so in 1976 he is guaranteed his cushy presidency through 1980.

In the case of so-called "independent" producers, the major film companies to which they are affiliated actually take on all their financial risk. They call themselves independent mainly for vanity, Murphy told me, and tax purposes. Owning a percentage of a film entails capital gains and other tax advantages.

Murphy's explanation of why there are so many fewer films per year than there used to be echoed Evans': People don't go every week to the movies as they used to. The same $40 or $50 million that once was enough to make fifty-two films every year is now enough to make only fifteen films. And, he asserts, the same proportion of these films are good, bad, or mediocre as when many more were produced.

☆   ☆   ☆

Otto Preminger, personally, is not really very popular in Hollywood. The story editor at one production facility comments archly that Preminger "is not one of our favorite people"; a bald studio head demands not to be compared with him; at least one

Film producer-director Otto Preminger

actress has blasted him in print. Nevertheless, from his offices in New York, the bald Viennese-Jewish producer-director is still a baronet of film. Directing and producing a string of successful, powerful-image movies, he has influenced the thinking of millions in the moviegoing generation. *Porgy and Bess* brought the song "Summertime" into the popular culture. *Stalag 17* remains the image of a World War II POW camp. *Exodus* is probably the single clearest statement of the Zionist sentiment in America.

Preminger has always dealt with sensational topics, manicuring them for popular consumption: dope addiction, prostitution, rape, racism, and homosexuality, for example. He brought the words "pregnant" and "virgin" to the screen in 1953, setting off a censorship fight that went all the way to the Supreme Court (which found for the movie). That picture, *The Moon Is Blue*, is still bringing in money. And last year Preminger put together a work about Arab terrorism, combining the kidnapped heiress motif with the actual presence of former New York mayor John Lindsay.

But for all his gaudy, controversial films (and some critics have dismissed them as "opportunistic," "safe and glossy," or even "boorish"), Preminger in real life seems to have a political stance that is fairly complacent and only faintly liberal.

Some of his recent political statements have included "Women's Lib is a put-on," "Everything somehow works out eventually," and "Young people should work on the improvement of this system rather than try to overthrow it."

He seems to be a bit of a hedger in his own behavior. He allows a Jewish organization to throw a large benefit dinner in his New York City apartment and then complains that their desire for kosher food is hypocritical. Questioned about his attendance at Leonard Bernstein's famous benefit gathering for the Black Panthers, dubbed by Tom Wolfe as "radical chic," Preminger affects a look of dopey innocence, ignorance, and excuses himself altogether.

I found Preminger in his large Fifth Avenue office, upstairs from Columbia Screen Gems, on the brink of leaving for Hollywood. There was a somber tone to the room: gray carpet on the floor, black designer chairs, two large inch-thick marble slab tables, one oblong, the other kidney-shaped. Fish-shaped black and white ashtrays on his desk. Numerous large oils on the walls— some looking like textured action painting, others like Klee-style antiques, all in the grainy secondary colors that suggested Africa or at least dashikis to me.

Behind the producer's bald dome two more paintings looked like inferior Picasso and/or Matisse still-lifes. Also flanking him back there were photos of him with F.D.R., J.F.K., and Mayor Lindsay.

Sitting with me in his office for ninety minutes, Preminger managed to look extremely busy, with subordinates running in and out on diligent errands. When one fellow, with longish graying hair and a natty three-color striped suit, failed to make a reasonable estimate of the cost of *Easy Rider* ("a million dollars?" he said), the producer-director-*auteur* barked, "Go back to sleep."

He and his secretary, Blanche, were mulling over some checks for $20 and $30 and a $900 phone bill for Sigma Productions. His nails were neatly manicured. His head would be "double shaved" later that day. Another aide was taking away a biography of the producer, "that old Rosenberg script," called, of course, *Otto!* to put into a binder.

Preminger is on a level, in the motion picture business, with maybe a dozen, certainly no more than twenty other men. Others in his class right now might be such as Francis Ford Coppola, Dino De Laurentiis, and Peter Bogdanovich. Because Preminger has a record of successes as an independent producer, his services are welcomed by the major film companies, which have, as he says, "no inherent styles or interests of their own." What this means to a scriptwriter or prospective filmmaker is that Preminger is one of the few men who have the power to bring a picture into being, who can get the funding from the large studios to make virtually any picture they want. All his pictures have been financed and distributed by Paramount, Columbia, or United Artists; these cinema orgs get their money, when they need it, from banks. Preminger said No, he does not reinvest his profits.

By directing as well as producing, Preminger takes a more active involvement in a picture than many independent producers who only put a package together and then let their director work with their writer. His staff boasts that he has never brought a picture in late or over budget—and that he himself performs all the functions of production manager, associate producer, line producer, and executive producer.

Born in Vienna in 1906, Preminger was hired to be a producer-director in that city by Max Reinhardt on the basis of a letter he wrote while a law student. He took over from the retiring Reinhardt in 1932 and in 1935 came to the United States on the invitation of the Schenck Brothers, Hollywood moguls. Eight years later he became an American citizen.

In the days of the movie studios' power, Preminger recalled, David Selznick was the only independent producer. Before 1959, six or seven big studios produced all the films. Nicholas and Joseph Schenck (pronounced "Skenk") between them controlled all the finances of Twentieth Century and Fox, which they merged, and Metro-Goldwyn-Mayer. Although Joe Schenck technically had the power, he did not in fact interfere with the creative end of the operation, which was run by Darryl F. Zanuck.

A few years ago the government sued the movie studios for monopolistic practices, forcing them either to produce and distribute or to run theaters, but not both. According to Preminger, this event opened the way for the independent producer. Previously even the worst Fox picture had ample playing time, for there was a double interest. Now only two or three showcases exist. For better or worse, the studios felt they had to finance the independent producers. In this way they got some of their power back, through creative control over stories or casts or directors.

But Preminger was reluctant to generalize in any way about the role of an independent producer or his own power position with respect to the studios. "In a democratic society, nothing is regulated across the board; it all depends on individuals." And later: "In this profession you cannot find two individuals with exactly the same power."

All he would say was that "to a certain degree, when you speak about power in motion pictures, theater, or book writing, it is very closely related to success. When somebody has a big success, he has a lot to say. No, not by contract, but there is competition among the studios. He gets final cut, instead of its going to the distribution company that financed the film.

"Paramount owned the property for *Godfather* for several years before they made the picture. Then because it was such a big success, they engaged the director for a whole string of pictures," Preminger said. And illustrating his own status, he recounted the speed with which United Artists had picked him up on his latest film, *Rosebud.* "We sent it to them Friday. Monday they invited me in to discuss the contract."

Preminger's current position derives from his enormous box-office success with pictures made in the 1950s and 1960s and he is still receiving on these accounts. Nevertheless, he distinctly did not want to discuss the past. "I usually forget my films," he said. "I deliberately detach myself from the picture after seeing it two or three times with the audience." He had no favorites among his own work; he said he didn't brood about what kind of producer he was.

Despite this, he communicated a subtle, if veiled, dissatisfaction with the system he works under. An independent producer's status apparently hinges on whether he has not even one unsuccessful picture. First Preminger acknowledged this; then almost immediately he hedged: "It's not quite that bad."

"There is a lack of something in the U.S.," he averred. He was impressed with what he saw at the Moscow School for Film, when he visited there on the invitation of the Union of Russian Picture Makers. "There were no 'teachers,' " he said, "only prominent directors, cameramen, writers, and actors—great craftsmen." He has incorporated this principle into his own operation, he claimed, inviting five or six boys and girls to observe every stage of the process when he makes a film. "I feel it is almost a duty in a profession like mine to listen to young people—without being sentimental about it—because I got my career started with just a letter to Max Reinhardt."

Several young people were in evidence around Preminger's office even as he spoke to me. His male secretary, Eric Barnes, turned out to be the former minister of public information for the Scientology Organization, an electronic-mystical sect. He was wearing a stylish imitation of a red flannel shirt, and he told me that he had made ninety-one industrial film shorts (for salesmen) and what a kick it was to talk like equals with the vice presidents of Coca-Cola or Lincoln-Mercury.

Another young man was evidently doing a script for Preminger. "Ted Gershuny, one of the great writers," said the older man, smiling. Then he asked why Ted was giving him only fifty pages. The writer was incredibly unflappable. "I have managed to conquer my exhibitionism," he replied, with a nod to the galleries. Then they joked about calling the work "Complete Creative Control." "How do you like that title?" Preminger asked me. "It's terrific," I said. "How long have *you* been here?" Gershuny demanded.

A Miss Summer was just down from the staff of a certain Jack Lewin, who, it was established, was not taking over the *Hollywood Reporter*. Miss Summer spoke like an Englishperson and had smudgy eyes and a midi skirt. Together she and Preminger discussed the quality of the London theater where his new picture was about to open. "Do you mean a theater or a cinema?" she asked. Then she admitted it was the less classy of the two places he'd mentioned. Preminger fumbled to communicate his concept of the mass arena. She didn't understand.

He rushed her out in four or five minutes. "Give her anything she wants!" he ordered Eric Barnes.

Barnes later explained to me that his boss is very accessible. "He'll give anyone two or three minutes. If they're really interesting people, three or four minutes." He and another young man, named Alfred Morris, who had just begun "observing" that day and was wearing a tie with little fire hydrants on it about which he said, "Don't ask!," were sitting comfortably in the outer reception office, calling everyone by their first name.

The difference between independent producing and studio producing, Barnes said, is only that with a studio the offices remain there, and the people come and go.

According to the secretary, something like one thousand scripts come in to Preminger's office each year, ranging per week from as few as five to as many as thirty-five. The choosing of a "property," *i.e.*, a script, is definitely the first step in the movie-making process, he said. He and another man, named Bud Rosenthal, read them, eliminating Westerns and science fiction right away.

Preminger himself was very vague on the subject of how he selects which scripts to produce. "You can know almost from the title—what it's about—whether you'll be interested." But he preferred not to elaborate on what themes interested him or how he selects "the two boys" who read through all the incoming manuscripts. "When I get excited enough I make a picture. I hope to make other people as excited as I was," he said.

Eric Barnes amplified only slightly. "Otto gets a boot out of making a picture," he commented. He contrasted the "Mercedes–Cadillac–Rolls Royce work" of New York, complete with superstars, to the "subsistence economy of regional theater" in places like Minneapolis, Houston, and San Diego. Otto eats lunch either at "21" or La Caravelle, he reported; he himself repairs to the Columbia commissary on the third floor of the building where they work.

Because Preminger has produced and directed more than one film on the Nazis, I asked him what he thought of recent movies on them. "Well, I must tell you," he said, "that I saw *The Night Porter* in Nice with only a half-hour time before an appointment. I went to refresh my memory of Kirk? What's his name? Dirk

Bogarde. And I was so fascinated I missed my appointment. I liked it better in French.

"Seriously, though, it proved something that I thought was true: that a Nazi underground still exists in Vienna and other places in Austria and southern Germany, where the Catholic Church is strongest. If other people felt something about this who are not Jewish, a great anti-Semitic movement going on in the U.S. could be stopped."

And he went on to tell me about a woman member of the American Nazi party in Los Angeles who had been written up in a San Francisco newspaper story.

Meanwhile, in the outer office, Eric Barnes was addressing envelopes, inviting people to a Jewish organization benefit dinner at Preminger's East Sixty-fourth Street apartment. And tormenting a giggly woman secretary with his Nazi accent: "It iss hhhrrainink. Do you haff chhhyour Jack Boots on?!"

☆   ☆   ☆

When I first received a letter written on stationery with a seven-mouse logo I rushed right down to Soho's Spring Street bar to celebrate with a man who could play Scott Joplin rags masterfully. Together we reminisced about the Disneys of our youth— undead, it seemed! He had gone for Donald and Duckburg in a big way, while I loved Cinderella and Sleeping Beauty. The conversation soon became too emotional to continue.

When Walt Disney died in 1966, his seventy-four-year-old brother Roy was left in charge of the enormous fantasy factory, supervising the building of a sequel to the $17 million complex of Disneyland in the form of a $400 million, much larger, Florida complex called Walt Disney World. Since Roy's death Walt's son-in-law Ron Miller, and Roy's son, Roy E. Disney, are left in the top management, and decisions are said to be made very much by committee. The studios are still active, headquartered in Burbank, California, and net a nice $50 million a year from their various enterprises, including "theme parks," movies, and educational materials.

When I spoke to them in Burbank I was told that the movie *Snow White*—Disney's very first animated full-length feature, now thirty-eight years old—was about to be released to theaters again soon. "It'll probably make five or six million dollars, and that's all clear profit," commented a chuckling Disney archivist named David R. Smith.

"*Snow White* was the top-grossing film in Paris for five weeks last year," Smith went on. On his desk was a copy of *Harvard* magazine. Disney characters in every imaginable dignified pose covered his walls and crowded desk.

"We haven't done any of the classic fairy tales recently," Smith declared, "because we did all the main ones." His roster of the main classic fairy tales, a giggle in his authoritative pronouncement, ran: "*Snow White, Bambi, Cinderella, Sleeping Beauty, Peter Pan, Pinocchio, The Sword and the Stone*, and probably I've forgotten some."

No new characters comparable to Mickey Mouse or Donald Duck have been started since Walt's death ten years ago, the archivist reported, nor have any more classic fairy tales been done; the product has been mainly family films with up-to-date settings and all new characters created for each. The animation of *Winnie-the-Pooh*, however, was begun in the early '6os, and the "young people today know more about Winnie-the-Pooh than Mickey Mouse," asserted the keeper of the archives. This he proved by citing a statistic: At Disneyland, Winnie-the-Pooh figurines sell better than Mickey Mouse figurines; however, in Florida, at Disney World, it's the opposite. He and I agreed that more surveys needed to be taken.

By proxy for my pianist friend, I then asked whether Mickey Mouse is, relatively speaking, a proletarian character, and Donald Duck a bourgeois character?

Smith: "I've never thought of it that way—let me think a minute. . . . I don't know that I wouldn't put them in the opposite categories. Mickey Mouse started out perhaps in the working class. He held down many different occupations in his cartoons. But he became in later years the typical middle-class American with a home and a dog, living a life of leisure, really. For this reason it became very hard for the Disney story people to come up with stories for Mickey Mouse. He had become almost the Boy Scout character. If they wrote a story where Mickey was doing anything naughty or bad, the studio would get a lot of letters complaining about it.

"But on the other hand, we had Donald Duck. Donald Duck's character was totally different. He could throw a temper tantrum, he could get mad, he could fly off the handle. And so it was much easier to write stories for Donald Duck."

I asked, "What was Donald's occupational background?"

"Well, Donald Duck started out I guess more as an entertainer. In his first cartoon he didn't have a job; he was a loafer. It was called 'The Wise Little Hen.' The hen tried to get him to plant her corn and harvest her corn, and he wouldn't help. And then when she had it all harvested, he was more than ready to help her eat it. [Smith laughs merrily.] In the later cartoons of the '30s he was really an entertainer, or a member of the gang, with Mickey and Donald and Goofy. He was a performer in a revue or follies. He would recite 'Mary Had a Little Lamb' and get mad when the kids would make fun at him. That sort of thing.

"The Disney people sort of steered away from Mickey Mouse after about the beginning of the 1940s, and Donald Duck became much more popular. And there were a lot of Donald Duck cartoons made after the war and very few Mickey Mouse cartoons. The last Mickey Mouse cartoon was in 1953, and Donald Duck continued until 1956." Groping for the figures, he estimated that there are 140 Donald Duck cartoons and 110 Mickey Mouse cartoons. "Somewhere around there.

"We are the only movie studio," David Smith said, on the subject of his own crowded archives, "that has done anything about preserving its history. . . . It's because we're a family corporation; there's some feeling to preserve the history, to preserve the name. Great Western, when they come in, they don't care about the history of Paramount," he said recklessly.

"When new people come in to MGM, and they're now operating a hotel in Las Vegas and this is what's making all their money [MGM is now turning out five or six feature films annually, just like the Disney studio] and they think, 'What ever are these rooms of old files? Let's ship them up to our nostalgia shop at the hotel and sell them!' And that's what they're doing!"

Disney Productions plans to put the archives in a whole separate building, he went on, which should somewhat relieve the crowding.

Previous to his job at Disney, Smith had worked for the state at the UCLA research library. It was hard for him, when he first came to Disney, to call *everyone* at the company by first names, as was the rule. "It's a friendly, open atmosphere," he said, chuckling.

We talked a little about the theme parks, with their attractions and guests (not "amusement parks" with "rides" and "customers"), built because Walt wanted to have "a clean place to take the kids where he could have fun too." No, Smith said to a remark I'd heard at Playboy Productions in Hollywood, Hermann Goering was not in charge to enforce the cleanliness. He told me about the $17 million indoor roller coaster in Walt Disney World.

And I left feeling more benevolent toward a corporation than I can ever remember feeling before, nodding good-by to David R. Smith. And to one of the ubiquitous Eastman Kodak portraits of Walt Disney himself sitting sideways with his legs crossed and a note pad on his knee.

☆   ☆   ☆

Larry Turman, who made *The Graduate* and *The Drowning Pool*, is a man with an interesting amount of filmmaking power. He calls himself a "wild-catter" and claims he does not have much power. If he were a football player, he would be running with a ball he made himself, hoping to be given a stadium. Yet he has already made one picture for Joseph E. Levine's Avco-Embassy and another for Warner Brothers. And he is comfortably set up in an office on the Warner Brothers lot in Burbank, thinking about what he will do next.

Like a Polish journalist trying to reconcile himself to communism, Turman does not criticize the motion picture establishment or system. He is still on the way up.

He looks for scripts, he says, which are upbeat, nonesoteric, star vehicles (that is, terrific characters, not bland), and cheap. Making it, in the movies or anywhere, he sees as being due to intelligence, social connivance and contacts, sheer drive, and especially a combination of these.

The first step in his personal schedule for moviemaking is selecting a writer and working with him, next comes selecting a director, third comes casting. After that follows "music and the works." He subscribes to Harry Cohn's famous seat-of-the-pants rule: "I know the picture's good if my fanny doesn't wriggle."

Though he is strongly interested in finding central characters with whom he can be psychologically connected, whom he likes, understands, and cares about, he is also interested in morality in the movies. He looks for his characters (and so far his leading characters have been males) to be at a malleable point in their lives, a crossroads, making an ending that is also a new beginning.

One of Turman's colleagues whom he respects terrifically is Stanley Kubrick, whom Turman calls "focused and centered as a personality, therefore very effective. And fortunately he also has talent."

For Turman the phrase "good work" has a mystical, utopian connotation.

Values he seeks in his own work include clarity, strong emotional fulfillment, understatement, "and, yes, didacticism." He hopes not to be too exotic or unique.

Asked if the concentration of power in the movie business is a good or a bad thing, he replies, "I don't know. I'm stuck with it."

A native Angelino, Turman came to movies, like so many others, by way of the family textile business. Before producing he was an agent.

☆   ☆   ☆

Bert Schneider, producer of *Easy Rider*, *Five Easy Pieces*, and *Hearts and Minds*, is in the process of closing up shop at his little company, BBS Productions. That company had negotiated for itself a production arrangement with Warner Brothers which Schneider considers unique in movie annals. Now at an end, it provided for six pictures, with a fixed risk of $1 million each for the studio, all other losses to be absorbed by Schneider's end. In exchange for this fixed risk, this "guarantee of our own negative costs," Schneider and his associates, most notable among whom being director Bob Rafelson, freed themselves completely from any interference from or even routine contact with the studio hierarchy.

"I structured my business specifically to avoid interaction with those people," commented Schneider, an enormous hippy with a pool table in his office.

BBS guaranteed delivery, took small fees, reinvested its profits from the Monkees movie, *Head,* and Warner Brothers bit because "they were interested in the people around us." The studio didn't even get to read BBS's scripts. But after *Easy Rider* tapped into the previously untapped youth market—"there were fucking lines around the block!"—a flood of imitations followed— *The Last Movie, Silent Running, Getting Straight,* etc.

Schneider says he invests his money in people whose minds he wants to spend three dollars to see laid out on a screen, people he himself wants to hang around with for a year.

On his wall was leaning a huge poster-graph entitled "Input Output Structure of the U.S. Economy," which had been designed by Nobel Prizewinner Wassily Leontief. Schneider didn't exactly understand it, nor was it up to date, but he got it because he liked the graphics, he liked the idea. On another wall hung the huge hexagram "Break-through" from the *I Ching.* He assured me it had no content; it was also bought for graphics value. He nibbled Tootsie Rolls as he spoke.

"Wasserman and Kerkorian still have that kind of power that Louis B. Mayer and Harry Cohn had," he said.

And Bert Schneider knows whereof he speaks. He's had three other movie chieftains in the family. His father, Abe Schneider, ran Columbia Pictures (as chairman of the board) along with his famous uncle Harry Cohn. After Abe's death, brother Stanley Schneider inherited the position.

A *Glossary of* Variety *Words*

acad	Academy of Motion Picture Arts and Sciences
anni	anniversary
ayem	morning
biz	business
bow	introduce
cleffers	musicians
coin	money
disk, diskery	record, recording
fem	women
gig	performance, job
hack pack	junketeering journalists
hardcore	pornography

hub	Boston
kidvid	children's television
lensing	shooting a film
pact	contract
pix	movies
praisers	publicists
prexy	president
seg	segment of a TV series
spec	spectacular
tabbed	elected
tveepee	vice president for TV
vidscripter	TV writer
webs	networks

ROCK:
Dividing Up the
Aquarian Age

Remember—the public doesn't make the hits. I make the hits. I tell the disc jockeys what to play.
>   —Hilton to reggae musician
>   in *The Harder They Come*

Until blacks wake up themselves, they can never have reall power. like regisrating to vote for people Percy Sutton Manhattan Burrough Getting together owning more busines's like Berry Gordy Motown brought 46 million dollas lasted year, George Johnson AFO
>   —Graffito in Eighty-sixth Street
>   IND subway station, 1974

The emancipation of women means Muzak in billiard parlors.
>   —Mel Cohen,
>   Muzak research manager

Power in the record business lies with accountants, soulless and unmusical, who control the conglomerates the record companies are a part of, checking out the investment figures.
>   —Dan Morgenstern, former jazz consultant,
>   National Endowment for the Arts

In Gotham, the major booking agencies deal primarily with Ron Delsener and Howard Stein.
>   —*Variety,*
>   February 19, 1975

248

TRYING to track down Bill Graham after the start of an evening concert at Madison Square Garden, I discovered the passion and blood of art (or is it combat?) one misses at Lincoln Center. Girls were flinging themselves at gatekeepers, glazed-eye youths and sponge-limbed drunks were clustered around the Garden's outer checkpoints trying to insinuate themselves inside, and Christmas and violence were competing for precedence over an otherwise normal cold, dark night. Scalpers were angry, there were no profits to be made.

As I chatted with the head usher ("If there's anyone I trust less than producers, it's newspaper people," he said, in response to my journalistic needs), a young man in denim was strong-armed out the door by three cops. All disappeared down the escalator to the subway. We heard an enormous crash. The cops came back up. "Did they kill him?" I asked the usher's doorman.

"No," he said, with apparent sincerity, "when they kill someone they don't take them through the front lobby."

But hearing himself say this, the youngish underling launched into a monologue alluding vaguely to army experience and ending with a blanket indictment of the system. "Disappear into the crowd; don't come back out this door!" he told me, and suddenly, ticketless, I found myself inside the George Harrison concert.

In the late 1950s and 1960s, rock 'n roll overthrew pop music. Pop had been a continuous and dominant strain in American music for the prior twenty to fifty years, having begun, it is said, with Victor Herbert in the early twentieth century. It was the mainstream, though there were mutual tributary influences with jazz. Jazz influenced the pop composer George Gershwin; pop in turn had an influence on jazz, since it provided the basic pop melodies that were the recognizable tune base for hotel dance bands and fancier jazz improvisation.

ASCAP, the American Society of Composers, Authors, and

Publishers, was an organization that existed mostly to protect the copyrights of musicians. Because it controlled the work of Gershwin, Porter, Kern, Rodgers, and the others, which formed the basis for the pop sound, ASCAP was one of the most influential opponents of the new sound in music—that is, rock.

Broadcast Music Incorporated, or BMI, on the other hand, was formed in reaction to ASCAP. BMI was instrumental in putting together the country and western opus from smalltown southern white music, and rhythm and blues out of big city black music. BMI was not opposed to rock 'n roll.

One of the most lasting effects of the rock revolution, then, may be the submerging of the pop tradition. Although pop has not disappeared altogether, it has certainly retreated. To Muzak. Every day sixty million people in twenty countries hear, if not listen to, the canned sounds that are engineered to fit the different moods of the hours of the day, owned now by the Jack Wrather Organization.

Rock music was not at first liked by the record companies, and they tried to resist it. But the popular pressure for it eventually convinced the corporation executives that it was unavoidable. Now who can argue about the pre-eminence of rock music?

The difference between a liberal and a radical on the subject is that a liberal says, "For nearly a decade rock has been central to our cultural experience" (Eliot Fremont-Smith), and a radical says, "The old music has been dead for fifteen years" (an employee at Warner Communications).

Rock is solvent. In 1973 it moved ahead of the movies as America's top entertainment medium, grossing $2 billion in domestic sales and another $2 billion abroad. The employees at Warner Communications, which leads the industry in record sales, were smug as a winning World Series team. They cleared $55 million, as much as the entire book publishing industry. At this point the top record acts are making $2 to $10 million a year. A top record executive can make half a million—approximately the salary of a sugar company president, not your usual Culture Baron.

But even in rock, as elsewhere in the nation's economy, signs of depression do show. Industry executives, according to the trade papers, are finding it hard to maintain the tradition of huge ad-

Pop Music Sales

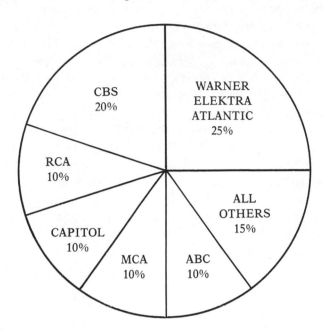

vance payments to performing artists, especially in the light of the increasing number of big stars.

A fistful of record companies dominate the business, especially the Warner Communications complex—now consisting of Elektra, Asylum, Nonesuch, Reprise, Atlantic, and Warner records, as well as Warner Brothers films and TV and Warner Paperback Library—and CBS' subsidiary Columbia Records (CBS also owns Holt, Rinehart, and Winston, the publisher, and manufactures Warner's records). Warner Communications is in addition responsible for two of Bob Dylan's albums, *Ms.* magazine, *Badlands*, DC comics (Superman, Batman, Wonder Woman), *Mad* comic, Joni Mitchell, the "Independent" News Company which distributes *Playboy*, and other units of culture too numerous to mention. One might venture to call Warner pre-eminent in the field of middle-hip. On Wall Street, Warner and the like are called Vertical Integration Companies; informally, people refer to them as "conglomerates." Another term that floated around business circles for a while was "congenerics," implying that all their varied activities were thematically related. At any rate, the Warner complex is responsible for one fourth of the entire pop music business, Columbia for one fifth.

At the head of Columbia Records from 1965 until 1974 was a lawyer named Clive Davis. Columbia at that time was doing the most business on the rock music scene, with profits moving into the eight figures. Davis didn't delegate any of his power. He effected some changes in the company which observers called "abrupt" and put his mark on everything, acquiring new performers like Janis Joplin, Blood, Sweat and Tears, Simon and Garfunkel, Santana, and Chicago, and even introducing a new kind of paperclip. He surprised others in the industry because he had come up through the ranks from the business end, and usually people who come from the business end don't have a lot to say on artistic matters.

In the late '60s the next largest companies were RCA, which had Elvis Presley and The Jefferson Airplane; and Capitol, which had the Beatles. RCA was the kind of company that periodically fired everyone and abandoned all projects. Artistic decisions were made by accountants directly responsible to former conglomerate chief Robert Sarnoff.

But in 1970 Warner-Reprise (Jimi Hendrix, The Grateful Dead, Joni Mitchell) merged with Atlantic (The Cream, Crosby, Stills, Nash and Young) and Elektra (Judy Collins, The Doors), and the new conglomerate moved into second place, from which it would eventually take the lead.

In the '70s, RCA was going with Nilsson, John Denver, and David Bowie; Ode (Carole King) was acquired by A & M (Tijuana Brass, Cat, Pie, Cocker, and Harum); and British Decca's London label owned the Rolling Stones. Davis at Columbia wooed Neil Diamond away from MCA (Elton John, The Who, Jesus Christ Superstar) with an offer of several millions of dollars—the first such breakthrough since the Beatles.

Sizable chunks of the pop music pie belonged to MCA (formerly called Decca), ABC (which bought Paramount Pictures' record company), and Twentieth Century–Fox.

As the record industry has become superprofitable, headquarters and offices of the record companies have been gradually shifting from New York to California. Even Motown Records, the

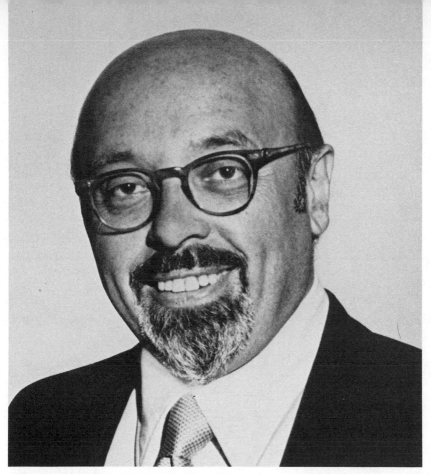

Ahmet Ertegun, president, Atlantic Records; member of the board of directors, Warner Communications

leading producer of black talent (with some exceptions, like Aretha Franklin) and identified with Detroit, has moved many of its top executives to Los Angeles.

The heads of some of the sister companies in the Warner conglomerate qualify as Culture Barons in their own right. At Atlantic the business is run by Ahmet and Nesuhi Ertegun, two sons of the Turkish ambassador to the United States, very rich, very hip, very knowledgeable jazz fans. Nesuhi was more drawn to traditional jazz in the '40s, when he owned a store called Jazzman, which his wife ran. Any jazz Atlantic does is done because of him. He is also on the board of the annual Newport Jazz Festival and runs Atlantic's overseas publishing division.

Ahmet was more interested in blues. He started Ray Charles

John Hammond, director of Talent Acquisition, Columbia Records. He signed Bob Dylan in the winter of 1961–62.

and then knew what to do with him. He is cool, the kind of man who is found in the social columns of the *News* alongside Mick Jagger and Penelope Tree. He has inspired at least one novel; one musician says he could be cast in a spy movie as a Turkish secret agent or hookah-smoking billionaire.

Clive Davis' real aesthetic interest, he once confessed, was in Broadway theaters and Johnny Mathis. In 1973 his head rolled professionally; just about the time Asylum Records' David Geffen wooed Bob Dylan off the Columbia label (where he had been since before Davis' tenure, signed by John Hammond), Davis was fired.

He left quietly, and immediately sat down and wrote his professional memoirs. In 1975 he was indicted by a Newark, New Jersey, grand jury for tax evasion to the extent of $45,000. A few of the axed lower-ranking staffers were found to have Mafia connections.

Davis went to work for Bell/Arista Records, a subsidiary of Columbia Pictures (no connection with Columbia Records). Ostensibly, CBS had resorted to the abrupt firings because any trouble in its record-producing subsidiary might endanger the network's FCC license. But many in the industry believed that Clive Davis had been made a scapegoat. Some thought his dismissal was a personal vendetta by CBS president Arthur Taylor. Others spoke of cocaine as being an integral part of the music business, as much as wining and dining and providing girls are to the larger corporate structure.

Because it is still a young, brash, very American art, the rock interests are concerned with dynamic content magnitude— with the hugeness of crowds, the loudness of sounds, the floods of money, and the fame of the "superstars." One almost sees iconolatry in rock, as, to a greater or lesser degree, in all the arts, in the elevation of certain individuals to positions of immense wealth.

There is a prevailing myth that the enormous success enjoyed by perhaps a dozen people in each art field is a mysterious windfall, a pot of gold at the end of the rainbow, the rightful due of talent. Stardom, according to Sir Rudolf Bing, has this character:

> If they are great artists they wake up one day to find themselves catapulted into enormous fame and riches. They have cover pictures in *Time* and *Newsweek*, their telephone never stops, they race from Vienna to Covent Garden to Milan to the Metropolitan, they have dinner at the White House, their income rises to $500,000 a year or even more. And for most, this apotheosis follows immediately upon almost total obscurity. Not everybody can take it.

In fact, stardom follows upon conscious decisions to produce it, by managers, impresarios, corporation executives, and Culture Barons. After Columbia Records' president Clive Davis startled the music world by offering a Bing Crosbyish singer named Neil Diamond $3 or $5 million for a contract (explaining, when questioned by the trade press, that he was merely matching a Warners offer), *Newsweek* magazine promptly began referring to "the Rolling Stones, the Beatles, Neil Diamond, and just about every other top artist. . . ."

This kind of price—equivalent to a Ford Foundation grant to Balanchine for ten years—is not uncommon in the rock industry these days. Sometime after the Neil Diamond windfall, Elton John renewed with MCA for $8 or $10 million. Bill Graham, the most successful rock promoter, informed a San Francisco newspaper columnist that he's now grossing $7 million a year.

The purpose of the production of superstars by the Culture Barons may be to dazzle the many inevitably unsuccessful artists with the big winnings of the few, and with the implied possibility that they might make it too, in the manner of a lottery. Radicals feel that the Establishment elevates those who present no threat to the class system, to consolidate its own power and defuse real opposition. Critic Pauline Kael feels that the superstars of television, radio, literature, academics, politics, and women's liberation feel anger and self-hatred because of the system they are caught in, and contempt for the audience that makes it possible for them to keep going. In sum, she says, the superstars are playing to the artist hatred of the Culture Barons, who perniciously undermine real art in this way.

As in the realm of visual arts, sentiments toward rock music are politically polarized. There are those who include rock in the high culture of America and exclude grand opera. And there are also those many who still refer to "rock music and real music." Depending on which side of this fence you stand, you will assess the contribution to culture of men like Bill Graham and Ron Delsener very differently. Graham might be said to have been the initiator on the national scene of the institution of rock concerts, now as in the late '60s a gathering point for youth; Delsener did the same thing but in New York City rather than on a national scale. Though Delsener was actually in the business earlier, the scope of his work does not equal that of Bill Graham, who monopolized the limelight as owner of the Fillmore theaters, the most famous auditoriums in rockdom.

When the Aquarian Age went out with a whimper in about

1970, it became problematic what the future of rock would be. Graham quit the business and returned several times. He did shut down the Fillmores, which have stayed shut; instead, he promotes rock musicians in various places around San Francisco and sometimes nationally. Many of the youth who had seen him as an evangelical angel earlier in the decade began to complain about the quantity of money he had made and his refusal to hearken to the creed of the counterculture and contribute his money to the community. Like the newspaper *Rolling Stone,* which similarly was successful and an emblem of the rock establishment, Bill Graham had gathered moss. Crowds of youth outside his concerts yelled at him to let them in free. Graham yelled back at them about the virtues of hard work.

Just about all that's really left, in 1976, of Graham's impresario-hood is the wealth and personal glory that came with it. He and the other Rock Barons agree that rock is no longer an integral part of a counterculture, that it has become simply youth entertainment. It didn't add anything of value to the culture to go see and hear the two concerts Graham promoted in 1974—Bob Dylan and George Harrison, neither of whom was at his best. Perhaps he could figure out a different kind of career for himself that would engage his sensibilities more fully.

☆   ☆   ☆

The word for Howard Stein is "smooth." He went to private school. He has almost unbearably regular features and ultrascrub manicured hands and wears his slightly receding hairline pushed wetly back. A huge mug of Marlene Dietrich looms out from behind his desk chair in his New York office; other Gable and Harlow-type posters adorn his front waiting room, which features an antique Victrola. At his fingertips are a bevy of electronic gadgets. And when the $250 act introducing his main feature gets a little too rowdy, threatening to make trouble if they're not allowed to go on, it is in the name of "smoothness" that Stein capitulates and lets them play.

Howard Stein confesses to being one of the "twelve to twenty" important promoters of rock music in the country. But his press agent, Roberta Burrows, contends he's the busiest, booking approximately three hundred rock, classical and pop shows a year,

Howard Stein, rock promoter, the Academy of Music, and executive director of the Westchester Premier Theater (Harry Sandler)

one quarter of which are in New York City's Academy of Music on Fourteenth Street, the others in seventeen other cities. He has offices in Miami, Atlanta, Houston, and Chicago.

In New York he's known as "the good-natured Howard Stein" probably because of the survival of the Academy of Music, which outlived its competition in Boston, Philadelphia, and Detroit and stands today as the last outpost of grundgy rock palaces. "The Academy is the reality level of rock," Stein has said, "scroungy, aggressive, violent, hard, scary, adolescent." And pot is smoked openly there.

How is it Stein has been able to keep such a sanctuary functioning, and without the interference of the police? "There has never been a drug sale or a death or a major injury," he answers smoothly, "and apparently the priorities of the police department in New York City do not include busting somebody for smoking a joint or sneaking a joint in the men's room. They're into parking instead.

"I think of myself as an impresario. Besides rock I am the executive director for the Westchester Premier Theater.

"Let me see if I can think of what I'm doing in terms of power structures," he muses. "It's not the way I see the music industry. It's performers that sell tickets. And the power really circulates around those persons who control the performers, either control their concert engagements or recording sessions. It's really the persons who've got control over the *heads* of the stars.

"Primarily managers. But very often agents too. Agencies. There are very very few major agencies in the music business, and each of these agencies really wields great, great power.

"I deal with agents and managers, sometimes with artists directly, sometimes with record company executives, which have a certain control or influence upon performers. But record companies participate very little, I would say, in the booking of acts on a regular basis. Occasionally a major record executive has a great influence on a performer and will sort of encourage him to go out on tour, encourage him to play a certain facility or even for a particular concert producer. But generally it's the artists and their managers and agencies that decide they want to work.

"Record companies and concert producers are sort of symbiotic. When somebody plays an engagement, that engagement usually has the residual effect of selling records. And when somebody's selling records, that usually has an effect of selling concert tickets as well. So both feed on each other—one doesn't really influence—they both operate in or function via that artist and via that performer."

Stein feels there are just a few strong, significant, aggressive contemporary promoters of rock music. Though he refuses to compare himself by name with any specific other concert promoter—in particular with Ron Delsener, who divides the New York market with him—he boasts that compared with "the others" he is more varied in the nature of material presented—"from Rolling Stones to classical, from heavy metal to down, dirty funk," he says—and more sensitive to and sympatico with the different needs of the different styles of acts. Others have said that Stein produces everything, Delsener only what he likes.

"It operates in two ways now," Stein says. "It has a kind of territorial overtone to it, concert producing. It's very hard for a major concert producer to get started in New York City and do battle with Delsener and myself. It's equally difficult for a major concert producer to establish himself against Frank Fried or myself in Chicago. In Miami, I virtually don't consider myself as having any real competition. In Atlanta, minor competition. In Texas, some competition. In New York there are three: Delsener, myself, and Jerry Weintraub. Bill Graham on the West Coast.

"Sometimes producers work territorially, and sometimes they acquire an act and take them totally across the country. The way Bill Graham did with Bob Dylan. In the past he decided to get George Harrison and do all the concerts for the entire tour. During that time I was operating differently. I was establishing major markets where I would operate on a weekly basis, as I do in New York City. Presently we are doing both; we both have the development of new acts on a regular basis, in a city, as well as some national tours.

"This territorial thing works two ways. One is that simply to produce concerts effectively, and to make an artist feel comfortable in a particular city, you have to be able to move well in that city, you have to be able to handle certain problems that come up in a particular locale, you have to be able to handle them smoothly and expeditiously. So I have to know how to operate in New York. I have to know the subtleties, the peculiarities of being a concert producer in New York. The other thing is, since I've been here so long I've been involved with groups since when they were beginning to burgeon. I've been involved with hall managers for years. I've reciprocated, I've given agents all kinds of opportunities for their attractions in New York, I've developed new acts on a weekly basis for five years at the Academy of Music, for ten years at the Port Chester theater. So I've developed all these relationships, all these associations. And if somebody comes along and says, 'I think I want to do Elton John,' my associates and contacts in New York City would say, 'Well, why do I need you to do Elton John? Howard has done this act'—not this one particularly—'when they were nobody.' That's one way, associations.

"Another way is that some people have exclusivities on halls. The Academy of Music is mine. The Chicago Stadium is Jerry Weintraub's. So other territorial rights are acquired by acquiring a facility."

Stein says he has no favorite musician or musicians in the field of rock and pop, because he's seen so many. Rather, his tastes run to the whole complex of '30s and '40s styles (witness his office décor and Jean Harlow logo), and when he goes home to Park Avenue in the evening to his wife, Helen, and their two children, he is liable to turn on Ruth Etting instead of any psychedelic or acid rock.

"I never really sit down and watch three hours of a concert," he admits. "I just sort of float around the theater. There are moments, as in a Dylan set, that offer me real enjoyment. A spark during a Grateful Dead concert. A moment or an expression of Shirley Bassey's. It's moments of performers, or at best a single tune, or a phrase, that really excite me now."

He professes a deep interest in the romance of the melodies and lyrics and films of the depression era.

About choosing which acts to present, Stein says, "I have to be careful not to afford myself the luxury of producing something that I like. That's why I don't like to think in terms of who my favorite group is. It becomes a bad habit. You start presenting what Howard Stein likes," says Howard Stein, "and very often the public doesn't agree with me personally. One must take the attitude of servicing the entertainment needs of the public, not only of oneself. And you have to think of yourself not only in the high-falutin' terms of an impresario or a concert producer but also as ticket seller. My income is created one way: when I sell a ticket.

"So when one begins, one looks for charts and calls record stores or record distribution or takes polls; but at this point in my career you work from the feel. I know basically what's going on, what's happening in New York or Chicago or Nashville. I know that Robin Trower, which is an act you probably never heard of, is going to be an English superstar guitarist. It's in the air. Young people know it. I know that Tom Jones and Englebert Humperdinck sell out all their suburban theater engagements. I know that—I totally exist within the flow of conversations and data regarding the music industry. It's just in the air for me.

"The power of an impresario or a concert producer is through associations. It's very political. It's very personal. It's building relationships. I have relationships with managers and agencies. They know that I have for the last five or ten years invested my time and dollars in their new acts. If they're part of that small group of people in this industry who do reciprocate, when those acts do become superstars, they'll reciprocate by having those acts play for me. So you try to build up, you know, a reciprocal relationship. And sometimes it takes years, and sometimes it's for naught.

"I can't afford to try and judge the artistic quality of an act. That way I would become the censor. If I don't like the political overtones of an artist, if I don't like the social or cultural, then I, Howard Stein, would be blocking off an entire area of music that the public or a historian or a musicologist might say is important. That would be misusing my position.

"If people took that standpoint, there would probably be no rock.

"What I'm doing is the most democratic. Every time I do a concert, my box-office statement is my public's vote.

"Big acts, not the biggest, get twenty-five thousand dollar guarantees per night. A hundred and fifty thousand a week, guarantee. Plus they get a percentage of the gross—lots of major groups are making thirty-five to fifty thousand a night. And then when they play for festivals, there are groups that are making a quarter of a million to three hundred and fifty thousand per night.

"There is very little middle class. And it's even becoming less of a middle class now, with the financial climate in America. It's the middle class that's really feeling the sting of inflation, and it's the marginal act that really can't make it and is going out of business. So I can get thirty acts that'll play for nothing, for the exposure. It's like actors. Give a new actor his first role in a movie and he'll pay you. No, not literally for nothing. We have acts that'll work for as little as the union scale—for a regular band, two hundred and fifty dollars, five hundred dollars, seven hundred and fifty dollars.

"I've lost seventy thousand in one night, in my life."

Stein calls the middle reaches of payment scale "good money" and the other, higher brackets "make-believe money."

His Howard Stein Enterprises grossed $6 million last year; this year he says he will gross $8 million. And he expects even more to come in at the Premier Theater in Westchester. Eight to $10 million. But because his is not a public company, he will not reveal what proportion of these huge takes are profit, or the size of his own must-be-sizable personal income.

Stein recalls his own perseverance in not falling down and dying any of the three times when his fledgling companies—"money hustled up by brokers"—went bankrupt. There were nights when losing only $5,000 was reason for celebration. He adds that he made every possible mistake so many times, in the beginning of his career, that finally the law of averages was in his favor. From program salesman on a Herman's Hermits tour to multimillion-dollar impresario—he credits, somewhat tautologically, his "survival."

And rock is not dead, he maintains, despite a contrary sentiment that has been attributed to him by reporters. "What I had said, and it was misinterpreted, was that rock has changed. There's always going to be, there are new rock 'n roll acts that are doing superwell. There's Bad Company, there's Robin Trower, there's a whole new wave of important rock stars. People like Led Zeppelin and the Rolling Stones and The Who are still doing bigger grosses than any performers in the world. So rock is hardly dead, it's hardly over. What I was saying was that the significance of rock has changed. It no longer has all the cultural, social, political affiliations that it used to have. The Woodstock Generation is no more. The new consciousness, the alternative culture—these are not things that are irrevocably intermingled into rock 'n roll. So rock 'n roll is not dead, but it's lost these accoutrements that were always as much a part of rock 'n roll as the music itself. Rock 'n roll is still a very major force in the music industry. But it's a force based on a *young entertainment medium.*

"Once upon a time if a guitarist was long-haired, you knew his political views, you knew his social mores, you knew a lot about him. Right now you don't know anything about him except that he's a guitarist."

Asked for an example of some lasting changes from that cultural revolution of the 1960s, Stein cites women's liberation, which he feels originated in the teen-age men and women of that period, the college protester and radical female, who not only wore jeans and T-shirts but also marched and spoke out with her men and changed her sexual and social mores as well.

"And I think the Nixon purges would not have happened if it weren't for the music and rock 'n roll protests and peace movements that were tied into this music in the sixties."

People are starting to dress again, with an interest in the '30s and '40s, he notes, but not with that old formality, nor with the extreme casualness of the recent period. It is a kind of "middling off."

"I don't know what the next new young thing will be. I only know that there will always be a young musical movement. Sometimes it will be political, sometimes it will be more innocuous, or inane.

"My political identification is none, absolutely none. I voted only once, the first year I was old enough to. And I don't register. I'm not a politician groupie. If people call up and say, 'Listen, this Presidential candidate wants Howard Stein to produce this benefit in the Garden,' I'm not interested. I don't want to be friends with any President. I have a particular disrespect for politicians, quite honestly. I am an admitted mercenary. I'm in business to make money. I'm in business for my personal needs, and so long as they don't hurt the needs of the public—and in my case I'm kind of proud because they service the needs of the public—I am what I am. But politicians, who are more mercenary, more personally interested, take on a pretense of not being. It's absurd! That's the strongest power-motivated people in the world, politicians. They live and die for power. That's why billionaires go into politics instead of reigning over their financial palaces—because they want power. More than anything. They thrive on it. They live on it. I'm not fond of politicians.

"I think I'm more of a Cultural Barometer than a Baron. If you want to know what's going on in the culture, you can look at my listings and see what kind of rock concerts I'm doing and where. What kind of pop and suburban attractions. What kind of classical attractions. Unfortunately, I don't think I create the culture. I think I'm something of a director—to make a comparison with films—something of an intermediary doing interpretive work more than creative. I interpret cultural phenomena, I put it on stage, I condense it. I take an aspect of society and put it in a two-hour composite for you."

☆   ☆   ☆

Ron Delsener would like the other promoters around the country to blackball Jerry Weintraub. Delsener is owner, with Howard Stein, of the New York territory—for rock concerts. He has been promoting rock concerts ever since Jimi Hendrix, The Doors, The Jefferson Airplane, and The Cream played at Hunter College in 1966. Howard Stein came in a little bit later, and so did Bill Graham.

But Jerry Weintraub, who has been actively promoting only for the last three years—Frank Sinatra, Elvis Presley, Moody Blues, John Denver—is not respecting the territorial rules that govern the rest of the shaky, semibarbaric, caveman ethic world of live rock. Weintraub has been going directly to the big-name talent and booking them for national tours without the benefit of agents, managers, or even (!) local promoters. Rock impresarios in every important city in the union are up in arms.

Bill Graham was guilty of the same practice, on his Dylan, George Harrison, and Jethro Tull tours. But at least he was amenable to compromises.

When Graham came through the country with Bob Dylan in early 1974, Delsener coproduced the New York concerts with him, for a cut. But in Weintraub's case the big promoter will brook no such abnegation—except in the case of San Francisco, where he lets Graham present. Howard Stein does not complain of these practices, apparently having some nationwide ambitions himself. But Delsener argues bitterly that small agencies are only too willing to cut out the big agencies on a $10 million tour by accepting a nonstandard five percent or even two percent. "There never really is a dispute, because the one guy who's in control is the guy who's got the whole tour. All the blame is on his shoulders. He's the boss that night."

Two years ago promoters from all over the country got together for the first time ever in Long Island to try to make big boys like Bill Graham and the newcomer Jerry Weintraub snap into line. "We told them, 'We've got to do it this way if we're all going to survive,'" says Delsener. Graham put on a show of cooperating—from the comfortable vantage point of having by far the most power and leverage in the live rock field.

Delsener called him "hypocritical," but Weintraub did not even show up.

Last year the promoters got together for a second time, at a *Billboard*-sponsored conference, where Delsener made the suggestion, not seconded by any of the others, that Weintraub be blackballed.

Delsener's plan was for local promoters all around the country to refuse to book the acts that Weintraub manages—such as Michael Murphy and Kinky Friedman—unless and until Weintraub returns to the time-honored methods of making rock tour deals.

At the *Billboard*-sponsored convention in Los Angeles, Bill Graham chaired a panel on "Who Owns the Territories?," which made the whole internecine turmoil sound like sweet nothings. And he gave a keynote address, purportedly on "Where the Power Lies," in which he admitted to three hundred agents, other promoters, club owners, and managers that "I cheat sometimes." On the number of security guards, he explained, the cost of the pastrami backstage, the color of the limos at the airport. He poked fun at the "Mafioso" who had come to the previous year's meeting, full of complaints, and, pantomiming his supremacy by jumping up on top of a stool and yelling about being "king of the mountain" who could push anybody he wanted off, Graham urged the other promoters each to stay in his own territories and not covet one another's.

Weintraub made an appearance at the L.A. confab, smiling broadly and unctuously over his dark shirts and white ties, always appearing in a cluster of ten or eleven men, slightly chunky, similarly attired. He took no part in the meetings, formal or informal, apparently coming just as far as he had to without being blackballed and not a step further.

☆   ☆   ☆

Ron Delsener is like a fragile wire. He is the kind of comedian who leads off by putting you a bit off with a put-on put-down.

"How did I start in this business? Oh, that damn dumb question!" he says with a brilliant electric smile.

Ron Delsener, promoter of the Central Park Schaefer Music Festival and other rock productions (Raeanne Rubenstein)

He tells his story in a middle–Bob Dylan idiom: ". . . went to Europe, came back, I was running up and down along the beach one day and . . ."

The main thing about rock musicians is their body type. They are skinny, energetic, decorative phallo-ectomorphs. And Ron Delsener at the age of forty is as skinny as, and as insane as, any rock musician (some of them are his best friends), though he is an impresario, a producer, a promoter, or, as he says, a presen*tor* of rock acts, everywhere in New York City from Central Park (courtesy of Schaefer beer) to the Metropolitan Opera, and including midnight shows at Radio City and Roseland in between. He has dozens of grudges. He enumerates them like a quick mumbled imprecation. He weighs in at about ninety pounds, soaking wet, his office girl Kathi Gorringe estimates. As an associate he has John Scharer, twenty-eight, a Yale graduate who's been working with him now for twelve years. If Stein's office is decorated á la "We're in the Money!," Delsener's is straight depression era. An inch of dust obscures a murky Oriental rug folded up at the edges haphazardly around an ancient bar-refrigerator. Elsewhere there is gray asphalt tile, a dartboard, the usual posters and awards, and a 1967 fan letter from Thomas Hoving. Delsener says he is moving offices soon, to a larger suite elsewhere in the same Upper East Side townhouse building.

As he described the situation with the Schaefer-sponsored concerts in Central Park, 1975 was to be their last year. Though Mayor Beame and the *Daily News* were supporting them, he said, as well as "some beautiful ladies" appointed by the Mayor to community planning boards, there was also a strong opposition, notably from "Joseph Papp's people—the ones who live around there and don't want those kids standing around," from Parks Commissioner Weisl, who apparently has cited damage being done to the Park, to which Delsener pleads not guilty, and from *The New York Times*, whose publisher's wife, Mrs. Sulzberger, is "socialite buddies" with Commissioner Weisl.

Delsener claimed that the socialites from the neighborhood just want to shunt the minority group kids uptown, back up to Harlem. He praised the Mayor by saying that he was "totally stoned—on our side." And he anticipated coming back into Central Park after two years, when there would have been another city election and Weisl, he hoped, replaced. Indeed, Delsener likes his ten-year-old program so well he feels it should be nationwide, with comparable outdoor summer pop concerts in every city in the United States. "It would only cost about a hundred thousand dollars per city," he says.

"[Bill] Graham called me the other day and said he wants to do it in San Francisco," Delsener bragged. "He said, 'Tell me on the phone how you do it.' I said, 'Send me a check.'"

Ron describes the kind of musicians he promotes as "classy," or "tasty," citing Carole King and Laura Nyro and Barbra Streisand and the Moody Blues—and deliberately omitting such as the Blue Oyster Cult and Black Oak Arkansas. "If they were never performing again," he says, "I would still like to be their friend." No, he says, he is not a mercenary. And, "I'm not a millionaire," though he admits he makes six figures, "not nearly so much as Bill Graham or Jerry Weintraub."

There are about ten rock supersuperstars, Delsener estimates, who earn more than a million dollars a year. Then there are a whole lot of acts that can make $5,000 a night. Among this second type of act, the latest trend in the rock world is the doubling up of headliners, to maximize the kids' shrinking concert dollars.

The Schaefer Music Festival is about one third of Delsener's entire operation. At $150,000 per year, that brings his company net up to about $450,000.

"I've never used anybody's money except my own. I don't have any backers," Delsener went on. "The first money I used was three thousand dollars I had saved from working all my life, and I made forty dollars' profit. Then I lost a couple of bills. Then I started making a profit, and that was it."

He thought the question of lasting effects of the cultural revolution of the 1960s was a tough one. Delsener had, after all, just started working during that cultural revolution. "In rock 'n roll and the music business there are a lot of effects," he laughed. "You see them running around the streets now. There's a lot of freaks still out there. I think rock 'n roll did have a lot of lasting effects. Without a doubt."

At this point Ron Delsener began ranting and rambling on in a way that was positively disorienting. At first I thought he was a left-winger, then a right-winger.

"I definitely think that a lot of rock music contributes to a lack of social graces, or whatdoyacallit, a lack of habit, good habits, or violence, or drugs, or sex, or the mores today. But I think that the whole breakdown of the whole system contributed to that; you can't blame it on rock 'n roll one hundred percent, but I think it had a lot to do with it. Yeah.

"I think it's going to get a lot worse, the I-don't-care attitude, no one gives a goddamn. Maybe it would have happened anyway.

"Attitude, you know: I'm going to grab it today and screw tomorrow. We're just on a downhill slide. The pollution's gonna eat us all alive. There won't be any earth in fifteen hundred years from now because people don't give a shit about anything except money. And the music is an escape and all that. And the more violent, the more crazy——

"I don't know, I'm just a fatalist."

I asked him if he thought there was a political solution.

"Oh, you're asking heavy questions," he moaned. "I haven't voted in a long time. I've seen a lot of politics—business and government and what they do—and people are just machines. They believe what they read in the papers. They complain a lot, but they don't get together and organize. They do a few marches, but that's meaningless. We're going to have to have some tremendous, tremendous radical changes. I mean, it's going to have to be almost like a police state. Where you're gonna say 'You get shot if you throw any more chemicals in that water.' To the big business guys. Or, 'If you sell any more heroin, you're going to be electrocuted in Madison Square Garden like the fight of the week.' It's gonna be on television. People break laws, the laws don't mean anything, there's no one around to enforce the laws.

"It's going to be worse and worse for the average guy. And unless he gets off his ass and really makes a tremendous move to make a violent change, we're gonna be in a lot of trouble. We're going to go more and more socialistic. Maybe I'm a pessimist, but if anybody good comes along, he either doesn't get voted in or gets shot. So.

"I'd like to do something about it. I talk and I write letters. But that's not enough, because I'm involved in my everyday work. As long as you're involved in your everyday work, trying to make money, you forget about the other thing.

"The people who got me back in Central Park, they're women with a lot of money, so they have time to do good things. They said, 'Hey, you should be fighting to get yourself back into Central Park because they threw you out for bad reasons.' They're like gadflies and they're terrific, and we need more people like this. But we all can't afford to stop what we're doing to be that concerned. And the country knows that, and that's why they got us!

"I don't think socialism is the answer to the problems of the country. Unemployment and welfare rolls are swelling, and how much more can we be taxed? They keep saying, 'Take it from the rich,' but there's gonna come a point, man, where I just throw in a towel and say, 'I'm tired of paying.' And if we all organize ourselves and say we're not going to pay taxes, you see what would happen. But that's going to have to be done.

"There's too many local municipalities. There's not one big

leader. I'm not saying there should be a dictator, but sometimes I say maybe there should be a dictator. There's so many little governments, and everybody's taking a little money under the table, and by the time it gets up to the top where Ford is, he doesn't know what's going on all the way down here in a small community, out in New Mexico. There should be one guy who says, 'The law is, Everything is closed at two in the morning,' and that's it.

"The very thought of lobbyists to me is illegal. The National Rifle Association: 'Rifles are good, matches are bad.' That's what they're saying, you know. 'Matches start more forest fires.' I would outlaw all guns. I would make a search of everyone's house, and if they had a gun I'd fine them. I don't care—antique gun or whatever.

"Maybe a young leader will come along. Geraldo Rivera, I think, is going to run. He's with a law firm now. That to me is the first step, that he's going to run for politics. I'm not saying Geraldo's the best guy in the world—he's a good guy—but Geraldo could be the answer. A lot of guys like that—who come and know what needs to be done to make things good. We need fresh leaders and we don't need politicians.

"It's the best country in the world—don't get me wrong. I'm not putting it down, I love it, and I wouldn't live anywhere else. But I want it to be the best forever. Look what's happening to Italy and Portugal, there's no government there anymore. People are just running around, crazy.

"That's just my opinion, and I could be full of soup."

☆   ☆   ☆

Ages of Rock Royalty *

42	Yoko
40	Sonny
35	John
34	Linda
33	Paul
33	Mick
30	Carly

* Courtesy of *Viva* magazine

29   Cher
28   Bianca
26   James

☆   ☆   ☆

Bill Graham has a presence like no other rock promoter I have ever seen—and a dozen of the biggest were gathered in Los Angeles the summer of 1975, from California and New Jersey (it being frequently reiterated that John Scher owned New Jersey) and Philadelphia and Washington, D.C., and Atlanta and the recently merged Midwest or was it Far West?

Compared with him, they were all adenoidal kids who could probably not imagine what they would have been doing if there were no rock 'n roll, till Graham suggested they might have been headwaiters and office managers, heads of small businesses. It was easy to imagine most of them so, bright as their eyes were. But not Graham.

Bill Graham's features seem to radiate outward from or pinch together into the spot just over his nose, but it is a brilliantly pinched look some have called "antediluvian." On the contrary. Graham inspires pity and awe because he is a pebble that washed through the fearful tide of the Nazi extermination camp machine and came out whole and dry on the opposite shore. Though he doesn't mention it himself, it should be said that Bill Graham, born Wolfgang Grajonca in Poland, lost his parents in the camps and only walked to safety with a dwindling schoolful of French kids. Much later he rented and promoted rock bands at the Fillmore, the Fillmore East, and the Fillmore West, certainly the most influential gathering points for the cultural revolution of the'60s insofar as it was expressed in music. There were other concert halls, to be sure, like San Francisco's Avalon and New York's Apollo. But more than any other single individual, Graham is identified with the propagation of the rock sound, the care and feeding of its practitioners.

The official Graham talks with a City College, service-in-Korea slang: "I hope at this conference, people are not going to talk about only broads, dope, and booze." But he is also flashily versatile, even musical, in his own way, and can hike up the

Bill Graham, number one U.S. rock promoter, formerly of the Fillmores

hipness level of his chatter when he's conferring with just a few of his fellow promoters: "romance, A-lines, spoons, grams." No less than *Rolling Stone* magazine has praised the high-decibel idiom of Graham's bass, the inventiveness of his multiple genital-appellation insults. It's all still true.

His world is polarized: Is it a put-on? Are we even capable of understanding? Reporters who come to sit in on his doings are either safe or not safe. When he sits down at a tableful of people he asks, only half in jest, "Is this the enemy camp or friends?" Two words written in gold were dangling around his neck, "God" and also "Bad." On his legs a unique pair of pants one might describe as bell bottoms in sweatshirt material managed to look unutterably sexy, white: showing his print briefs slightly through. For good measure he rolls off his shirt for a quick change, revealing a middle made even sexier by its flesh rolls.

"Paris is by far my favorite city," he says.

And when asked what happened in the '60s he responds,

"Nothing." But surely . . . ! "The kids just woke up and saw that there was a difference between dream and reality."

Getting serious: "Rock 'n roll is no longer a religion to the young people; it is no longer a social force. That was the sixties, and they are gone. It is a form of leisure-time activity. It is entertainment. The hip kid now has stopped freaking out, he's twenty-five, he's got a wife and two kids, he's got a job. He may deal, but he's got a gig. And he doesn't go to his cathedral anymore. He goes to a place of entertainment, and he wants to see an artist on the stage. And he wants to be entertained. He's no longer entertained by his fellow freak. There are no longer enough of them that are willing to do that." (Graham does a quick shimmy.)

Graham refused to promise publicly that if the reunited Beatles were to phone him and ask to do a tour, he would necessarily involve any other promoters. He expressed his own feelings at the prospect by puffing out his chest like Charles Atlas and exclaiming, "My God!," and a chuckling audience of professionals who were supposed to deplore that sentiment seemed to be on his side anyway.

Promoters laugh, recalling that to irk Jerry Weintraub, who was forced to let Graham present John Denver in Graham's home territory of San Francisco, Graham had his stage crew wearing T-shirts that read "Bill Graham presents," picturing a large head of Weintraub. Larry Magid, the promoter from Philadelphia, was wearing such a shirt. Another man said, "I'll give you fifty dollars for that, right now." (Magid refused.)

They sat around making deals in the cement plaza L.A. sun, talking names like madams or slave marketeers. "The basis for our madness is the Why Him? sentiment," Graham said, "though it's not that easy or simple, and cheating pays."

"You know it's envy when people start saying that David Geffen is from the mailroom at William Morris."

"We're not real promoters," insisted Ron Delsener, flown in late for the conference but in time to sit with Graham just before they had to go on a panel. "Real promoters use megaphones."

When Weintraub and his ten cohorts arrived, even later than Delsener, Graham called out exuberantly, "Here's Canada! Here's Alaska!"

Carrying a centuries-old Gucci bag, Delsener indicated "the

biggest deal in town," pointing to a small scribbled-up scrap of paper.

Graham threatened people with "the shredder!"

Mostly the talk ran to statements of the form: "I played Ron Sterling when he was . . . ," with unambiguous demands for gratitude and returned favors. Sometimes the talk ran to the more weighty: "That's how I got Florida, by default of William Morris. . . ." One of Graham's favorite themes was "Us struggling promoters have been eking it out over the years." He also favored the phrase "getting even with." The best question anyone could ask him, he said, was a sympathetic, "How are ya really doing?" To which he would answer with lifted shoulders and rippling fingertips. Meaning, of course, "eh," or "eking it out."

In his area in San Francisco there are about two million people, Graham said. Was there a tinge of envy in his voice when he added, a moment later, that over Labor Day weekend in New York City there were eleven rock shows, all sold out?

When a gorgeous Hollywood nymphet passed by, Graham called out, "Good morning, I'm brilliant, how are you?"

Graham's favorite rock story: Remembering the young John Scher, who said he had a tremendous act, with a lot of corporation backing, for which he expected a three million audience. "Where're we gonna have it?" demanded Graham. And Scher: "Well, we've got Wyoming."

At the final banquet of the *Billboard* convention several of the top promoters agreed that there were six major promoters and about twenty-four minor ones, and except for a few gripes with certain agents, their main enemy, the bad guy, seemed to be Jerry Weintraub.

Jim Fischel, a *Billboard* staffer, cited Weintraub as the most powerful man in the business after Graham. After Weintraub, he named Dick Clark as next most powerful and said that New York's Stein and Delsener figure somewhere among the top fifteen.

Graham named the men he feels have done the most for pop music: composers Jerry Moss, forty, and Lou Adler, twenty-five, and producer Robert Stigwood (*Hair, Jesus Christ Superstar, Tommy* and *Sgt. Pepper's Lonely Hearts Club Band on the Road*).

There is a slightly different opinion of the power lineup in live rock as well. Several of the promoters sitting informally agreed with Graham's statement, "A Frank [Barsalona, head of Premier Talent, an agency] and an ICM [the newly merged superagency] can control the whole industry."

Frank Barsalona, who was apparently a friend of Graham's, Delsener's, Larry Magid's of Philly, Joe Cohen's (the building manager of Madison Square Garden), and Dee Anthony's (an ICM agent) (for they all chose to sit together at the final banquet, like the popular kids in a high school) has also been called, by rock critic Robert Christgau, "possibly the most influential man in the whole music business." He turned out to be a porky overweight blond man with a big turquoise ring, short hair and sideburns, and a raspy voice. Dressed à la Mafiosa, with a dark shirt open to expose a hairy chest, he said he changed his image when Howard Stein changed his.

"In the restaurant or the construction business," Graham declared, "anybody can make a fortune. But in our business anything you do purely, your competitor can make it by doing it dirty." When speaking to the assembled convention, he confined his remarks, elaborating on this theme, to the shenanigans available to a young and raw promoter, chiefly cutting prices. He did not discuss the tricks or cheating tactics available to the big promoters. In private he defended himself against charges from the others by reminding them that on the Harrison tour he had gotten an agent, and, as on the Dylan tour, copromoted with Delsener.

At the end of the convention, when Graham and Delsener were each awarded gold plaques proclaiming them Promoters of the Year, as voted by a panel of their friends, Graham gave the much smaller man a big hug, exclaiming, "It's me and you, Ron, not Weintraub!"

Delsener accepted his plaque with a brief comic speech, "I've been here twelve years; I've watched Bill grow," he began. "And I've watched Jerry Weintraub go past us. I'm just waiting now for Frank Sinatra to call me. Do you know, Weintraub gives out Yankee jackets? Forty-five-year-old men, wearing shirts that say, 'I love the Yankees!' " Referring to the fact that the L.A.P.D. had recently made five hundred pot busts at a Pink Floyd concert, Delsener concluded, "Pink Floyd is coming to the Nassau Coliseum soon. We're expecting a million busts out there—it's bust heaven."

Doug Weston, owner of the Troubadour club in L.A., then financially faltering, a man with shoulder-length yellow-gray hair, a flowered body shirt in blue and ivory, tall and skinny with a bad right arm from a 1972 car accident, and wearing a many-jeweled belt buckle, got up to say that Bill Graham was indeed guilty of not giving enough free concerts. Graham defended himself again: "Free shows are a pain in the ass. The same freaks, the same vacuums, come to each one; in between they 'just hang out.' " But, as compared with the L.A. pot scene, he added, "In San Francisco they don't deal; they don't use it out in the open."

"Bill Graham is a leftover from the psychedelic cult, as I am a leftover from the beatniks," commented Weston, and ended with a plaintive, "Remember the hungry i!"

☆   ☆   ☆

BILL GRAHAM'S DISCOURSE ON "WHERE THE POWER LIES"

Power. Where does the power lie? Power, the main power in our industry, in the end, we all know, belongs with the artist. More so than ever before. Somewhere along the line an agent gets the right from the artist or the artist's manager to determine where the act plays. A manager can relate to the promoter, and makes his deals. But the thing that we all know, in the end, you're looking at the ultimate power. The ultimate power is God, or our health, our spirit, fine. But as far as the power on the earth, on the ground—I think we can all accept that that artist, with his instrument, and based on what he has got, his weight in the industry, can dictate where he plays, when he plays, what he plays, for whom he plays, and for how much he plays. That's where the ultimate power lies.

A group that sells two million units is not told, they tell; a group that sells five hundred thousand units sometimes tells, sometimes is told, because they're still climbing, they will take the second slot on the outdoor show and accept the fact that they can only play forty-five minutes. Until they get to be the headliner, next year; then they tell the next second act, who is in their position, "You can only play thirty minutes." Once they become a star they become the way we become. They start using that power as we use our power. The way we talk to opening acts—we

*wouldn't dare talk that way to the headliner. The way the head-
liner talks to the promoter—he wouldn't dare talk that way to the
promoter when he was the opening act. "Yassuh, boss," when he's
the opening act; "YOU!" when he's the star. All power goes both
ways.*

*It is how we use the power that's really important, not who
has it. Because no matter who has it, if you use it properly, power
is great. If you use it positively. If I had one sentence to describe
power, I would probably say, "Power is respect, is a test of the respect you have for the other party involved." Respect for the audience, from the promoter, the promoter to the artist, artist-
agent, agent-promoter, promoter-manager. How do you use the
power that you have? Knowing that you can do this, do you do
that? Knowing that you can go to an opening act and say, "You
got fifteen minutes." And the manager says, "The contract says
forty-five minutes. I can hold you to the contract, Mr. Promoter."
Thinking that my act someday is going to be a major star and this
promoter wouldn't dare not having me come back to him in this
town. The promoter heard the soundcheck, and some agent asked
him to do them a favor and put that act on as the opening act.
"What a piece of shit, this act is never gonna make it. You got fifteen minutes or you walk!" All because the promoter doesn't
think the act's gonna make it, therefore he doesn't have to be nice
to them.*

That's power.

*How long does one producer wait in the lobby of an agency?
How long does another producer wait in the lobby of an agency?
How does your agent talk to you? Who calls whom in your business? And how quickly do they call back? How quickly do you
call back? The use of power is what really runs our industry.
Well, it probably runs any industry. But in ours, it's much more
devastating, because if it's misused, the shit and the abuse that is
put out toward us and away from us—when we put it out, they
have to eat it; when they put it out, we have to eat it. . . . When
the road manager says, after the soundcheck, "If you don't have
that avocado dip in the dressing room, man——!" Or when a
major artist that I have to compete for says, "Now you don't understand. The other guy says he can get a white limo." And I lost
that artist because I refused to look for a white limo. And the art-*

ist says, "well! We'll show you." And they found a white limo, and they found a promoter. All power.

To go into a little more the devastation of power: some of us are very very very powerful. In this industry. The things that we do for the star, or what he makes us do, knowing that he filled eighty thousand seats—hot food for a crew of nineteen for breakfast. This is a line that's in the center of the head of every promoter in this business: "If I don't do it, somebody else will." It's true! The best we can do is try to convince the agent, or the manager, or the star, to play a small facility. But fewer gates, bigger places, rather than more time on the road. Is the challenge to see how far the last guy in the audience can be from the microphone? I'm as guilty of this as anybody. Though there has never been a time when I didn't prefer to plan an act twice in a five-thousand-seater rather than once in a ten-thousand-seater, and take a little less money.

Because of the rapidity of the success of the industry, we are faced with staying with the demands of success. And if the artist wants to play a seventy-five-thousand-seat stadium, and he wants to be paid based on capacity, in advance—we do it. Because the next guy would do it.

The marbles are so much bigger now. It's 1975. Forty thousand dollars promotion money. Free trip to Europe. That's between the record company and the lawyer.

Seven, eight years ago there was excitement when The Doors were going to play the Garden, when somebody made twenty-five thousand dollars or sold a million units. Now it's part of our everyday lives. We hear a group made three hundred thousand dollars, it's ho-hum. We hear somebody's doing a tour for nine point two million, we say, "Eeyeah, did it work out?" "Did you hear the lead singer for Mott the Hoople electrocuted himself overseas?" "Oh, yeah. Hey, do you want to get the copies of the——?"

I'm trying not to want your territory; I would like you to try not to want mine. [He paused.] We're all Mafiosa.

You read in the trades that So-and-So is going to do a tour throughout the whole country. As we did some years ago, as other producers and promoters are doing now. And the minute the promoter in Peoria or San Francisco reads that, the computer goes through his brain saying, "What is my relationship with that per-

*son? Is he going to give me my city? How embarrassing if it says,
'John McGillicutty presents God in San Francisco' and I'm not involved. How devastating!" Devastating to who? The kid doesn't
give a shit, the patron'll go. The promoter says to himself, "It
won't be done right. Not in this town. They don't know. I know
the back doors and all the secrets about the stage, underneath
where they crawl and all that!" We're all pros. All the promoters
know how to do these shows.*

*A straight businessman would say Jerry Weintraub made a
smart move; so some of the other promoters don't like the vibes,
the aesthetics. Fuck the vibes! When it's three with a bullet, all
that matters is who's got the act!*

*A few years ago I was using all my energy to climb up that
mountain. And I have not found nirvana. But I've gotten to a
place where I feel I'm very lucky to realize how very lonely you
can get when you have all that power, and all those connections,
and people are looking up rather than standing next to you. And
the tragedy of people fearing you for who you are. "I can't approach him with my tape. He'll eat me. That's madman Graham."*

*So I've tried to relate to those things and get back down
where I should be.*

*Well, I think I am very lucky. I was raised in New York City,
was fortunate enough to get a good education, went into the service, came back, finished my education, came to the Coast.
Worked as a paymaster with a truck company, got into statistics,
got into office managing. Got into theater, somehow—the radical
mime troupe of San Francisco, did a benefit, got to know some
artists. Ten years later here I am.*

*I have the good fortune to roll dice every day of the week, to
be afraid of the weather: will there be a door? will the record hit?
what will these new costumes do for my act? Only in the last few
years have I been able to feel how lucky I am to be in this business. 'Cause I'm not in the garment business, which is, you know,
rags and broads and showrooms. Or car manufacturing. Or sani-
tation. Or furniture. I'm in the business of putting people on a
stage and putting people on wax. We've got this great privilege to
take shots at what the public will want. And when we're right,
we've got the good fortune of being next to the most exciting feeling in the world. The most exciting one has got to be the artist*

that stands on the stage and has people tell him or her that they like what I do, they love me, they care about me, I make a lot of money. I live very well, I'm idolized.

I say to myself I'm responsible for that: fully, partly, half, twenty percent, whatever it is.

I'm lucky to be working in this industry. I know for a fact that I couldn't possibly live this well or earn as much as I do unless I married a very rich lady or unless I involved myself with illegal things. I have a position in my community that I could never have as a statistician or even if I started a small business and became the head of it. During the days of madness that everyone in this industry goes through, we don't stop to realize that there's no other business where we could get off the way we can get off in this one.

I no longer fear who's coming into my territory or trying to knock me off the mountain. Greed has been one of my hangups. And happiness at other people's failures. It's almost impossible in our society to look to our competitors with a positive nature. To go into somebody else's community as a positive competitor. It's been very very difficult.

There is no other gig in no other industry where I have the potential to go as far as I can in this industry. So I think to myself, "If I lose this star," or, "If I lose this gig . . ."

There is nowhere you can match what happens to you if you succeed in this business. The power. Fame. Money. Ego satisfaction. Security. So we all fight very very hard to get to that place and hold.

But I've gotten to a position, based on luck and skill and ability, of saying, "How much do I really need? Do I really want to conquer, to fight, to buy another territory or another tour?" And it's very very hard to turn it down. And I don't turn it down. Until I get a lot of it, I get ten pounds of caviar shoved down my throat—and we realize one pound might do it, or five pounds, but we don't need ten.

I've got the same motivations as any other rock promoter or agent or manager: competitive drive, challenges, control, power, ego, greed, some lust, a little of everything thrown in.

The superstar wants to play one ten-thousand-seater rather than five two-thousand-seaters because he wants to have more time to enjoy the luxuries that he's attained. And promoters are the same. We don't want to cover as many acts as we did five years ago. We want to be home with our color TV set and with our kids, or play with our boat or go golfing. So we look for the formula whereby we can retain the power and retain the relationships, not be there all the time but continue to succeed.

And I'm not talking about any religious trip, any spiritual trip: "I found God on acid in San Francisco."

I've gotten so big in my area that I'm not really involved with the selling of a show; it's gotten down to the second or third or fourth man. But at what price? I exchanged, some years ago, quality for quantity, until I caught myself. Not fully yet. Because the power's still there; it's hard to give it up.

For a producer the key is: What happens when you take the ticket from a patron, what happens to him then?

I've tried to be honest with myself in the last few years and to accept the realities of the business.

For those who have tasted success, go back and remember what it looked like when you didn't have it. I do that all the time, and it blows my mind. Just for openers: to sit with friends, as we did last night, and order another bottle, and order another drink, and another salad, irregardless of price. Not just to be a bigshot. There's a joy in being able to share with your friends. And part of sharing, that kind of thing, clubs and bars, takes money. We make money by being successful. We live in America.

And if a kid fresh out of college wants to be a bigshot and is willing to do what I did ten years ago, all I can think is, "Holy shit, now I have to work again."

I was in L.A. a few years ago, and somebody said one sentence about the rise and fall in the entertainment industry, what it's like, that I've never forgotten. He said:

"Who's Rock Hudson?

"Get me Rock Hudson.

"Get me a Rock Hudson.

"Get me Rock Hudson.

"Who's Rock Hudson?"

Every promoter is guilty of catering to the superstars on the basis of their power. We do things we can't believe we've done *when we're alone in our shower. We cater to power so that we can retain our own power.*

It's not easy to be honest about the price we're willing to pay for the things that life in America has taught us are the good things in life, the material things.

For the first time in my life I took an extended vacation—ten days. And I went to Paris, a couple of months ago. My first extended vacation in Paris. The first two or three days I came down, got to a relaxing point, went to the theater, a couple of sidewalk cafés, went to the tourist places. Met some people through other people that I knew. And all of a sudden—hit with a blockbuster—the heaviest in a long, long time—and I don't know if this business has affected any other promoters to the extent that it has affected me in this area. . . . People at the table had a few drinks, talked about horse racing, painting, fixing up their houses, a book they'd just read, a play they'd just seen, whatever. All of a sudden I realized I wasn't in the United States of America. I wasn't [an octave lower] "Bill Graham." Nobody was trying to lay a tape on me. Nobody had some eight by ten glossies of some freaks in New Zealand. I was just another American. And I didn't have the comeback I always have here, that I can always throw into a conversation whenever I'm in trouble: "WellIhaveMasoninSanJoseandathomeIgottwooversixtyandninety-two—" And all of a sudden we are always safe with the shticklach that we have in this industry, because of who we are. And I couldn't use that. And I realized, with a wallop, the main price that I've paid, that I've become pretty much one-dimensional.

I've never been an intellectual, but I had a pretty good education, in the streets and in the schools, and I used to go to the theater, I used to go to the galleries, I used to read books. But now I realized that for ten years it's been, compulsory in the bathtub, Newsweek, Saturday Evening Review, Time magazine. That covers it. So you become the conversational waiter in the mountains: you can talk about anything, on the surface.

The big price I paid was that I couldn't talk to the average guy.

Graham said he had made an announcement of farewell to his home office, right after he got back from Paris. Some thought it was just Graham going "crazy bananas" again. But he promised them that this time it was not. They were going to have to take over for him, he recounted (though he was not closing the door on them altogether, with an 'I found God'), to the best of their ability. And if his staff couldn't handle so many shows as well as he, Graham, could—well, then they were just going to have to gradually slacken off.

"I'm going to try not to pay the price anymore, of staying on that mountain at all costs," he said.

☆   ☆   ☆

Dave Busch is the kind of young man who resents Bill Graham's position in the rock industry. He hesitates only a second before answering affirmatively that he's a Socialist. Ten years ago he would have been a part of the National Student Association (financed, they later found to their dismay, by the CIA) or student council president. In 1975 he is concerts chairman on the campus of his small Texas college; last year he was president of the Student Services Council. And he has $70,000 to disburse on concerts under a faculty adviser's signature. He thinks it is very possible that the only lasting change effected by the cultural revolution of the 1960s was the transfer of control over college money from faculties to students.

Busch sees Graham not as an enemy but merely as a capitalist. According to the intelligent, bearded youth, the collusion between promoters like Bill and the four big agencies that control the few hundred biggest names in rock music is "choking off the colleges." Why should an agency book an attraction in one of the nation's three thousand colleges—and the colleges certainly want them—when they can sell fourteen dates at once to a promoter like Bill Graham, the Safeway of the rock field? And why should Bill himself bother with Texas? Busch asked him that directly: "How come you never come and work with us in Texas?" And Graham allegedly replied, "I had a car accident one time when I was driving through Texas; I don't care to go back."

Busch says, "Even Graham doesn't know how much Graham's worth."

And: "The other promoters crowd around him because he can hurt them, but also so they can learn how he made his money and get some."

But Busch has not thought at all about a solution, or about "the ideal political economy of art."

☆   ☆   ☆

I first encountered the reputedly nefarious Clive Davis at the preview screening of *Godfather II*—not at the classy première showcase on Broadway but at the subrun Loew's around the corner and out of the way from spotlit Times Square, rather more in the glow of the sleazy Sun Luck, as befits such unlucky ex-riders of the golden storm as he. He was sitting almost directly behind me. Thoughts of the Roman legions were filling my head as Coppola and Paramount intended. His face was impossible to miss; he looked, as he looks in 99 out of 100 of the photos taken of him, like a smiling lightbulb.

I hailed him: "Mr. Davis!" and volunteered two pleasantries: that I was enjoying his book, that I had found the movie "fascinating." Mr. Davis merely upped his face-wattage a point or two and continued walking.

At that juncture my companion paused to look for her gloves, and I lost sight of the erstwhile steward of the Bob Dylan and Janis Joplin music contracts.

When I next caught sight of him he was stationed directly aft the main front doors of the Loew Astor, performing such rites as one expects from premières: greeting, discussing with, being there. The men speaking statesmannishly with him were notoriously unmemorable. I walked by him once. But then, outside, I remembered my obligation to Culture Barony. "Should I go back and ask to interview him?" I asked Kathie, the inventor of Consciousness Raising. "Is he a Culture Baron?" she asked. I told her he'd overseen Dylan's belonging to CBS-Columbia and been fired approximately the same time Dylan had gone to Elektra-Asylum. Kathie is no rock buff, but she did have some special associations with Dylan, and so she was already leading me back to the crowd.

Outside Loew's again, we could have been anywhere, except that the mixture of blacks and whites was more thorough and unobtrusively harmonious than in your usual sidewalk scene.

Clive Davis, former chief administrative officer, Columbia Records (Ken Regan/Camera 5)

I bopped back in to see Clive. And lo! he flashed some imaginary *paparazzi* the same glad-to-be-here-with-this-person smile I'd seen on his face when photographed between George Harrison and Richard Perry! (not to mention literally dozens of lesser luminescences). Clive and me! for the benefit of the *paparazzi* of the imagination. I wondered hard, very hard, where I was; and laughed a little inside at this man's obvious goof-ball pleasure at seeing me again, an old friend—of scarce long enough a time period to be measurable to man. Or had he so few friends?

The rest of the encounter was less interesting. I mentioned my desire for an interview—book on Culture Barons—name of publisher Thomas Y. Crowell. To which he said, "Who?" and I amplified: "Crowell, a subsidiary of Dun and Bradstreet." An imperceptible nod. A scarcely recordable positive gesture. To call him at his office.

☆　　☆　　☆

Ernest Leogrande, entertainment columnist for the *Daily News*, repeated Bob Dylan's comment on the new head of Columbia Records (replacing Clive Davis). Apparently the minstrel found Irwin Segelstein "politically liberated."

☆   ☆   ☆

THE LABOR COUNTERFORCE

I. PHILIP SIPSER is one man whose business it is to confront the Culture Barons. He dislikes the arrogance of the few individuals who dominate the money and power in the arts. And he spends his time working—in forty-two symphony orchestras around the country, at the New York City Opera and Ballet, at the Metropolitan Opera, in the Museum of Modern Art—to increase the extent of participation by the musicians and other artworkers in their own management.

Sipser is a trade union lawyer, senior partner in the firm of Sipser, Weinstock, Harper, and Dorn. One of his clients is the International Conference of Symphony and Opera Musicians (ICSOM), which covers, for starters, all the orchestra members in all the various houses at Lincoln Center.

He has also represented, with his associate Leonard Liebovitz, the Professional and Administrative Staff Association (PASTA) at the Modern.

His involvement with trade union law especially in not-for-profit cultural areas (he also represents hospital workers in some eighteen states, technical engineers, and various other blue-collar industrial unions) began seven or eight years ago when lawyer Leonard Boudin asked him to mediate in a contract negotiation for the New York Philharmonic. Since then he has focused more and more on the cultural employees' unions, even though that aspect of his career is less profitable than the other. He prefers to call his a "trade union law firm" rather than "labor law," since he says the latter term might cover both sides of the table.

Trade union lawyer I. Philip Sipser, representative of the International Conference of Symphony and Opera Musicians and of the Professional and Administrative Staff Association at the Museum of Modern Art

After his successful experience with the Philharmonic, one of the orchestra's violinists, Ralph Mendelson, took him to lunch and presented him with a pen set inscribed "To the Heifetz of negotiators."

"It was better than a fee," Sipser says.

Shortly afterward he was asked to represent ICSOM, then a young union.

One of Sipser's provocative ideas is that the management of the New York City Opera and New York City Ballet should merge. He has suggested this annually to City Center's president, Martin Oppenheimer. Of course the Center's management is shocked at the idea. But Sipser calls its reluctance merely "vested interests," and costly, inefficient overhead. He concedes that some of the organization's administration would be out of a job, and perhaps one or two conductors. He is nevertheless pulling for his orchestral clients, who should, he says, that way be guaranteed job security and a full working year. At present about fifteen musicians play overlapping positions in the City Opera and the City Ballet.

On a panel of representatives from arts unions and management sponsored by Volunteer Lawyers for the Arts in late 1974, Sipser said, "Everyone blames labor for everything." He pointed out that there is "a great deal of distrust and bitterness among the rank and file of the symphony orchestras." In 1973 this bad feeling had erupted in a horrendous series of strikes in nonprofit cultural institutions throughout the country, for instance, locally at the New York City Opera, the New York City Ballet, the New York Philharmonic, and the Museum of Modern Art. But during the course of the negotiations at the Philharmonic, Avery Fisher made a large grant of money to that organization. Exacerbating the employees' bad feelings, the management of the Philharmonic and of Lincoln Center made it impossible for the unions to find out the nature and size of the grant. Instead they continued to plead poverty, as they do today. And as a result, maintains Sipser, there is a great deal of distrust among the musicians toward the Philharmonic management centered around the Fisher grant.

The Fisher grant, says Sipser, "is symbolical of the problem we have in all the arts. Nonprofit institutions are run by boards of directors, when in reality their management should be a matter of public information." Unlike private institutions, he contends, arts organizations are run for the public interest and so "there should be full disclosure of how much money is paid to whom."

Culture Barons and their representatives, on the other hand, defend the right of wealthy individuals to prescribe, in secrecy and confidence, just how their money is to be used. Two who take this position are Tom Hoving, director of the Metropolitan Museum of Art, and Alan Jaffe, attorney for City Center, Inc.

Sipser identifies his chief professional innovation as being an outgrowth of the fact that workers in the arts, unlike most of the labor scene, are intensely interested in their work-product, in its criticism and public reception. Classically, the trade union stance is, "We do our work, and it's your job to find the money." But because of the passion of musicians and artists, Sipser is leading his flocks into greater participation in the management and funding of their work.

Three years ago the PASTA–MOMA (Professional and Administrative Staffs of the Museum of Modern Art) struck, demanding staff representation on the Museum's rather distant board of trustees. The board found the experience "extremely distressing" and were glad that "relationships were repaired" and the strike settled within only three weeks. They raised all PASTA workers' salaries by 7.5 percent, and they agreed not to raise the admissions fee for senior citizens. But they refused to let one staff person onto the all-powerful governing board of trustees.

Asked for his comment on why they did this, Sipser opens Russell Lynes's book *Good Old Modern* to the last page and points at the scholar-critic's words (quoting the Art Workers Coalition, with his qualified endorsement): "rich, dictatorial trustees." "Mrs. Rockefeller and the others regard the institution as their playthings," Sipser amplifies. "They think, 'To hell with the public.' "

Mrs. Blanchette Rockefeller, president of MOMA, had a different explanation. She said, "The request for more actual authority in the running of the Museum was opposed by the board because that union [PASTA] does not represent the top staff of the museum, the management staff, like the director and the director of administration and the heads of all our departments and the chief curators. And *they* do not have a representative on the board. They come to board meetings and confer with the board and report to the board, but they don't have a vote or a standing representative. Neither do the guards, who are also a union. They've never asked for one; I don't think they'd think it was useful, particularly, to have someone come to every board meeting. So we just felt it was not appropriate and would cause all kinds of problems of representation for everybody. But I think we do have, and I think the union now feels that they do have, access to the board."

Sipser goes on to explain his musicians' involvement in fund raising. It began right after the Ford Foundation announced a cutback in funds (due to a fall in the Foundation's stock) for all programs, in late 1974. The musicians, who are very aware of their service to the public—especially under circumstances like free concerts in the parks in summertime—officially decided then to get involved with raising money. At that time the Ford Foundation also reported on the 166 most significant arts organizations in the country and projected huge operating deficits. Sipser thinks the figures are "phony," though they might have some basis in truth, given the stock market decline and the re-ordering of social priorities. But this is another of the reasons why he is getting into fund raising. "Assuming there is some basis for that report," he says, "we concluded that fund raising is too important to leave to management."

Members of ICSOM (International Conference of Symphony and Opera Musicians) consequently went into fund-raising in the government sector, writing letters to every congressman and senator in Washington, urging them to introduce a bill making a provision on the income tax form for every citizen to check off an automatic, deductible contribution to the arts.

Sipser's and others' feeling that this would bring in a lot of money was based on the Harris poll that found that sixty-four percent of the adult public would be willing to pay an additional five dollars in taxes if the money was directed toward arts and culture.

Representative Fred Richmond (D-N.Y.) responded affirmatively to ICSOM's mailing, writing to ICSOM'S chairman Irving Segall in March 1975 that he was in fact working on just such a bill based on the same study, and in July he filed the legislation.

In 1974, Sipser, along with Schuyler Chapin for the Metropolitan Opera, went to City Council president Paul O'Dwyer and got $150,000 from New York City, thus saving opera-in-the-parks. From O'Dwyer the fund raisers had to go to all the borough presidents; ultimately the Board of Estimate made the grant. Sipser crowed briefly: "As many people see opera in the parks in two weeks as see it in ten years in the Opera House."

At the Philharmonic, Sipser says, chairman Amyas Ames (who is also chairman of Lincoln Center) insisted that the musicians' salaries be raised to the level of the Chicago Symphony, which amounted to a fifty dollar increase (Chicago had recently raised its musicians' pay by sixty dollars). Their morale high, the New York orchestra organized a tour of Spain for themselves, without the help of management.

Sipser praises Ames as being "genuinely interested in the arts." However, the double chairman is seen as having some "resistance to input in the areas he considers to be management concern." These points of contention include the scheduling and content of the music, the auditioning of prospective new players, the firing of older players, and the allocation of funds.

Sipser claims he is fighting, on behalf of his unionized instrumentalists, merely for *input,* not *determination,* in these areas. "The musicians merely want their opinions taken into serious consideration."

As he spoke to me the trade union lawyer was energetically consulting lawbooks, negotiating on a long-distance phone call ("without admitting the issue is arbitrable . . . we are prepared to enter into expedited arbitration"), and orchestrating a busy host of interracial employees and a hippy son. He expressed his negative opinion of the 1974–75 New York State Council on the Arts' allocation. By prescribing a *per capita* distribution it was inequitable, he said; "New York City is not like any other city." He went on to compare both the Metropolitan Opera and Lincoln Center to the United Nations, both being "supermunicipal," belonging to the world.

He assented to my essential Culture Baron proposition—that there are a small number of men with enormous power in the arts—as "absolutely true." But he placed it in the larger noncultural context. "The arts have got to be considered in the same vein as all the institutions in the country," he said, "electoral, educational, corporate, health. Institutions in general are not responsive to the people; they have hardened arteries. It's not that their administrators are mean or unconcerned but just that they don't understand the cultural revolution in America and the generation gap. Arts are a reflection of the whole operation," he said.

Sipser began to represent the orchestra members precisely at the height of the cultural revolution, in 1968–69.

The only example of a Culture Baron he mentioned whose interests in addition to being vested were also pernicious was one of the directors of the Kansas City Symphony, who refused to raise the matching funds required and thus forfeited a Ford Foundation grant. Allegedly he said, "Why should we raise all that money? It would just go to the players anyway."

A wave of younger men are beginning to take over the directorships of orchestras, however, who are able to get along with the members better and in general take a different view. He cited Nick Webster, the general manager of the New York Philharmonic, Dick Seizak in Minneapolis, and Peter Pasreich in St. Louis.

"In part," Sipser has said, "the union activity of players is part of a professional revolution in America. They looked around and saw truck drivers getting good pay and excellent fringe benefits, and they realized that collective bargaining is an essential for them too.

"The wages they were getting would be like paying Joe Di-Maggio twenty thousand dollars a year instead of one hundred thousand. There is this nonrecognition of the performing arts in this country in monetary terms."

Eventually, Sipser believes, orchestras and the other arts will have to become more cooperative, as they are in most European countries. Rich patrons will no longer be able to say, "This museum is ours, we work for nothing; if you don't like it here, scram!" The staffs' or players' opinions will be listened to, instead of their being considered upstarts or subversives with crazy ideas. It's not that he can't understand the managements' reluctance to share power; no, he can almost sympathize, putting it in terms of his own office. It's just that "I am a very partisan fellow across the table."

From his long experience he summarizes: "When it's a money issue, they tell you there's no money. When it's a nonmoney issue, they say, 'Oh, but that is a management prerogative!'"

☆   ☆   ☆

The major labor unions connected with the arts include Actors' Equity (which negotiated its first collective bargaining contract in 1917 with a producers' group that has since disbanded), AGMA, or the American Guild of Musical Artists (singers and dancers), the American Federation of Television and Radio Artists (AFTRA), and the Screen Actors Guild (SAG), all of which are affiliated under the figurehead organization Associated Actors and Artistes of America (4As). Then there is the American Federation of Musicians and its sub-division, the International Conference of Symphony and Opera Musicians; the Dramatists' Guild; United Scenic Artists; Society of Stage Directors and Choreographers; and the Association of Theatrical Press Agents and Managers. The IA, or International Alliance of Theatrical Stage Employees, which represents stagehands, electricians, carpenters, propmen, soundmen, treasurers, ticket sellers, and wardrobe attendants, may be the most economically powerful of all these unions. Least powerful are the semi-unionized professional organizations such as the American Society of Composers, Authors, and Publishers; the Authors Guild; and Poets, Playwrights, Editors, Essayists, and Novelists.

At the Metropolitan Opera alone, the general manager negotiates with sixteen different unions. *The New York Times* calls the labor situation in the arts "chaotic" and "a jungle." Throughout the United States, there are a few million people working in the arts in this way, with their trade union as a power base and potential starting-point for collective action. In the American Federation of Musicians alone there are 330,000 members around the country, with 30,000 of these in New York City. A fiction editor at a leading publishing house estimates that 250,000 books are written each year—out of which a mere 25,000 are published—which implies that there are at least a quarter of a million serious writers working somewhere in the nation at any one time. *Fortune* magazine estimates there are 107,000 visual artists working actively, of whom about 4,000 can actually support themselves at it. Next in size, nationwide, after these three groups is the IA (stagehands, etc.), with 60,000 members.

Trade-unionized actors are not quite so numerous, but of all the groups they may be the most highly concentrated around New York City; one half of all the members of Actors Equity are in the New York area, and even one third of all the members of the Screen Actors Guild. Though it's hard to tell precisely how many actors are doubling up in both unions in New York City there are at the very least 10,000 separate individuals of the acting profession in New York, of whom New York City theaters employ only about 600.

Artists and Artworkers

FIELD	ORGANIZATION OR SOURCE	N.Y.C.	U.S.A.
I. Musicians	Amer. Fed. of Musicians Local 802	30,000	330,000
Songwriters	Broadcast Music, Inc. (BMI)		35,000
	Amer. Soc. of Composers, Authors, and Pubs. (ASCAP)		16,000
Soloists	Amer. Guild of Musical Artists, (AGMA)	1,924	4,400
II. Writers	Crowell editor's estimate of no. books written each year		250,000
Professional Writers	No. new books published each year		25,000
	Authors Guild		2,200
	P.E.N.		1,600
III. Visual Artists	*Fortune*'s estimate of active professional artists		107,000
Professional Artists Making a Living	*Fortune*'s estimate		5,000
IV. Stagehands (electricians, carpenters, soundmen, propmen, etc.)	International Alliance of Theatrical Stage Employees (IA)	1,452	60,000
V. Actors (all categories)	*New York Times*' estimate	25,000	
TV & Radio Actors	Amer. Fed. of TV & Radio Actors (AFTRA)	10,500	31,500
Film Actors	Screen Actors Guild (SAG)	10,000	29,000
Live Actors	Actors' Equity	10,000	20,000
VI. Film & TV Directors	Directors Guild	2,000	4,000
VII. Costume, Lighting & Scenic Designers for Theater, Film & TV	United Scenic Artists		900
VIII. Choreographers	Society of Stage Directors & Choreographers		500
IX. Press Agents	Assn. of Theatrical Press Agents & Managers		500
			1 million +

In every art field there is a large working class, earning low or even marginal salaries, and there is a small upper class, enjoying enormous wages and employed in a few budget-popping extravaganzas upon which the whole stock of the industry is gambled. There is no artistic middle class. America's culture industries are feudal.

This is as true in the motion picture industry as it is in rock music, as true in book publishing as it is in classical dance. *Godfather* was budgeted at $9 million, the unimpressive *Day of the Locust* at $4 million. We have already discussed the handful of people in the rock music field who are earning in seven or eight figures. Meanwhile, there are tens of thousands of musicians and actors who can't get work, owing to the unhealthy economic structures of their industries. Some film critics explain the hit-or-miss syndrome in films as being caused by television; but then what explains its presence also in publishing? Publishers blame the bookstores for concentrating on best sellers. But the problem goes deeper than that.

Where there are unions, the situation is occasionally better. Until recently AGMA members of the corps de ballet could not expect to make more than $150 a week starting salary at the nation's top dance companies, while film projectionists, protected by the International Association of Theatrical Stage Employees, were pulling a weekly $420. "Artists are underpaid almost beyond belief," commented the outgoing director of the New York State Council on the Arts. But his administration did nothing to change these proportions.

And where there are unions, there are also the issues of trade unionism, of communism, of labor leaders who are tyrants in their way, like Herman Patrillo, former head of the A.F. of M. Others, like Herman Kennon, Patrillo's successor, have lobbied like any proper Culture Baron for government money to the arts; Sam Rosenbaum of the Music Performances Trust spent ASCAP and BMI funds for more performances in the communities and for youth.

Artists as a class are still oppressed. But whether their redemption is to be the work of the Culture Barons per se or of the barons of the counterforce, which is cultural labor, remains to be seen.

POSTSCRIPT:
The Ideal Political Economy
of Art

I T's not easy to be articulate about the arts. Boundaries are shifting all over the place. Television plus computer becomes "mixed media." Rock is compared to classical music, to jazz, to theater. Jazz in turn is seen as classical, rock personnel as movie stars. Film has become, among the avant-garde, a form of graphics. Painting and sculpture are used as stage set and architecture. Radio is called "theater of the mind." Journalism aspires to literature, televised politics to drama; the "caper" is what we call our trivial epics. And then there is always the Steppenwolf Factor, the Magic Theater of psychedelicism, electronic light and sound with no holds barred.

It has not been within the scope of this book to analyze the content of artistic productions in the United States at this time, though to do so would surely have been interesting. But even a superficial analysis reveals that by and large the themes of Broadway plays have been dismal when they were not perverse; yet a full 36 million Americans went to see a live, professional Broadway musical within the past year (see accompanying chart). This kind of mass audience should not be trifled with. Plays worthy of their attention should be produced. Movies, furthermore, are seen in theaters by 138 million Americans each year, and at home on television by 186 million—nearly every single one of us. Can we leave all the decisions about the content and style of this artistic fare up to the Culture Barony that is now operative?

The Art Audience

Percentage of 6,000 respondents in twelve cities around the U.S. who have been exposed in the last year to:

	%
Live Amateur Opera	2
Live Amateur Ballet	4
Live Professional Ballet	4
Live Professional Opera	4
Live Amateur Symphony	6
Live Professional Symphony	10
Opera on Records/Tape	10
Live Amateur Broadway Musical	11
Opera on Radio	12
Opera on TV	14
Broadway Musical on Radio	14
Live Professional Play	16
Live Professional Broadway Musical	18
Ballet on TV	22
Live Amateur Play	23
Symphony on Records/Tape	25
Live Professional Jazz, Rock, Folk Music	25
Broadway Musical on Records/Tape	27
Symphony on Radio	28
Symphony on TV	30
Broadway Musical on TV	38
Jazz, Rock, or Folk Music on Records/Tape	52
Jazz, Rock, or Folk Music on Radio	65
Jazz, Rock, or Folk Music on TV	66
Movies in Movie Theater	69
Movies on TV	93

From *The Finances of the Performing Arts*, Vol. II (Ford Foundation, 1974).

It has been said that 750 families own all the wealth of this country.* And that less than five percent of the people in the United States have ninety percent of the wealth.† But not everyone realizes the impact of such statistics. Among these 750 families, these 10 million people, are the rulers of our hearts and minds, the Culture Barons. By cleverly opting for control not over gross material things like steel and wires but rather over the airy and spiritual provinces of the muses, they wield power over what we will sing and dance, what we will hear and see, what we will know and do, just when we think we are escaping from the clutches of The System. There can be no doubt that the extreme centralization of cultural power which exists in the United States is a bad thing. Why should everything of artistic value center on New York City (with the official counterculture in California)?

It may be provincialism, but I have a vision of cultural centers as majestic as Lincoln Center in maybe a dozen places around the country—and in every city twenty-five miles apart an orchestra or a ballet or a film studio—so that there would be both leadership and also a very highly evolved audience, so that there would be competition for that leadership, and strongly competing alternate forms of high culture.

David M. Keiser's response was to say, "I think twenty-five miles is a little bit close. I was born and brought up in the city of Milwaukee, which is eighty miles from Chicago. Even then, Milwaukee had a symphony, and of course Chicago has. There was always a lot of rivalry. . . .

"A lot of it has to do with whether you can afford the luxury of having so many symphony orchestras."

I: "Oh yes, of course, it would all have to be paid for. And so many people would be involved. But (coyly?) it gets into more economics than I am expert at."

In the ideal society, power would be distributed differently from ours. And because political power would be different, cultural power would also be different. The arts would be bread and butter in the public schools, with so many talents blossoming under this care that serious competition would arise among the

* Panther Field Marshal Don Cox, quoted by Tom Wolfe, *New York* magazine, June 8, 1970.
† Gerald Lefcourt, lawyer for the Panther 21, *op. cit.*

dozen regional metropolitan centers for cultural pre-eminence. There would be opera in every town, of course, and legitimate theaters, and a ballet school. Perhaps every fifty miles there would be a substantial film studio, with school, a TV studio, and a record-cutting plant. So many artistic outlets would be available that millions of people would be employed in the theaters, orchestras, schools, and production and distribution facilities, and they would not earn significantly less money than the "stars" of the works. To make such serious reforms, serious steps must be taken.

Some will dismiss this vision and deride the people of the towns as Babbitts impervious to culture. But that is not true about America. The people of the richest, most technological nation in history are well educated, and they are universally open to television, film, and publicity, which represent forms of further education. Opera, theater, and serious dance have demonstrated their value by enduring hundreds, even thousands, of years. When the mechanisms are set in motion by which old and new forms of the high culture are far more widely available then they are now—to express oneself through participating, not only to appreciate—the natural vitality of the people will reawaken and fertilize the growth.

INDEX